ICFA Continuing Education
Innovations in Fixed Income

April 19–20, 1994
New York, New York

Susan D. Abbott
Carl O. Bautista
Dwight D. Churchill, CFA, *Moderator*
James Grant
Theresa A. Havell
Jerome J. Jacobs, CFA
Andrew B. Jones
James A. Kaplan, CFA
Martin L. Leibowitz
Amy F. Lipton, CFA

Kris Mahabir
John V. Malvey, CFA
Sharmin Mossavar-Rahmani, CFA
Gregg N. Patruno
Glenn L. Reynolds, CFA
Michael R. Rosenberg
Isabel Saltzman
John F. Tierney, CFA
Francis H. Trainer, Jr., CFA
Tracy L. van Eck

Edited by Dwight D. Churchill, CFA

To obtain an AIMR Publications Catalog or to order additional copies of this publication, turn to page 132 or contact:

AIMR
P.O. Box 3668
Charlottesville, VA 22903
U.S.A.
Telephone: 804/980-9712
Fax: 804/980-3634

The Association for Investment Management and Research comprises the Institute of Chartered Financial Analysts and the Financial Analysts Federation.

This publication is designed to provide accurate and authoritative information in regard to the subject matter covered. It is sold with the understanding that the publisher is not engaged in rendering legal, accounting, or other professional service. If legal advice or other expert assistance is required, the services of a competent professional should be sought.

ISBN 1-879087-43-X

Printed in the United States of America

December 1994

Table of Contents

(continued on next page)

Foreword

The composition of the fixed-income market has changed significantly in the past two decades. Mortgage-backed securities, which did not exist 20 years ago, now account for one-third of fixed-income securities; corporate bonds have declined as a percentage of the market from more than one-half in 1975 to less than one-fifth today. At the same time, credit quality has deteriorated. In order to alter portfolio risk exposure and return patterns, many strategists for institutional portfolios are incorporating derivative securities in their plans and the use of global bonds is rising. Fixed-income managers have responded to these significant developments by seeking out and embracing a variety of research approaches, valuation techniques, and portfolio management practices.

To survey the fixed-income managers' current analytical techniques and investment strategies, AIMR developed and sponsored an ICFA Continuing Education seminar in the spring of 1994, from which this proceedings resulted. The seminar examined an array of approaches to valuing individual securities and to structuring domestic and global fixed-income portfolios. Speakers provided insights into applying tried-and-true approaches and evolving new techniques. A particularly useful section was devoted to the incorporation of derivative securities for capturing market opportunities and controlling portfolio risk. This proceedings is intended to make a selection of those collected insights available to the reading audience.

The changing interest rate environment makes this seminar proceedings particularly timely. As many investors have discovered, the strategies and techniques used during a period of declining rates must differ dramatically from those used in periods of rising interest rates. This proceedings challenges the assumptions of conventional fixed-income investing and provides readers with suggestions for varying techniques to meet the times.

We wish to thank all the speakers at the seminar; we are particularly grateful to those who assisted in the time-consuming task of helping with preparing their presentations for the printed form. Special thanks are also in order for Dwight D. Churchill, CFA, Fidelity Management and Research Company, who moderated the seminar and contributed the Overview.

The speakers participating in the seminar were as follows: Susan D. Abbott, Moody's Investors Service; Carl O. Bautista, Bankers Trust Company; James Grant, *Grant's Interest Rate Observer*; Theresa A. Havell, Neuberger & Berman; Jerome J. Jacobs, CFA, The Vanguard Group of Investment Companies; Andrew B. Jones, Duff & Phelps Credit Rating Company; James A. Kaplan, CFA, Capital Management Sciences; Martin L. Leibowitz, Salomon Brothers; Amy F. Lipton, CFA, Aetna Life and Casualty; Kris Mahabir, Fidelity Management and Research Company; John V. Malvey, CFA, Lehman Brothers; Sharmin Mossavar-Rahmani, CFA, Goldman, Sachs Asset Management; Gregg N. Patruno, Goldman, Sachs & Company; Glenn L. Reynolds, CFA, Lehman Brothers; Michael R. Rosenberg, Merrill Lynch & Company; Isabel Saltzman, Scudder, Stevens & Clark; John F. Tierney, CFA, Lehman Brothers; Francis H. Trainer, Jr., CFA, Sanford C. Bernstein & Company; and Tracy L. van Eck, CS First Boston.

Dorothy C. Kelly
Assistant Vice President
Education

Biographies of Speakers

Susan D. Abbott currently serves as associate director in the Electric, Communications, and Speculative Grade Group of the Corporate Department at Moody's Investors Service. She formerly served Moody's as associate director in the Industrial Group and in the Financial Institutions Group and as a vice president of International Operations in Moody's London office. Previously, Ms. Abbott was a senior investment analyst at Aetna Life and Casualty. She is a graduate of Syracuse University and holds an M.B.A. from the University of Connecticut.

Carl O. Bautista is an associate in the Investor Group of Bankers Trust's Global Investment Bank. Mr. Bautista is responsible for structuring and marketing derivative products related to dollar and nondollar interest rates and foreign exchange. Mr. Bautista earned his M.B.A. from the Kellogg School.

Dwight D. Churchill, CFA, heads the Taxable Fixed Income Investments Group for Fidelity Management and Research Company. Prior to joining Fidelity, Mr. Churchill was employed by Prudential Insurance Company of America as a managing director with Prudential Fixed Income Advisors and, most recently, as president of CSI Asset Management. Prior to joining Prudential, he was a fixed-income portfolio manager with Loomis, Sayles and Company and managed the fixed-income segment of the Public Employees Retirement System of Ohio. Mr. Churchill currently serves AIMR as vice chair of the ICFA Candidate Curriculum Committee. He holds a B.A. from Denison University and an M.B.A. from Ohio State University.

James Grant is founder and editor of *Grant's Interest Rate Observer*, a bi-weekly financial publication. Before founding *Grant's*, he was capital markets editor of *Barron's* and originator of its current yield column. Mr. Grant is the author of *Money of the Mind: Borrowing and Lending in America from the Civil War to Michael Milken*, which was selected the best financial book of the year by *The Financial Times*. He has frequently appeared on national television news shows, including *Wall Street Week with Louis Rukeyser*. His articles have been published in the *New York Times*, *Forbes*, the *Wall Street Journal*, the *American Banker*, and other publications. Mr. Grant is a graduate of Indiana University and holds a master's degree from the

Columbia University School of International Affairs.

Theresa A. Havell is a partner and director of the Fixed Income Group of Neuberger & Berman and serves on the executive committee. She is also president of ten Neuberger & Berman fixed-income mutual funds. Previously, Ms. Havell served as director of the Liquid Asset Group at Lehman Management Company. She began her career at Citibank in foreign exchange and liability management, where she was vice president/treasurer for the Latin American region. Ms. Havell has appeared on CNN-TV's *Your Money*, CBS-TV's *Wall Street Journal Report*, and PBS's *Sound Money*. She received a B.A. from Manhattanville College and an M.A. from New York University.

Tracy L. van Eck, director of Fixed Income Research at CS First Boston Corporation, specializes in asset-backed securities. She is a member of the Market Research Department, a group that analyzes relative value among fixed-income securities and publishes frequent research reports, including the monthly *Relative Value Review* and *Mortgage Market and Prepayment Review*. Prior to joining the Market Research Department, Ms. van Eck specialized in risk-controlled arbitrage in the Portfolio Strategies Department. Recently, she was selected for *Institutional Investor's* All-America Research Team for her work in asset-backed securities. Ms. van Eck is a graduate of the Plan II Honors Program at the University of Texas at Austin.

Jerome J. Jacobs, CFA, is a vice president of The Vanguard Group of Investment Companies and senior portfolio manager of the Vanguard municipal bond fund long-term and high yield portfolios. Additionally, he is the head of the Tax Exempt Division of the Fixed Income Department. Mr. Jacobs holds a B.S. in economics from the Wharton School of the University of Pennsylvania.

Andrew B. Jones, group vice president at Duff & Phelps Credit Rating Company, is responsible for the Mortgage-Backed Securities Rating Service. Prior to joining Duff & Phelps, Mr. Jones worked for Moody's Investors Service as a senior analyst in the Residential Mortgage-Backed Securities Group and subsequently as head of the Home Equity Team. Mr.

Jones had previously worked as a tax attorney in structured finance for Cadwalader, Wickersham & Taft and for Milbank, Tweed, Hadley & McCloy. He holds a B.S. in economics from the Georgetown University School of Foreign Service and a J.D. from Yale Law School.

James A. Kaplan, CFA, is president and founder of Capital Management Sciences. He has expertise in portfolio management system software design and an extensive background in the practical application of investment management systems gathered from his career as a portfolio manager for Bank of America and for Title Insurance & Trust Company. Prior to founding Capital Management Sciences, Mr. Kaplan was vice president of Gifford Fong Associates.

Martin L. Leibowitz serves as director of research at Salomon Brothers and as a member of the firm's executive committee. He joined Salomon Brothers to form the first research unit directed toward portfolio analysis in fixed income. Dr. Leibowitz is the author or co-author of several books and more than 100 articles on topics ranging from immunization techniques to total portfolio duration to surplus management for pension funds. Dr. Leibowitz serves on the executive council of The New York Academy of Sciences, the Board of Overseers for New York University's Stern School of Business, and the board of directors of the Institute for Quantitative Research in Finance. Dr. Leibowitz received his bachelor's and master's degrees from the University of Chicago and his doctorate in mathematics from New York University.

Amy F. Lipton, CFA, portfolio manager for Aetna Life and Casualty, directs a portfolio of Life Company General Account assets and is the mortgage- and asset-backed securities specialist for the Life Company. Ms. Lipton joined Aetna from Greenwich Asset Management, where she was a portfolio manager responsible for U.S. Treasuries, agency debt, and fixed-income derivatives for a variety of corporate and public clients. Previously, she was an assistant portfolio manager at First Boston Asset Management. Ms. Lipton holds a B.S. in economics with a concentration in finance from the University of Pennsylvania.

John V. Malvey, CFA, senior vice president of Corporate Bond Strategy for Lehman Brothers, was previously director of Corporate Bond Research at Kidder, Peabody. Mr. Malvey has lectured at Georgetown, Wharton, and Columbia graduate business

schools. In 1993, he was elected to *Institutional Investor's* All-America Research Team for corporate bond strategy. He received an A.B. in economics from Georgetown University and did graduate work in economics at the New School for Social Research in New York.

Sharmin Mossavar-Rahmani, CFA, partner and chief investment officer for Goldman, Sachs Asset Management, is responsible for overseeing all dollar-denominated bond portfolios, including U.S.-government, mortgage-backed, corporate, municipal, and asset-backed securities. Ms. Mossavar-Rahmani joined the firm after six years with Fidelity Management Trust Company, where she most recently served as chief investment officer responsible for all separate and commingled fixed-income accounts. Ms. Mossavar-Rahmani is the author of two books and numerous articles on customized benchmarks for measuring fixed-income performance and risk and return in the Treasury market. Ms. Mossavar-Rahmani is on the advisory board of *The Journal of Portfolio Management*. She received a B.A. from Princeton University and an M.S. from Stanford University.

Gregg N. Patruno is a vice president in the Fixed Income Research Department at Goldman, Sachs & Company. As head of the Mortgage Modeling Group, he is responsible for the mathematical and statistical analysis of mortgage security behavior. Previously, he served at First Boston. Mr. Patruno received a B.S.E. from Princeton University and M.B.A. and M.S. degrees from Columbia University.

Glenn L. Reynolds, CFA, is managing director and head of the Credit Research Group for Lehman Brothers. Prior to joining Lehman, Mr. Reynolds was a senior analyst in the credit research area of Prudential Capital Management and a Certified Public Accountant at Deloitte Haskins & Sells. He has been selected for *Institutional Investor's* All-America Research Team for the past four years and is involved in coverage of such industry groups as manufacturing, energy, and transportation. Mr. Reynolds holds an A.B. in history and economics from Harvard College and an M.S. in accounting from New York University.

Michael R. Rosenberg is managing director of the International Fixed Income Research Department at Merrill Lynch. Prior to joining Merrill Lynch, he was director of International Bond Management for Prudential Insurance Company of America. Mr. Rosenberg holds a B.S. in accounting from the State University of New York at Albany, an M.A. in economics from Queens College, and a Ph.D. in economics from Pennsylvania State University.

Isabel Saltzman, principal for Scudder, Stevens, and Clark, currently works in Scudder's High Yield Bond Group, with specific responsibility for credit and investment analysis for the Venezuela High Income Fund N.V., the Sovereign High Yield Investment Company, the Sovereign High Yield Investment Company N.V., and the Latin America Dollar Income Fund. Previously, Ms. Saltzman served in the International Finance Department at J.P. Morgan, where her work included Latin American corporate finance. Ms. Saltzman received a B.A. from Tufts University and an M.I.A. from the Columbia University School of International Affairs.

John F. Tierney, CFA, is a senior vice president in the Fixed Income Research Department at Lehman Brothers. He follows the mortgage securities mar-

kets and regulatory developments that could affect the capital markets. He writes frequently about new developments in the mortgage and regulatory arenas. Prior to joining Lehman Brothers, Mr. Tierney was a vice president in the Fixed Income Research Department at Kidder, Peabody and an analyst at the Federal National Mortgage Association. Mr. Tierney received B.A., M.P.A., and M.B.A. degrees from Cornell University.

Francis H. Trainer, Jr., CFA, is director of Fixed-Income Investments, a member of the board of directors, chairman of the Fixed-Income Investment Policy Group, and a senior vice president of the Sanford C. Berstein Fund. Previously, Mr. Trainer was a senior portfolio manager at Monumental Capital Management, and he also served as a fixed-income portfolio manager at United States Fidelity & Guaranty Company. Mr. Trainer is author of several articles. He received a B.S. from St. Joseph's University and an M.B.A. from Temple University.

Fixed-Income Management: An Overview

Dwight D. Churchill, CFA
Head of Taxable Fixed Income
Fidelity Management and Research Company

Analysis of fixed-income securities has evolved throughout the years from an apparently simple task, that of judging creditworthiness, to the complex task of combining sophisticated quantitative techniques with in-depth qualitative judgments to establish accurate valuation. In the past, fixed-income analysts did not worry about duration or convexity; they used rules of thumb to assess risk. As long as interest rates remained controlled and market volatility remained relatively low, this approach seemed to suffice and market participants had little reason to question the assumptions behind the rules.

In hindsight, we can see that this simplicity was largely an illusion—the result of assuming away a significant portion of the valuation problem. The rules of thumb oversimplified the issues. As interest rate controls faded and volatility picked up, the rules broke down, leaving analysts and portfolio managers with ineffective valuation measures.

In time, however, analysts began to develop improved forecasting, risk-control, and valuation measures to compensate for the shortcomings of traditional measures and approaches. This ICFA Continuing Education conference designed to explore the techniques and practices of today's fixed-income managers presented an opportunity to review the variety of analytical processes being applied to fixed-income investments. The discussions in this proceedings range from the current approaches being taken by the rating agencies, to interest rate forecasting approaches and models, to new market sectors, to accounting issues in fixed-income portfolio management. The analytical needs introduced by globalization are a particular focus of the proceedings. In the global markets and in all the market segments discussed in the proceedings—and particularly when dealing with derivative securities—the seminar speakers stress the importance of risk analysis.

When viewed as a whole, fixed-income investing is not a difficult business. A portfolio manager or analyst must simply consider a stream of cash flows and assign a weighted probability to receiving those flows over time. The market provides discount rates to allow a translation of expected future flows into a present value price. Complexities arise in the calculations when the securities being analyzed are subject to significant default potential or optionality—as

is the case with mortgage-backed securities. Valuing the components of such securities and determining the effectiveness of each security in representing an investment viewpoint are difficult indeed without the appropriate tools. Several presentations in this proceedings contain discussions of tools for valuing and comparing MBS.

The primary message of the conference was that analysts and investors must understand the tools required to analyze the different components of each fixed-income security. The speakers provided a picture of the scope of the analytical challenge and discussed the details that need to be considered in creating or fully developing a framework for modern fixed-income analysis. A comprehensive framework is critical. It allows an analyst to establish a set of securities on the efficient frontier. Dependence on outdated tools or traditional rules of thumb leads to inefficient decisions, and a portfolio of fixed-income instruments based on such decisions will pay the costs associated with the inexorable pull of market efficiency.

Consider the following situation: A portfolio manager receives a telephone call and a fax detailing a transaction to sell a U.S. AA-rated corporate purchase. This offer is one of several alternatives. The first is a BBB-rated security for which the portfolio manager will gain a 30-basis-point advantage in yield to maturity. The second is a current-coupon mortgage that provides a 50-basis-point advantage in cash flow yield (based on the previous month's prepayment speed) to the yield to maturity of the corporate bond. The third alternative is a structured note issued by a AAA-rated corporation with the cash flows tied to the performance of short-term yields relative to long-term yields in the Canadian government market. The coupon on this note is 40 basis points higher than the coupon currently being received. The fourth alternative is the floating-rate component of a commercial MBS offering a 70-basis-point spread as measured by discount margin. How does the analyst compare these choices?

Deciding which, if any, of the four investments should be made requires a full understanding of the most current analytical tools because a reasonable comparison begins with establishing the probable stream of cash flows of each alternative. The analyst must make use of the most sophisticated tools available to assess the optionality in the investments and judge how that optionality affects the probable cash flows. Without an appreciation and understanding of the tools, a fixed-income portfolio manager is destined to be swayed by incomplete arguments. In the worst case, the portfolio manager may be persuaded to sit down to a "free lunch," but as numerous speakers at this conference demonstrate, when the correct measurement tools are used, any apparently free lunches disappear.

The tools fixed-income analysts and portfolio managers use are constantly evolving and improving in response to globalization and to changes in model-building, market participants, and investment products. Using the tools effectively is the responsibility of anyone charged with analysis of fixed-income instruments.

Introduction to Fixed-Income Analytical Techniques and Management Practices

Francis H. Trainer, Jr., CFA
Director, Fixed-Income Department
Sanford C. Bernstein & Company, Inc.

Today's fixed-income managers focus on total return rather than yield, and today's sources of information focus on strategic and analytical material rather than simple descriptions. Managers use the information with portfolio management tools that have become increasingly complex in response to the evolution in model building, the emergence of third-party vendors, and the growth of derivative securities and international fixed-income investing. One cause for concern in modeling and management practices is the volatile effects that the mutual funds can have on market liquidity.

This presentation traces the major developments in fixed-income techniques and management. The principal change for fixed-income investment managers in the past 10–15 years is a shift in orientation. In the past, managers focused on yield; they were yield buyers. Today, the focus has gravitated to total return.

The main reason for the shift is the growth of pension funds. In 1975, private corporate and union defined-benefit pension plans controlled about $186 billion; by 1993, they were controlling $1.3 trillion, and the estimate for 1998 is growth to $1.9 trillion. Pension funds evaluate investment managers on the basis of the returns they achieve relative to some benchmark. Therefore, managers must concentrate on total return.

Another reason for the orientation toward total return is changing regulations. Financial Accounting Statement No. 115 is having a profound effect on the U.S. financial institutions that are classic yield buyers—banks, insurance companies, and savings and loans. They must now mark their assets to market for the purposes of calculating book value; thus, for the first time in the industry's history, they are taking a serious look at the total rate of return they expect to achieve—not simply looking at yield but also looking at the effect on market value.

The third factor behind the change in orientation is the growth of the mutual fund industry and its increased focus on performance. This factor affects the taxable market as much as the tax-exempt segment, and it manifests itself in several ways. One is

that managers must show net asset values (NAVs) to clients. In the past, investors simply bought bonds and held them; they did not pay much attention to them on a daily basis. Today, they see NAVs listed daily in the newspaper, and they focus on those values and their fluctuations; they may see the value increase 2 cents or decrease 5 cents in one day. In addition, the *Wall Street Journal* grades bonds with an A, B, C, D, E, or F. When a fund has an F next to it, clients begin asking questions about the management of that fund. Similarly, every Saturday, the *New York Times* publishes rating numbers—2, 3, 4, 5, or some combination. Such ratings raise questions about total return and shift the focus away from yield.

Effect of the Shifting Focus

As the focus changed, Wall Street responded appropriately. Investment banking firms moved away from the descriptive analysis that once dominated research material on fixed-income securities to analytical or strategic research. A comparison of 1983 and 1993 bond market year-end reviews published by First Boston highlight this transition.

For example, in 1983, in a descriptive mode, the analysis proceeded month by month to show the yield curve, how it had changed from the previous month, and the month's economic conditions. This review contained an enormous volume of information on Treasury issuance—how many bills, notes, and bonds were issued and how the volume compared with the past.

In the 1994 review, the analysis shows the current yield curve, postulates a number of possible yield-curve changes, calculates the corresponding expected total rates of return, including the value of rolling down the curve, and then, by applying probabilities, comes up with the weighted expected return. In addition, the review looks at the yield curve from three months to two years, two years to five years, five to seven, seven to ten, ten to thirty—all of the possible variations. It indicates current spreads, average historical spreads, and standard deviations. The review also discusses the implications for portfolio management and what a manager should be doing with a portfolio's maturity structure. In summary, the Street research today is reaching out and saying, "Do something with your portfolio" and "Here is how you ought to be investing," not just "Here is an attractive investment."

In 1983, state-of-the-art mortgage analysis assumed a constant prepayment rate, which would provide a stream of cash flows, and then calculated the internal rate of return. Today, prepayment models and option-adjusted spreads (OAS) are available. Analysts now use scenario analysis within the mortgage market, examining not only shifts in the yield curve but also differing assumptions about spreads, to come up with an expected return that is weighted across a variety of scenarios.

The analyses of corporate fixed-income instruments in the 1983 and 1994 reports had few differences. In 1983, the review gave a complete credit overview and a recap for each instrument—sort of a score card of the upgrades and downgrades. It then provided a detailed analysis of spreads by quality class, maturity, and sector, including where the spreads had been in the past. Today, spreads are not emphasized; perhaps researchers are realizing that measuring spreads is difficult. Otherwise, the two reviews are the same, covering trends in credit quality and major industrial themes, such as the impending deregulation of the utility industry.

Major Changes in the Industry

The transition described in the previous section was accompanied by three major developments. First came a major wave of model building. Every Street firm hired quantitative analysts to create detailed OAS and effective-duration models. However, several problems accompanied this development. One was incompatible assumptions. Some analysts would assume the volatility of interest rates to be 10 percent; others used 15 percent. Some models used a mean-reverting assumption that allowed interest rates to vary but assumed they would run into a

ceiling and come back down. Others simply let interest rates vary forever. The problem with such incompatible assumptions is incommensurable output. For example, because the model assumptions were often different, an investor could not tell if one brokerage house's bond with a spread of 100 basis points was truly better than another house's bond at a spread of 80 basis points.

This problem led to the second, and perhaps most important, development in the industry of the past ten years: the emergence of third-party vendors. The critical element of this development was that it provided independence from brokerage research; it put analytical power on investment managers' desktops so that they no longer had to rely on Wall Street. Third-party vendors chased the fox out of the hen house by removing the analysis from the hands of the parties doing the securities offerings. Vendors have allowed managers to manage money in a more effective fashion than previously.

The third development, and one that has dominated the newspapers recently, is derivatives. These instruments started with futures and options; then, almost exactly ten years ago, the first collateralized mortgage obligation (CMO) was created. Today, almost 45,000 tranches of CMOs are outstanding, and they cover every possible variation of splitting up cash flows. The degree of complexity in the derivatives and swap markets is incredible. Not surprisingly, complexity often overwhelms the users, and many firms have experienced significant financial losses as a result. Recently, a prominent mutual fund failed because the managers thought it had a duration-neutral strategy—until interest rates went up by more than 100 basis points in a very short time. Then they discovered that duration apparently deviated materially from zero.

Changes in Portfolio Management Methodologies

Not only have the instruments changed, but so have the ways in which people manage money. In the past, the basic framework for managing money was to start with a macroeconomic outlook. Managers would get a handle on "the big picture" from Street economists, or perhaps their own firms' economists, and then they could start to make the important portfolio decisions. If the economists thought the Federal Reserve would push up short-term interest rates, then the managers would conclude that the yield curve would flatten and would barbell the portfolio. If the economists thought the economy would be strong, the managers would invest in cyclical companies. If the forecast was for rising interest rates, the managers would not be worried about bond calls, so they would buy callable bonds, and in the mortgage market they would worry about extension risk but not prepayment risk. In short, managers could use a macroeconomic forecast in an intuitive way to construct an entire portfolio.

The problem with this methodology is that it is only as good as the manager's macroeconomic forecast. If the forecast is wrong, everything the manager does will turn out wrong, leading to volatility in results.

Therefore, alternative methods have been developed that provide managers with some diversification within the overall process. Managers using these methods do not have to make numerous forecasts. For example, rather than making an assumption about future interest rates, managers can simply set up a potential band of volatility of interest rates—that is, use a stochastic process in which rates may go up or down and vary in between, much like the weighted expected-return measure.

For spreads, managers can simply assume a reversion to the mean. If they have measured the spreads over a long enough period and they think the world has not changed, they can simply assume that, wherever the spreads are, the chance is greater that they will move toward the average than away from it (the only two directions possible). These sorts of techniques take some of the volatility out of the money management process.

The Future

There is no end in sight to the increasing complexity in fixed-income investing. Innovative products are a profitable business for the securities industry. Elements of that complexity will involve the following issues related to international and emerging market growth, derivative securities, the swap market, and financial intermediation:

▪ *International.* The continued development of global fixed-income investing seems assured. Hence, managers who do not have international capability will be considered second tier.

▪ *Emerging countries.* This extension of international fixed-income investing is similar to (or another version of) the junk bond market. It is not part of mainstream fixed income but will stay on the periphery, much as junk bonds did for so many years. This market is here to stay, however, and it will be a very exciting one.

▪ *Derivatives.* One of the effects of complexity is that it can lead a variety of customers to overpay for derivative products. Therefore, Wall Street man-

agers will no doubt continue to create more and more variations.

▪ *Swap market.* The swap market provides managers with another way to capitalize on their interest rate forecast or credit risk outlook. It can be quite valuable to someone managing individual funds or working for an insurance company, a corporation, or a bank. For someone who has multiple client relationships, however, the swap market is currently quite limited. A firm that has, say, 200 clients cannot be expected to write 200 swap contracts.

▪ *Financial intermediation.* Newspapers recently have raised issues related to what might be called the dark side of financial intermediation. The term "intermediation" here refers primarily to mutual funds that have invested individuals' money and, as a result, have created an enormous amount of liquidity for individuals in both the taxable and tax-exempt markets. Because of that liquidity, any client can move from one fund to another—from taxable to tax-exempt, from cash to long bonds to intermediate bonds, or from bonds into the equity market—simply by picking up a telephone and making a call. Clients have costless liquidity.

The problem is that the liquidity of the funds does not match the liquidity of the underlying instruments. The municipal bond market does not have the same amount of liquidity as has been given to the holders of—the individual investors in—these mutual funds. The dark side of this situation was clear when the municipal bond market sank in the last two weeks of March. The municipal contract sold off four points relative to the bond contract, and the reason was very simple: Net flows out of the municipal bond funds required them to raise money. The mutual funds did not have a choice, and in raising funds, they crushed the municipal market. The markets sold off. The bid side completely disappeared. Selling bonds was impossible. Liquidity was gone. The municipal market did not recover until the situation settled down and some money started to return.

The cost of this liquidity mismatch, therefore, is spikes in volatility. The only answer that seems reasonable is to institute exit fees in order to somehow take away the mutual fund investor's costless transfer. The major impediment is the competitive pressure to sell the funds. So, the battle is between marketing and finance. The finance people are saying, "Wait a minute. I need some exit fees," and the marketing people are saying, "Yes, but I have to sell our funds." Only the future will decide which side wins.

Question and Answer Session

Francis H. Trainer, Jr., CFA

Question: Aside from increased liquidity, how are changes in the large pension fund, insurance, and mutual fund businesses altering the direction of investment?

Trainer: Perhaps the most dynamic shift in pension funds is away from defined-benefit plans toward defined-contribution plans. Historically, defined-contribution funds have been dominated by insurance companies with their guaranteed investment contracts (GICs). The GIC premise was yield and stable value; participants received a competitive interest rate without any fluctuation in principal. When Executive Life failed in 1990, followed by Mutual Benefit in 1991, the market became rattled. The stability of principal was called into question, especially because portfolios that are invested solely in one industry are inherently undiversified. The creative juices began to flow, and synthetic GICs emerged.

The difference between a synthetic GIC and a standard (net-of- fees) GIC is that, with the synthetic, a bond portfolio passes through its entire return to participants, whereas with a GIC, the participant receives only the yield. Today, as more pension administrators take over GIC business, they are starting to say, "Wait a minute. If I hire an active manager on my defined-benefit side, why don't I hire an active manager on the defined-contribution side, too?"

The synthetic GIC business is thus exploding. GICs are a $250 billion market, of which synthetics are now about $15 billion, and synthetics are expected to grow to $100 billion within the next five years.

Question: The bond market has experienced a fairly high level of volatility recently, as you noted in connection with mutual funds. Will the volatility in the bond market be as high as equity volatility?

Trainer: Volatility in the bond market has returned to the level of the mid-1980s, which is much higher than it has been in the past several years. Interest rate volatility is primarily a reflection of economic volatility, however, and from about 1986 through 1992, GNP grew at roughly 2–3 percent. The economy was fairly stable, so the Fed really did not have to change directions very often. The result was that volatility during this period was at its lowest level since the 1970s, when the financial markets were regulated.

The fourth quarter of 1992, however, brought about a 5.5 percent growth in the economy, followed in the beginning of 1993 by almost zero growth, and then by a 7 percent growth rate at the end of 1993. Now economists are forecasting 3–4 percent growth in 1994.

Such volatility in the economy causes the Fed to worry about what it should do: Is it too late to raise/lower interest rates? Has it raised/lowered them too far? Enough? The resulting volatility in short rates has translated into volatility in long-term interest rates. My best guess is that economic volatility is here to stay, as it was during the 20 years leading up to the recent placid period.

Question: With respect to the corporate bond market, please shed some light on the debate between absolute and relative spreads.

Trainer: Absolute spreads are calculated by subtracting the yield on a comparable Treasury from the yield on the corporate; relative spreads are derived by dividing the corporate yield by the Treasury yield.

Empirically, spreads appear to be somewhere between relative and absolute but much closer to absolute. Theoretically, they should be absolute, because spread is primarily a compensation for risk, and this risk does not vary systematically with interest rate levels.

A high-interest-rate environment may generate a great deal of concern and angst in the market, so that component of risk may expand. People sense less risk in a low-interest-rate environment and demand less spread.

Question: You noted that the analysis of mortgages and Treasury notes has changed significantly but that the analysis of corporate bonds has not changed to the same degree; what should be happening in corporate bond analysis?

Trainer: It's not surprising that little research has been done on corporate bonds (although some has been done on defaults) because corporate bonds are simple when compared with mortgages. The challenge in mortgages is predicting prepayments and duration, which is, to say the least, difficult. Aside from callability, the basic issue with corporates is simply credit risk, which is straightforward.

Question: The press has been whipped into a frenzy over derivatives. How is the trend toward increasing use of derivatives going to be reconciled with press criticisms of their danger?

Trainer: The term "derivative" is a catch-all phrase for any security that is derived from another instrument. Derivatives range from the simple to the esoteric.

In order for investors to sort out the differences among derivatives, we must be able to explain to our clients the risks of the various alternatives and the steps that we have taken to limit those risks.

For example, my company took a 1 percent position in interest-only STRIPS (separately traded registered interest and principal securities) last year. At first, we lost some money, but now the market value has doubled and we have liquidated the position. Today, we look like heroes. If we had taken a 10, 20, or 30 percent position, we would have been destroyed; the initial negative experience would have knocked us out of position. The challenge of derivatives is more than simply knowing what you have; you must resist getting carried away by taking huge positions in what can be incredibly leveraged instruments.

Interest Rate Uncertainty and Forecasting

James A. Kaplan, CFA
President
Capital Management Sciences

Two major issues analysts must decide in forecasting are what kind of interest rates they want to forecast and how to handle uncertainty. A stochastic model can be useful in revealing the aggregate thinking of the market about the future of interest rates. In basing forecasting on stochastic models, a speedy Monte Carlo-type analysis called "representative path" is effective.

In the fixed-income investment management business, expectations about the future relate directly to the process of forecasting—specifically, forecasting interest rates. The term "interest rates" must be narrowly defined, however, to be of use. One of the first questions analysts should consider is what they are forecasting: Are they forecasting long-term rates or short-term rates? For what time horizon—one day, one year, a market cycle? For what market?

In addition, forecasts are made in a world of uncertainty. Thus, the second issue analysts must decide is how to handle uncertainty in their forecasting procedure: Does the future hold a lot of uncertainty or very little?

Methodologies to Predict Interest Rates

Analysts use three general methodologies to predict interest rates—the econometric, the technical, and the stochastic, or statistical, methods.

Econometric Method

Every analyst has his or her own definition of economic forecasting and opinion of its effectiveness. Econometrics is certainly a comforting way to look at the world, but when the Federal Reserve raises its discount rate by one-quarter of a point, and the market reacts by increasing the long rate by one-half of a percentage point and driving stock prices down 50 points in one day, then analysts know that the market is not successfully using this econometric information to predict future rates. Successful prediction would not have such instability or uncertainty associated with it.

Technical Method

The technical method investigates where rates have been in order to deduce where they may be going. If the focus is on riskless rates, for example, technical analysts would examine the history of Treasury-note rates and the volatility, or changes, in that history.

Many analysts examine technical aspects of the market; the market itself is at least a reflection of everyone's thinking in the aggregate. However, the market may not be right; it is merely an aggregate of opinions. The problem with technical analysis is that the information is often quickly dated; thus, deducing future interest rates by looking at the technical aspects of the market is difficult.

Stochastic or Statistical Method

The third method was developed because of the lack of useful methods for forecasting interest rates. The approach uses a statistical process, or mathematical framework, to determine where interest rates are going, and it requires some assumptions about the efficiency of the market, where rates are today, and how rates will evolve in the future. Understanding the statistical method of forecasting is critical to modeling the future behavior of interest rates.

Key Elements of the Stochastic Method

The most basic starting point is the pattern of interest rate behavior in the past. As shown in **Figure 1**, approximately 500 basis points (bps) separate peak from trough for both long- and short-term rates. For a ten-year-duration instrument, that 500-bp change is equivalent to a 50 percent change in the price of the

Figure 1. Yield on Short-Term and Long-Term Interest Rates

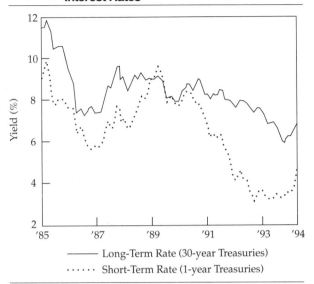

——— Long-Term Rate (30-year Treasuries)
· · · · · Short-Term Rate (1-year Treasuries)

Source: Capital Management Sciences.

Figure 2. Spread between Short-Term (1-Year) and Long-Term (30-Year) Treasury Yields

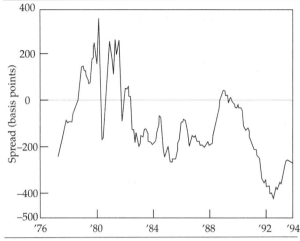

Source: Capital Management Sciences.

security, so it is not a trivial change. Analysts would be hard-pressed to find securities of ten-year duration when rates are 12 percent, but this example nonetheless provides a nice rule of thumb. As shown in the figure, when long rates fell, short rates generally fell, and when long rates rose, short rates generally rose. From 1989 through the early part of 1994, short rates fell considerably. As the rates began to come back up, they followed the same pattern, so there may be a long-term correlation between short and long rates.

This pattern is an analytical starting point, but it is not as important as spreads. Analysis of the spread (the difference between the short and long rates) shows that the differential is a function of time and can change dramatically, as shown in **Figure 2**. The longer time frame in Figure 2 shows how dramatic the spread differences have been since 1977.

The second important observable aspect in Figure 2 is the range around an average. That is, the yield curve may be positively or negatively sloped. In fact, some range over this time period captures the relationship between short-term and long-term Treasury rates. Not only is an estimate of an average rate over time possible, but the dispersion around that average is identifiable and is not unbounded. Indeed, a look at a longer history than depicted in Figure 2 would show continuous reversion toward some mean.

The next element, volatility, is the factor in the stochastic method that deals with uncertainty. Volatility measures the dispersion of interest rates, or more precisely, the standard deviation of interest rate change. The measure is used to try to capture the uncertainty associated with the market. If ana-

lysts knew with absolute certainty what tomorrow's interest rate would be, then the market's volatility would be zero. Increased volatility in the market reflects the greater uncertainty among market participants.

Volatility in any month can vary substantially from the prior month, and over time, volatility can be very high or very low. In addition, it changes regularly, although it does not change in a regular way. As can be seen in **Figure 3**, the actual month-by-month volatility of a ten-year Treasury note never exceeded 17 percent during the 1985–94 period. A longer period of observation would show about 20 percent as the maximum volatility, and it has never dropped lower than about 7 percent. Thus, much like the relationship between short and long spreads, volatility exhibits a tendency to revert to some long-term average. Ten-year Treasury volatility—that is,

Figure 3. Ten-Year Treasury Volatility

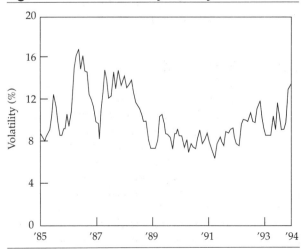

Source: Capital Management Sciences.

the change in rates—has been, on average, 12–13 percent a year, and it has ranged from 7 percent to 20 percent.

For analysts attempting to forecast week by week or day by day, the likelihood of detecting volatility reversion toward some long-term mean is remote. Although yesterday's volatility was 22 percent for ten-year Treasuries, today's volatility is unknown. It may be correlated with yesterday's volatility, because things are uncertain now and the uncertainty may persist, but it may not. So, the tendency to revert to an average is not a concern for the very short run, but over a more reasonable time frame, a generic average for volatility is likely.

In the past, analysts who looked at the interest rate pattern shown in Figure 1 would be unwilling to say anything about the pattern. The industry has come to realize, however, that embedded in that historical information are some kind of reversion and some kind of expected dispersion over the long run. With the proper tools, an analyst can take today's Treasury yield curve, convert it to a series of spot rates, make an assumption about volatility, and use a forward-rate model to create a set of possible future interest rate projections over the next 30 years. The problem is that most of these models do not provide for mean reversion (the average time it takes after an interest rate shock to revert to the mean), which leads to some unrealistic interest rates.

A more reasonable set of future interest rates can be developed on the basis of how rates behave over time and how they tend to revert. For example, the model might include the assumption of 11 percent short-rate volatility and 20-year mean reversion. If rates jump up 100 bps at the beginning, then an analyst would expect them to revert 5 bps a year. The whole purpose of modeling is to emulate how the markets behave. Therefore, the most useful model will include reversion.

Model Applications

Application of stochastic modeling can be illustrated with a planned amortization class (PAC) bond. **Figure 4** is a representation of an actual set of Monte Carlo paths created to value a 15-year PAC bond. This process of generating a series of prepayment expectations from interest rate expectations comes from term-structure modeling and the introduction of uncertainty. If the direction of interest rates were known, then by definition, there would be no risk—and no need for simulating possible interest rate scenarios. The value of the security is determined by a PSA (Public Securities Association) vector chosen to represent interest rate expectations. If the analyst picks the right path, the assessment of risk associated

Figure 4. Random Monte Carlo Method for a 15-Year PAC

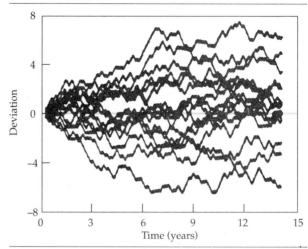

Source: Capital Management Sciences.

with acquiring that security will be correct. If the analyst picks the wrong path, the amount of risk will be misassessed.

In a random Monte Carlo analytic, the more paths generated, the better, because numerous paths help reveal where interest rates could go. The number of paths included is limited, however, by two costs: the cost of the tools to perform the modeling and the cost of the time to do it. The cost of tools is minuscule compared with the time cost. Performing a stochastic analysis for a mortgage-backed security (MBS), for example, takes a great deal more time than picking a few vectors. Generating enough prepayment paths to remove statistical bias can be quite time consuming. Using Monte Carlo methodology to value a PAC might take 1–5 minutes, for example; to value an inverse floater, 10–20 minutes.

The high cost of effective Monte Carlo analysis sparked a search for a more practical approach. Although the Monte Carlo paths appear to be random, they have certain distributions and behaviors that can be built into the modeling process. An alternative approach, therefore, uses a sample of the possible distributions rather than generating all of the possible paths. It thus reduces the number of paths required to get the same answer and saves a considerable amount of time.

The approach, called the representative path (RP) method, accelerates the Monte Carlo process to make it practical to use on desktop computers. It is illustrated in **Figure 5**, which applies the RP method to the same security as in Figure 4. Whereas computation for a single security may take 10–20 minutes in the full Monte Carlo model, that computation takes 2–3 minutes in the RP model. The widths of the distribution and the shape of the RP scenarios are governed by volatility and mean reversion. The ef-

Figure 5. Representative Paths for a 15-Year PAC

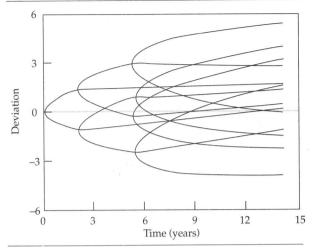

Source: Capital Management Sciences.

fectiveness of the RP method is clear from **Table 1**. The security was a 100-tranche Fannie Mae (Federal National Mortgage Association) MBS deal with various tranches—PAC, accretion directed (AD), second PAC (2PAC), floater (FLT), sequential (SEQ), and principal-only PAC (PCZ). I selected some random vectors to calculate the effective duration for each of the securities and used three approaches—the vector approach, an approach using a 32-RP Monte Carlo

Table 1. Comparison of Durations by Methodology

Tranche	Vector	Bond Edge	RP Monte Carlo Analytics (32 paths)
PAC	2.52	2.02	1.94
AD	5.85	5.63	4.91
2PAC	8.61	5.11	3.93
FLT	−0.10	−0.17	0.30
SEQ	8.41	8.13	5.37
PCZ	12.11	10.33	8.05

Source: Capital Management Sciences.

analytic, and a nondynamic approach (BondEdge) that uses a forward rate and vector methodology but does not incorporate volatility as does the Monte Carlo analysis—to determine how differentiated the results were. In the vector approach, the duration was 2.52 years; in BondEdge, 2.02 years; and in the RP, 1.94 years.

The sensitivity of each security to the approach selected varies significantly. A PAC would not be adversely affected by the modeling procedure because the cash flows, regardless of how variable they are, will not have huge effects on the riskiness of a PAC, which is intended to be protected within certain boundaries. Even so, the duration shifted. Therefore, incorporating a much more robust modeling procedure picked up some big tails in the dis-

tribution of possible events. We started to break the PAC and thus to change its duration. We went from 2.5 years to 1.94 years—a half-a-year change—in the effective-duration measure.

The PCZ security was very sensitive to the estimation process. In the vector approach, the duration was about 12 years; in the RP Monte Carlo approach, it was about 8 years; and in the BondEdge approach, it was about halfway between the other two, 10.33 years. The 4-year difference between the vector and RP Monte Carlo numbers is dramatic.

This aspect is important for fiduciaries subject to the Federal Financial Institutions Examination Counsel testing for commercial banks because the security would fail under the vector analysis and pass under the Monte Carlo analysis. It is also useful for insurance companies. The mismeasurement of this risk has serious implications in terms of insurance companies' capital, as well as the expected return they might earn on a given security. In addition, the difference is important to investors who index because using a 12-year duration when the duration should be 8 years is grossly misleading in terms of how to structure a portfolio.

One can take the analysis one step farther by showing the results of running 256 RPs with the Monte Carlo analytics to calculate duration. The values change only minimally as the paths increase, which means that the considerably faster RP methodology captures the bulk of the riskiness.

If portfolio managers use a more robust model, they end up with different results than if they used a very limited number of estimates (vectors) in predicting the riskiness of a collateralized mortgage obligation (CMO). This outcome is true for an interest rate swap or any kind of contingent-claim security for which a probabilistic approach must be used to measure riskiness. The differences are shown for the Fannie Mae sequential in **Figure 6**. The dotted line represents the results of a vector approach to measuring risk and return of this security. The solid line represents the results of a 32-path RP Monte Carlo approach.

The vector method clearly overstates the return for the amount of risk in this tranche, as evidenced by the tangent of the vector line, which is much steeper than the tangent of the Monte Carlo line. The tangent of the lines is the duration. The curvature of the vector line is much greater than that of the Monte Carlo line. Because curvature is a measure of convexity, a vector analysis indicates that the duration of this security is longer, and its convexity is much more negative. Correctly measuring its riskiness or sensitivity to interest rate changes and taking into account numerous paths and uncertainty, as in the Monte Carlo analysis, will indicate the true riskiness

Figure 6. CMO Vector and Monte Carlo Price Curves: Fannie Mae 1983–144–C Sequential Tranche

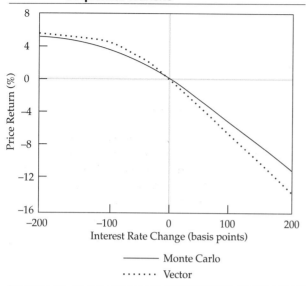

Figure 7. CMO Portfolio Price Curves: Vector and RP Monte Carlo Analyses

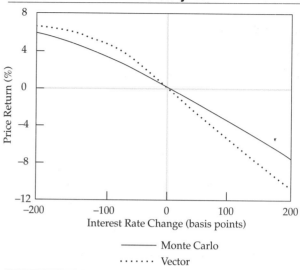

Source: Capital Management Sciences.

Source: Capital Management Sciences.

of this security. The Monte Carlo line is bent quite differently from the vector line; it is much straighter and less negatively convex.

Vector analysis generally overestimates risk because it does not account for uncertainty, the optionality that is associated with a given tranche. The results shown for the security in Figure 6 may not be the same for another security, however, because the results will be dependent on the structure of the deal (the collateral, the tranche, and other factors).

The difference between the two results is significant when a portfolio rather than a single security is examined. **Figure 7** shows a portfolio of 30 equally weighted CMO tranches taken from various deals. They range from PACs to target amortization class bonds to sequentials to ADs and so forth. For this large random sampling, the result is similar to Figure 6 only magnified. The duration of this portfolio found by the Monte Carlo approach is far less risky than the duration found by the vector approach.

Conclusion

In order to assess risk effectively in a security or a portfolio of securities, the assessment must recognize the degree of uncertainty associated with the measurement. In the case of complex securities, such as mortgage-backed securities, the analyst must incorporate future interest rate expectations, including volatility and reversion. This set of forecasts must be integrated with a mortgage prepayment model that includes numerous estimates. Given the high level of uncertainty associated with the forecasts, the analytical tools used must be robust enough to incorporate the associated uncertainty. Monte Carlo analytics were developed to deal with the uncertainty investors face.

Interest Rate Forecasting

James Grant
Editor
Grant's Interest Rate Observer

Certain financial, political, and business signs are more useful than others in forecasting markets and interest rates. In the United States, the automobile business and auto financing, actions by the Federal Reserve, and commodity prices raise significant flags. In Europe, unemployment and French monetary policy have proved to be good predictors of interest rates. In reading the omens, fixed-income analysts need to be careful not to equate economic growth with inflation.

Investors can watch for a number of landmarks to draw conclusions about where U.S. business activity and interest rates might be headed. This presentation focuses on financial, political, and inflationary omens. It also explores the distinction between price inflation and benign, noninflationary growth in the real economy.

The great issue today is whether the rise in interest rates is going to be self-correcting. Wall Street contends that it will be. The argument goes that interest rates will rise, business activity will flag, bond prices will then recover, and therefore, stock prices will rally. I propose a different notion: Business activity will continue to surprise on the upside, and therefore, interest rates will also surprise on the upside. The supporting evidence for this proposition includes the strength on Main Street and in the commodity markets.

Financial Landmarks

The automobile market and auto financing are wonderful bellwethers for both the economy and the bond market. The U.S. auto market is a laboratory of financial innovation and improvisation. In the beginning was the Ford Model-T, which was plain and black. Then came the car loan, which was plain and short—one year. Not until the end of World War II could consumers obtain two-year loans. Then, despite the anguished cries of the mossbacks of the 1950s, three-year loans became available. Nobody in the lending business was happy about this trend, but auto financing lengthened even farther. It reached its temporary apogee in August 1988 with the unveiling of the five-year loan on the Yugo—the short-

lived, tin-can, Yugoslav import. The top of the long-dated auto-loan phenomenon had been reached.

By the early 1990s, another, much less bullish, phenomenon had developed: upside-down auto financing, the state in which consumers owe more on their loans than their cars will fetch on a car lot. According to the National Automobile Dealers Association, in 1991, about 40 percent of the people in the United States were upside down, and this situation did not advance the cause of economic growth. It was little appreciated at the time, but it was tangible, and car sales simply rolled over.

Skeptics were wondering what Detroit could possibly do to improve new-car sales; increasing loans to six or seven years would not reduce the size of monthly payments by much and would turn people even more upside down. Thus arose the question of whether the market had reached some sort of mathematical barrier. Of course, it had not.

The next financial breakthrough was the lease. Without reviewing the arithmetic of lease financing, suffice it to say that, by selling only that portion of an automobile's life that the consumer actually expects to use, a lease can reduce monthly payments immensely. Moreover, most leases require no down payment. The combination of lower monthly payments and no down payment has set the domestic automobile market on fire.

I learned during the last credit expansion that merely because something appears to be unsound and antipuritanical does not mean it is bearish. Rather, it means it is bullish. Easy credit is bullish until the day it stops. Few people think easy credit in the auto market will stop soon. In time, however, the used-car market, which is now white hot, will cool, because 2 million or so vehicles will come off lease every year and residual values will decline. People without equity in their leased vehicles will be hard-pressed to acquire new ones—until the next financial innovation in automobile financing occurs.

In the meantime, leasing is a wonderfully stimulative financial arrangement in the automobile market. This arrangement is one of the underappreciated spark plugs of the business expansion, and people who sell it short may well be surprised.

What about the overall state of credit? Is the tide of credit coming in or going out? Is the United States more liquid today as a society than in the past or less? Is the burden of debt easing, or is it being made heavier?

Traditionally, analysts start with the Federal Reserve: Is the Fed tight or loose, drunk, and disorderly? In such an analysis, a key distinction should be made between what the Fed professes and what it actually does. Currently, the Fed is professedly tight. Several press releases and many hours of congressional testimony attest to this stance. In addition, the Federal funds rate has risen. The Fed is a bank, however, not the Interstate Commerce Commission or a government bureau, and it discloses a balance sheet every Thursday. Therefore, rather than listening to the chairman's speeches, you can examine his footings and see what the Fed is really doing.

The Fed is buying securities. Treasury securities bought outright for the system account are, using a four-week moving average, up 12.4 percent in the past year. You may ask, "So what?" Currency demand is brisk overseas. The domestic banking system has lost market share. The monetary base is obsolete. You may also wonder, however, whether the Fed has to grow its footings at 12.5 percent a year simply to suppress the Fed funds rate. This interpretation suggests that the credit-creating machinery has more vigor than some disinflation-minded analysts contend. Indeed, a quick look at credit indicates how frothy the situation might become; many institutions have returned to solvency, liquidity, and prosperity because of the monetary policies of the past several years. Citicorp has just reinstated its dividend, for example, and the Bank of Boston is resuming lending against the collateral of office buildings.

The credit cycle is closer to a beginning than to an end. If analysts use the ratio of capital to assets, or if they check the standard ratios of liquidity and profitability, they will find that banks are ready, willing, and able to perpetrate the next excess. To bet against that outcome is to bet against long and venerable experience.

To summarize, this tour of important financial landmarks has shown so far that the automobile market is thriving, thanks in part to the leasing boom; the U.S. central bank is monetizing the public debt at double-digit rates despite its claim that it is stingy; and the banking system is advancing lending once more. From 1991 through 1993, the Fed was easy but the banks were tight. The result was the brilliant financial prosperity analysts remember so well. Now, however, the banks are opening up, which is good news for Main Street, if not for the people who speculate in bonds.

Some evidence of a slowdown does exist, of course. Rates are up. Commodity prices have pulled back; some commodities are down dramatically. Refinancing activity is vanishing. Fiscal policy is tight. Taxes are increasing. You may wonder why analysts should look beyond that evidence for strength in the economy and, therefore, continued weakness in long-term bond prices.

One reason can be found in some humble, commonsense evidence of economic well-being. Consider, for instance, the market in gypsum wallboard. Wallboard is a principal commodity in the home-building business. Wallboard prices have increased substantially during the past year or two, but the wallboard companies report that business is terrific. The collapse in interest rates did not particularly benefit new-housing activity, so the wallboard companies have concluded that an additional 150 basis points will not hurt business. This attitude makes some sense.

Consider also some contradictory evidence in the languishing commodity markets. Commodity prices have come down hard. The Commodity Research Bureau (CRB) Index dropped from 230 to 220 in early April 1994 and is still falling. The prices of gold and platinum have fallen. Is the bull market over? No one knows, of course, but one reason to stay bullish comes from "commitment of trade" reports, which are filed routinely and disclose what the various participants in the futures markets are doing. From these reports, analysts can see what moves the large hedgers, traders, and speculators are making.

The people to watch are the hedgers. They represent commercial interests. When they buy, they do so because they need the stuff and believe it is cheap. They sell when they think the stuff is dear. Interestingly, as the CRB Index moved up from 195 to 230, the hedgers bought. Buying has also been strong during the pullback from 230, which indicates that somebody is bullish on commodities, and that "somebody" happens to be an important group of users.

Whereas grain prices are substantially down this year, the oil market, which is far more vital for industrial activity and far more important for the inflation rate than a portfolio of grain prices, is actually up. The Goldman Sachs Commodity Index is doing far better than the CRB Index, and the *Journal of Commerce* Spot Index, which is a barometer of mundane, and very important, industrial goods, is also doing well. In conclusion, the commodity markets, although movements are mixed, suggest that the bull trend in things, stuff (as distinct from paper), is intact.

Political Landmarks

People who deal in the securities markets are frequently somewhat cold-blooded about the consequences of financial market valuation on human beings. That cold-bloodedness has been especially visible and especially jarring in Europe. Unemployment rates in Europe are not only high; they are seemingly intractable. Many U.S. investors, believing that interest rates must decline, have been speculating in the European bond markets. They contend that Europe will reenact the period of downsizing and general disappointment experienced by the United States from 1991 to 1993.

Is there any reason to believe Europe will be different from the United States? For an answer, consider an important European economic bellwether—France. French policy toward monetary matters is different from policies in the Anglo Saxon world. Since 1984, France has had a policy called *"franc fort,"* meaning a strong franc, low inflation, and *la gloire.* It has also meant institutionalized unemployment. Thus, as the streets periodically fill with protestors calling for more jobs, the government frequently gives in. The result is that the franc has been trading right at (or even through) the old European Monetary System (EMS) target for the German mark. The spread between three-month Eurofranc and three-month Euromark instruments has widened from the approximately 30 basis points it was in early 1994 to 50 basis points and up. Moreover, Philippe Séquin, president of France's National Assembly, recently called for a national bond issue to boost employment.

Putting all these elements together indicates a potential for an important sea change in politics in France and perhaps throughout the continent of Europe—that is, a change away from disinflation at any price toward "reflation" and toward increased activism on social matters, increased government spending, and great indifference toward the consequences for creditors. Only 7 percent of French business leaders recently polled by the Bank of France view rates as an impediment to economic growth. The standard hedge fund bet of last year was that European rates should decline because rates declined here. That bet may turn out to be wrong.

Inflation Markers

Analysts are inclined to lump growth together with inflation. For many generations, however, the United States enjoyed robust growth and not much inflation. So, although under a regime of pure paper money the two are frequently linked, they are not, in fact, synonymous. You cannot say, "Ah, let's see, 4 percent growth this year; therefore, more inflation."

Indeed, for the past five years or so, the world has been suffering from a kind of deflationary undertow, with too much debt and widespread downsizing. A kind of viral condition has infected the economies of Japan, Europe, and the United States, and the disease has been primarily deflationary rather than inflationary.

The important question for bondholders is: When will this condition lift? When will a more familiar tendency (i.e., toward rising prices) reassert itself? Analysts can look at a rapidly growing central bank balance sheet and a very liquid, willing, and compliant banking system in the United States as a heap of dry tinder. You cannot know exactly when an outside spark might ignite a new inflationary cycle, but you can be alert to the leading indicators.

Perhaps the easiest and most commonsense kind of inflation bellwether for U.S. inflation is the inflation rate in the United Kingdom. In the fall of 1992, Britain devalued massively and, in an undignified and forcible exit, left the EMS. Some analysts immediately thought that this development meant a new cycle of depreciation for the pound sterling, that it was bound to be devalued again, and that the result was bound to be increasing domestic inflation. (The United Kingdom has lurched from one inflation crisis to the next in the postwar world. It is truly an inflation laboratory.) However, Britain's underlying retail, or consumer, inflation rate for March 1994 was only about 2.5 percent—the lowest since 1975 (when this particular data series was invented) and probably the lowest since 1967. In short, 18 months after a truly titanic devaluation, inflation in the devaluing country is lower than it was at the time of the devaluation itself. Thus, inflation is still prospective; it is still a notion rather than a palpable thing.

Conclusion

In summary, analysts can expect strengthening economies, rising interest rates, and bull commodity markets. They can expect increased inflation also, but it is not here yet.

Question and Answer Session

James Grant

Question: Please comment on Japan's trade policy and protectionism.

Grant: I have been mystified by the strength of the yen against the dollar, but in the context of an unresolved trade dispute, it is not so amazing. Lingering, and necessarily destructive, trade disputes are bearish for humanity and for markets.

The bond market has consigned Japan to indefinite stagnation. Japan is laboring under a debt problem similar to that of the United States but has failed to come out of it. It does not have workout artists. It does not have the zany, improvisational, makeshift approach that has characterized the exit of so many U.S. banks from their problems. The rigid society and rigid financial structure in Japan have not made much headway in solving the debt problem.

What people think they know, however, and what is actually under way are sometimes different matters. I am struck by the growing signs that the Japanese economy is bottoming—has stopped getting worse and has begun to get better. If so, the bond market will have to take notice. The bond bulls contend, for example, that although Detroit is running up against its capacity in automobiles, fully 2 million vehicles a year can be imported into the United States from Europe and Japan. Well, if Europe's economy is turning up, and if Japan's is bottoming, an excess of 2 million vehicles will not soon be offloaded at U.S. ports. Therefore, car prices might strengthen.

Question: Where are the excessive valuations of today, as opposed to the excesses of yesterday, that we can identify?

Grant: One extreme valuation is the Mexican peso:U.S. dollar exchange rate. The peso has been pegged to the dollar for many years. The Wall Street odds-makers will sell you a put on the out-of-the-money peso for next to nothing, but the odds are that history will repeat itself and Mexico will soon devalue—as it did in the election cycles of 1976, 1982, and 1988. Maybe the computer models of the Wall Street odds-makers do not know their Mexican history. In any case, the derivative securities desks are eager to bet against historical precedent.

Investors may look back and see that financial assets collectively constituted an extreme valuation in the spring of 1994. Maybe bonds were as grossly mispriced last fall as oil was in the early 1980s or silver was in the late 1970s. Many of the valuations accorded stocks and bonds during the latter part of this cycle will appear to be truly lunatic when investors look back.

For example, a prospectus arrived recently from a packaging and linerboard company that is part of the Morgan Stanley leveraged family of companies. Like so many other businesses that have been in the supposedly tender care of the merchant bankers, Jefferson Smurfit Corporation has not been much improved by the experience. It is fantastically leveraged; cash flow does not cover EBITDA (earnings before interest, taxes, depreciation, and amortization) less capex (capital expendi-

tures)—neither historical EBITDA less capex nor a prospective EBITDA less capex that gives effect to the recapitalization. The fees to Morgan Stanley, moreover, constitute a meaningful percentage of last year's operating income.

This information will become public, and people will no doubt speak well of the deal. Then they will note such propitious cyclical omens as an increase in linerboard prices. Linerboard shipments are up, so this conclusion is, in fact, on track, but note the extreme, the excess, in the structure of this deal. The extreme is that people look at the hideous capitalization and the scandalous fees and are not repelled. They have been sedated by the bull market.

All these extremes creep up on investors. I personally was an extreme in the early part of 1991. I had been bearish on the debt predicament and bearish on the banks. I should have known the bear market was over because I, a journalist, was making money on my short selling. The stock market increased dramatically on January 15, 1991, and it kept rising. I lost everything I made in 1990, and afterward, I realized that I had been an excess. That identity is difficult to recognize at the time; nobody takes you aside and says, "By the way, you're an excess."

Today's excess will turn out to be the past several years' yield curve. It has been this lush, prosperous, enriching thing that has given so many banks the opportunity to heal themselves. When short rates are 3 percent and the two-year note is 4 percent, traders can leverage up tremendously because "short rates only go down and bond yields only rally," which is what occurred from 1991 to February 3, 1994. The "carry trade" has been the great excess, and what is afoot in the bond market is not simply the reappraisal of fundamentals. It is not people coming to terms with, perhaps, a vibrant lease market in cars or a bull run in soybeans or in crude oil. It is a great global margin call. The yield curve has itself been an excess, and people who think about what the Fed has done sometimes muse, "Well, in raising rates, maybe the Fed was not going after the real economy; maybe it was trying to prick this bubble. Maybe it knew about the excesses."

Question: Can we also attribute the destruction of value in the emerging markets to the yield curve?

Grant: The emerging markets phenomenon was about yield groping. People would suffer anything except $2\frac{7}{8}$ or 3 percent on their money, so they did not suffer it; the Street, as it always does, happily assisted them. Not only did investors find yield, but they were able to achieve it through leveraged structures.

Yield groping is a recurring story in the markets, and because the yield curve continues to be positively sloped in emerging market debt, people have contin-ued to grope—as they continued to buy Krugerrands in 1982. People do not stop merely because somebody says, "It's over."

The collapse in these debt markets is not merely the result of an orderly and detached appraisal of a changed set of fundamental circumstances. It is a forcible and quite emotional response to receiving a call for collateral. The Swedish bond market did not decline merely because somebody calmly decided the run was probably over. That may have been one reason, but the deciding factor in the collapse was investors' needs to raise cash for other positions. The margin call of 1994 has swept far and wide.

Credit Analysis: A Case Study in the Utility Industry

Susan D. Abbott
Associate Director
Moody's Investors Service

In deciding and revising bond ratings, a rating agency analyzes the issuer's fundamental characteristics, financial data, and strategic position. Changes in competitive forces in an industry require careful re-analysis—based on which changes make a difference to company ratings and which do not.

This presentation is designed to provide insight into the purpose of a rating agency, how it rates, and how ratings change as an industry—in this case, the utility industry—changes. A fictional utility company is used to illustrate the rating process.

Perspective of a Rating Agency

Moody's goal as a rating agency is to provide accurate, fair, impartial, and independent opinions to investors on the ability of issuers to meet their obligations. The agency evaluates the protection a company's sustainable cash flow is likely to provide, enables investors to compare various investments on a global basis, and ensures that investors pay the appropriate price, based on the issuer's credit quality, for the investments they make.

Moody's rating scale, from Aaa to C, is broken down in **Figure 1**. The range Aaa to Baa3 is considered investment grade; below that range is speculative or noninvestment grade. The ratings for short-term commercial paper and some other short-term instruments are approximately correlated with this system. The overlaps indicate some leeway in the rating; that is, an issuer with a senior debt rating of A2 might receive a Prime 1 or a Prime 2 short-term rating.

Analytical Construct

Moody's analysis of a company consists of three parts: fundamental analysis, financial analysis, and analysis of strategic position.

Fundamental Analysis

The fundamental analysis of a company explores its historical and current position. The basic intent is to determine what the company is and what it does. Elements explored for the utility industry would be the following:

- service territory,
- revenue classifications (sources of cash flow),
- energy-generating sources (nuclear, coal, oil, hydroelectric),
- reserve position (does the utility have, or will it have, enough power to build something soon if it is running out of capacity?),
- cost position,
- transmission capacity,
- diversification efforts,
- regulatory and political environment, and
- management capability.

The last two elements may be the most important because, in them, Moody's is trying to understand and quantify something that cannot be quantified—the behavior of human beings. Behavior is often unpredictable, but it is the driving force of a company.

Financial Analysis

The financial analysis of a company provides an idea of how much strength it has to meet the obstacles facing it in the future. The most useful indicators are capitalization ratios and cash flow indicators, such as cash flow interest coverage, cash flow for construction, and cash flow as a percentage of debt outstanding. These uses of funds are what a company has to pay, and it has to pay in real money; thus,

Figure 1. Moody's Ratings

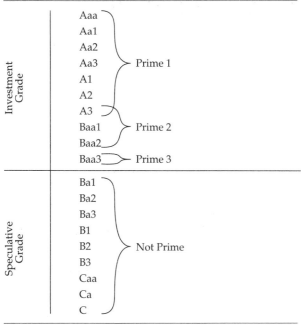

Source: Moody's Investors Service.

the analysis focuses on cash coming in and cash going out.

Strategic Position Analysis

Analysis of the company's strategic position determines where the company is today, the challenges it faces, and how it will overcome future obstacles. For electric utility companies, territorial growth, construction and resource requirements, regulatory matters, the changing competitive environment (which is extraordinarily important in today's industry), and organizational issues are part of understanding the company's upcoming challenges.

For this part of the analysis, Moody's obtains a strategic plan from management. Moody's reviews the plan to determine, essentially, whether management has recognized all of the issues it faces.

Because it specializes by industry, Moody's rating perspective covers a whole industry. Exposure to the 140 electric utility companies' plans provides a good idea of the problems companies face. The problems differ from region to region, but if two companies in one region view a situation totally differently, Moody's assesses which view is realistic and which is not.

A company's strategic plan indicates where the managers want to take the company and how they plan to accomplish their goals. Moody's assesses the following aspects of the strategic plans:
- appropriate recognition of issues,
- plans to deal with those issues,
- whether organizational and management

skills are sufficient to attack and overcome barriers to success,
- how aggressive the plans are,
- how realistic the expected outcomes are (some companies are very ambitious and others are not ambitious enough), and
- the impediments to success.

The third aspect of strategic position analysis is financial projections—what a company thinks it will gain, from a financial standpoint, when it accomplishes its goals. A company's current and projected capital structure, cash flow, and interest coverage are extremely important. Financial projections often depend on factors such as getting rate relief on a specific date in a specific amount of money. That kind of assumption is extremely important because the assumed activity may not take place, or it may occur but not on the date or to the degree management expects.

Also important in a company's financial projections is how much cushion is allowed in the assumptions for the unexpected. Some companies are extremely conservative and may not include projected returns unless the company is certain of them. By analyzing financial projections, Moody's gains an idea of whether the financial projections are actually the downside (the worst a company can do), a likely scenario, or pie in the sky.

Moody's corporate memory and a history of analyzing many of these issuers allow Moody's to establish a track record for each company. That kind of history provides an understanding of how much Moody's can depend on management projections. Many companies hit their projections on the nose every year.

Competitive Forces

Moody's major concern about the utility industry today is competition. The industry is in the advanced-beginning stages of evolution from a monopoly structure to a competitive structure, which has created great uncertainty in the financial world and in the industry. Managers and investors are not comfortable; they do not know where the industry is going. As a result, Moody's has changed the way it looks at various factors in the industry.

Essentially, five factors constitute the driving force behind change in the utility industry. First is the accelerating globalization of trade and the pressure this trend places on the competitors in utility customers' markets. In the automobile industry, for example, the U.S. customers used to be the Big Three (General Motors Corporation, Ford Motor Company, and Chrysler Corporation); they were the market. Then came Japan, Germany, Sweden, and so on—competitors working in environments and economic structures different from those of the U.S. manufacturers. These competitors have different levels of support from government, different wage structures, and different tax structures. The U.S. manufacturers found that they needed to reduce costs, including energy costs, to compete effectively around the world.

Indeed, many industries believe their energy costs are too high. The first area an energy-intensive company, such as a steel manufacturer or a chemical company, will address in cost-cutting efforts is energy costs. The National Energy Policy Act of 1992 was essentially the result of widespread focus on energy costs by industrial customers. Companies were demanding lower rates, and they wanted to buy power from other providers if they could not get it cheaply enough from their local utilities. The National Energy Policy Act codified changes in regulation that had been taking place for some time.

Among a variety of its features, the National Energy Policy Act allows open wholesale access, permitting power to be sold to wholesale purchasers through transmission lines belonging to other utilities at a fair price without those utilities being able to block the sale. The act also addressed the issue of retail wheeling—the practice of selling power directly to others. Although Congress decided the Federal Energy Regulatory Commission would not mandate retail wheeling (that decision would be left to the states), the threat of a federal mandate has changed the way companies think and operate. Moody's expects the rate of change in the industry to accelerate during the next five years.

As industrial customers continue to demand lower rates, electric utilities will face several dilemmas. One issue is whether utilities should lower rates to maintain their industrial clientele, who have choices for the first time in 100 years. Because they have choices, these companies can no longer be treated as "rate payers"; rather, they must be treated as customers. The utilities must listen to them, understand them, and find out what will satisfy them. If a utility loses one customer, its huge fixed costs must be spread over the remaining customers.

Regulators are not inclined to allow the utility companies to compensate for lower margins on industrial business by hiking the rates of "captive customers" (consumers who do not have a choice, such as residential customers). Thus, when a utility negotiates lower rates with its industrial customers in order to retain them, its margins will be squeezed. To maintain financial strength and flexibility, the utility must reduce its costs.

Cost reduction is a difficult task for electric utility companies because they do not have the neces-

sary mind-set. The industry has operated as a cost-plus, regulated monopoly since the 1920s, and managers have not worried about how much something costs. Instead, they worried about reliability; they worried about whether they were providing the best service possible to their customers. The new competitive situation requires balancing reliability against the cost of service, and it is changing the way companies think.

Changes in the Basic Analytical Approach

The industry changes have affected Moody's analysis of utility companies a great deal in some areas but not much in others. The aspects that Moody's analyzes have not changed; the questions Moody's asks, however, are different.

Territory and Revenue Classifications

Moody's is still interested in territorial growth and in the economic and political conditions of a territory. These factors are the primary determinants of a utility's revenue-producing opportunities.

How Moody's views revenue classifications, however, is changing. In 1977, a typical electric utility's revenue classifications would have been 35 percent from residential customers, 30 percent from industrial customers, and the remainder from commercial customers. The residential customers were the steady customers, and the industrial customers were the large users. The industrial customers were big, cheap to serve, used a lot of electricity, and paid more than their fair share, in effect, subsidizing the residential customers. From the rating agencies' perspective, in short, they were great customers.

Today, because the industrial customers are the ones that have the choices, Moody's carefully examines the nature of a utility's industrial customers: How much of the utility's revenue flow is from industrial customers? Who are those industrial customers, and what do they do? Is a customer's industry energy intensive? A commercial customer may be large, but if it is a shopping mall that uses only heat, lights, and air conditioning, the customer may not care much about energy cost because that is not one of the customer's biggest expenses. Are the customers likely to find other sources for their electricity? For example, if a customer is a chemical company, where 60 percent of every dollar is spent on electricity, is the company likely to self-generate or cogenerate electricity?

Although tempting, and better than providing no analysis, Moody's believes that looking at a utility's average industrial rate to determine if it is at risk of losing industrial customers is not the best way to analyze this risk. Rather, analyzing *who* the customers are is most important.

In addition, the number and diversity of industrial customers may offer more protection from loss of customers than merely a small percentage of revenue from industrial customers. For example, a utility with 3,000 industrial customers accounting for 30 percent of revenues is much better off than one with only 3 industrial customers representing 15 percent of revenues.

Generating Sources

With respect to generating sources, Moody's examines a company's fuel type, reliability, cost, and diversity. Nuclear power has been an issue since 1979 when a major accident occurred at the Three Mile Island (TMI) plant near Middletown, Pennsylvania. No new nuclear plant construction is on the horizon; so, the questions about various utilities' nuclear plants differ. Are the plants post- or pre-TMI? If they are pre-TMI, they are probably relatively inexpensive plants. To run a nuclear power plant and sell power on an incremental basis is the cheapest form of electricity from a fuel-cost standpoint. If the plants are post-TMI, they are expensive plants because, after TMI, the Nuclear Regulatory Commission (NRC) demanded a higher level of safety assurance at nuclear plants, adding tremendously to costs. Plants that were to cost $1 billion ended up costing $4 billion. A company must charge a great deal to recover those fixed costs, which will skew the utility's competitive position. The post-TMI nuclear plants are not worth today nearly what they cost to build. Many utility companies have written down their investments in nuclear power plants because, if they tried to sell them on the open market, they would never earn book value for them.

The disaster scenario, in which a plant must cease operation, is one ever-present consideration of Moody's. A TMI-type failure could happen again, or a plant could simply stop operating properly. The company would then have to compensate elsewhere for the losses or write them off completely. The immediate focus, however, is how competitive or uncompetitive owning a nuclear plant might be.

Purchased power is another issue that has become important in recent years. Many companies would rather not build a new plant to provide for growing customer needs because building is expensive, risky, and may not match the area's growth pattern. For example, if a company builds an 800-megawatt plant, demand may not grow to match it for six-to-ten years, and regulators are not inclined to allow utilities to put a plant that is not totally useful in its rate base. In this case, the company must carry the plant without earning revenues from it. Thus, the ability to purchase power from companies that have excess is important. Total reserve margin in the country is about 30 percent, so excess power is available.

Moody's considers agreements to purchase excess power a financial obligation. The situation is similar to raising debt to build a plant; that is, a company has agreed to pay X amount of money year after year to purchase power. Moody's reviews those capacity payments when analyzing financial statements to determine how much financial flexibility the payments consume.

Cost Position

A utility company's cost position is an area of growing importance. In the past, neither utility companies nor regulators cared much about costs. Efficiency did not affect a company's position except in cases where a company made bad decisions, forcing it to raise rates significantly and resulting in an outcry from its customers.

To cut costs, the utilities have had to reengineer everything they do. Companies can eliminate many costs by cutting staff, but they must also reorganize and reengineer how people do their jobs. Cutting staff alone does not suffice because it simply results in fewer people doing the same amount of work, which leads to low morale. Moreover, when the work is not getting done, staffing starts to creep back up.

Rethinking and reengineering require a bottoms-up management structure, pushing down responsibilities to those on the front line. The people who decide how to do the work are those who actually do the work, know exactly how the work should be done, and know why things may not be working. If a company challenges its employees to take that responsibility, empowers them, and offers them the tools they need, the company can generate some interesting cost-saving ideas. For example, one company discovered that, through the years, so many administrative layers had been added to the process that 14 steps and three months of time were required to sign up a new customer, although the actual labor to do the job took only four days. The company was able to reorganize the whole process by having the people who performed the work decide how it should be done.

If it is allowed, retail wheeling will open the market completely and enable free-market competition for any large user of electricity (probably not at the residential-customer level because the option would be technically too complex). What will happen concerning retail wheeling is uncertain, and Moody's is studying this factor carefully. Michigan recently agreed to allow a limited retail wheeling experiment to start in 1995. Within a narrow range, certain third-party providers will be able to provide electricity directly to customers. If a provider comes into the market, however, it will come under the jurisdiction of the Michigan Public Service Commission, which no company really wants to do, so the experiment may have little effect. Nevertheless, somebody has taken the leap. The questions now are: Who will be second, and what will their plan look like?

Because of the possibility of retail wheeling, the relative positions of neighboring utility companies are extremely important in analyzing credit quality today. Only neighbors will be competitors (a company will not be selling power from New Jersey to southern California, for instance, but from New Jersey to Maryland), so the issue is regional. With all the utility companies striving to bring costs down to improve their competitive positions, the company that wants to stay ahead of the competition must make sure it knows what others are doing and can adjust its own strategy to keep in front. This mindset of watching the competition, as with cost cutting, is very different from the industry's past mind-set.

Transmission Capacity

Perhaps the major issue for utility companies today concerns the pricing of transmission capacity under the terms of the National Energy Policy Act. The act mandates that, if utility company A wants to sell to utility company C, utility company B in between them cannot deny transmission. Company B must, for a fair price, provide that transmission from A to C. The questions to be asked are: What is the fair price? How will this more competitive wholesale market be implemented? These questions have no answers yet.

Not knowing how the competition will work, Moody's simply puts companies into two unofficial categories. The "haves" are those companies that have a lot of transmission capacity; the "have nots" are those that will be seeking open access. Who will benefit from the act is hard to predict because the pricing is unknown.

Diversification

In the past, utility companies could be criticized for diversifying into far-flung industries—such as drugstores, insurance, savings and loans, or real estate—about which they knew little. The utilities have finally gotten or are getting out of such enterprises because they have learned that they do not know how to run those businesses. Today's version of diversification focuses on something they do know—building power plants. The question for the rating agencies is: Where? Building power plants where they are needed abroad may require operat-

ing in a different culture and through an unknown language. Companies must consider how to motivate unfamiliar workers and contractors and what the common practices are in the industry in a different country. Having the right partner will be extremely important to help with the morass of regulations and tax issues.

Most of the utility companies have not yet spent much money outside the United States, but many companies have ambitions to spend up to 10–20 percent of their equity overseas. The risk of failure is significant for these companies; they could lose 10–20 percent of their equity. Thus, Moody's examines where the companies are going, who their partners are, how much of a profit they are taking, and what the project entails.

Regulatory Environment

Does traditional rate-of-return regulation make sense in a deregulated, free enterprise environment, or will all the regulators soon be out of a job? Regulation probably has a place in the industry for quite some time, at least on the distribution and transmission side. The residential customer who has no choice needs the protection that regulation provides. Power generation, however, is almost a natural for eventual total deregulation.

Currently, another major issue is how much flexibility regulators will allow the companies within the regulatory framework. For example, suppose an industrial customer tells a utility that it no longer likes its rates and wants something different. The utility may respond that it has only three industrial tariffs to offer. The customer may not like any of them because they do not suit its needs. The utility can then offer to talk to the regulators and try to make different arrangements. If the regulators refuse, or if it takes them 12 or 18 months to think about a decision, the customer may become dissatisfied and look for power from another source. The better regulatory situation is regulators who are willing to provide flexibility to companies in order to respond to their customers in a timely manner.

Management Capability

Since 1940, a successful utility has usually been one with management that knows how to deal with the regulators—can maintain good dialog with the regulators, can read the political tea leaves and understand what it can ask for, and knows how to go about getting what it wants. Managers must understand the political dynamics of the environment in which they work. They must understand that regulators, being people, do not treat every company the same. A regulation in one state can differ from one company to the next. The rules are not different, but the application of the rules may vary.

What is needed now for good management in an electric utility company is people who understand the market and who can deal with customers—not rate payers but customers. What do the customers want? What do they need? What are the challenges? What are other people doing? How can this company gain an advantage? In particular, the company is not merely providing electricity; it has several different services to offer a customer. Can it unbundle its services? How inventive can the company get in terms of what it can provide? Can it convince customers to go on a night schedule so that peak demand can be flattened, the company can work more efficiently, and costs can be lowered?

Those are the kinds of questions companies need to ask and managers need to address. Interestingly, many companies have recognized that they do not have customer-oriented skills and have sought help from people who do. They can bring people in from the telephone industry, for example, who have already experienced this environmental change, or they can bring in people who have no experience dealing with regulations but offer a perspective on and understanding of what makes a free market work.

Tomorrow's Winners

Based on the previous discussion, the company that will do well in the more competitive environment in the utility industry will be not only a low-cost producer today but will also not face additional costs on the horizon. Some companies appear to have low costs, but they have many capital expenditures that they need to make in order, for example, to comply with the Clean Air Act. These costs will change their competitive profiles.

A winning company will have adequate supply to serve its native territory and excess to sell extraterritorially. Building a new generation plant is expensive, and timing it right is hard to do. Circumstances can change dramatically during the two-to-six years required to construct a new plant. Winning companies will have low levels of at-risk industrial customers in their home territories. Transmission capability is important because a company needs to get power in and out and have the flexibility to buy from somebody else. Some companies' strategies are to buy power from other companies because buying is cheaper than running their own plants. Those companies need to have transmission capability into their areas so that they can then distribute that power to their customers. Finally, winning companies will have capable, flexible management and will operate in an environment of reasonable, flexible regulators.

The companies that will be at a disadvantage are in many ways the mirror images of the winners. They will be in a poor cost position, with overvalued assets; they may have post-TMI nuclear plants; and they will be facing Clean Air Act compliance. Excess high-cost reserves are deadly. Nobody will buy this supply from the company, yet the company must support it with the rates from current customers. In the end, that combination is not going to work. Companies with a high proportion of energy-intensive industrial customers also face problems.

Companies that are slow to respond will suffer. Some companies recognized long ago that competition was coming, that they had better seek a low-cost position from which they could compete. Other companies are only now waking up.

Companies lacking clarity in strategy will also suffer. If they do not have a good plan, they will not recognize what they have to be to get where they need to go in the future.

Protective regulation limits companies. Regulators who seek to regulate companies as they have always regulated them will deprive the companies of flexibility. Regulators who will not consider more flexible regulatory paradigms because of inability or because they are uncomfortable with other practices can be destructive.

Case Study

The following case study of a fictional company, Northeast Consolidated Power & Light, is intended to illustrate how Moody's applies these ideas to rating an electric utility.

Fundamental Analysis

Northeast serves territory in northern New York, parts of Vermont, and parts of western Massachusetts. Approximately 45 percent of its revenues are derived from industrial customers, primarily shoe manufacturers, forest products companies, and agricultural processing plants. The company has 5,700 megawatts of generating capacity; 59 percent is oil fired, which is common in the Northeast, 25 percent is from a joint-ownership position in the Dragon's Breath nuclear plant, and 16 percent is gas fired.

The company's peak load last year resulted in a reserve margin of 34 percent. Demand growth is slow—expected to be only 0.6 percent a year during the next five years. Northeast, however, is counting heavily on economic development activities in its geographical region to boost growth to 1.2 percent a year. The company's cost position is the third highest in the region. Northeast is fairly well interconnected; it shares transmission ties with 14 of the 16 regional utility companies. Thus, it can obtain power from practically anywhere and send it to practically anywhere.

Northeast is subject to the three jurisdictions of the states in which it operates. In terms of how the regulators' actions affect the utility companies, the New York jurisdiction is considered to be average, and Vermont and Massachusetts are considered to be below average.

Moody's has had a file on Northeast for 25 years. In the regulated environment, the company management has been adequate.

Financial Analysis

Northeast's capital structure is as follows: debt to total capitalization, 48 percent; preferred stock to total capitalization, 9 percent; and common equity to total capitalization, 43 percent. Its cash-flow interest coverage is 2.7 times. Cash flow for construction, at 1.57 times what it needs, is very good. With 0.6–1.2 percent annual growth expected, the company does not have to construct anything, so all of its cash flow can be used in other areas. Cash flow to debt outstanding is 9 percent. The rating agency looks at that percentage to see how much debt could be paid off with current cash flow.

Strategic Position Analysis

Massachusetts and Vermont allow a low return on equity, and Northeast, at 9.75 percent, is below average. Northeast faces relatively inflexible rate regulation in all three jurisdictions. The company has started negotiations with industrial customers but will have to go through litigated rate cases to change its pricing structure. Forest products companies and agricultural processors are prime targets for cogeneration.

The NRC does not like the way Dragon's Breath is being operated. Thus, the NRC is watching Northeast very closely.

The company's all-in cost of producing power is $62.30 per kilowatt per year. A new cogeneration facility can produce power for slightly more, $64.58/kw/year. The lowest cost producer in the region is at $25.56, and the highest is at $94.03. (These figures are not exaggerations; some U.S. com-

panies can produce at much lower cost than Northeast, and others spend about $150/kw/year.) In its financial plan, the company plans to cut costs 10 percent the first year and 15 percent in each of the two subsequent years.

Financial Projections

The company's financial projections for 1994 through 1997 depend on regulators permitting it to change its rate structure and on area economic development to boost the weak demand growth. As shown in the **Table 1** projections, Northeast expects to shift its total debt to capitalization to 44 percent by 1997, to improve cash flow interest coverage to 3.6 times, to maintain cash flow for construction at about 155 percent, and to increase cash flow to debt to about 10 percent.

Table 1. Northeast Consolidated Power & Light Financial Projections

	1994	1995	1996	1997
Capital structure				
Debt/total capitalization	48%	46%	44%	44%
Preferred stock/total capitalization	9	8	8	7
Equity/total capitalization	43	46	48	49
Cash flow interest coverage	2.7×	2.9×	3.2×	3.6×
Cash flow for construction	157%	165%	148%	155%
Cash flow as a percent of debt outstanding	9	11	12	10

Source: Susan D. Abbott.

Moody's Ratings

Northeast's ratios can be compared with the average ratios for Moody's ratings. As shown in **Table 2**, for example, solely on the basis of current debt to total capitalization, Northeast's current ratio would garner the company a Baa2 rating; a 44 percent debt to total capitalization would command an A3 rating.

Based on its current ratios, Northeast may merit an A3 rating today. The company's projections and the

Table 2. Average Ratios for Moody's Ratings

Rating	Debt to Total Capitalization	Preferred Stock to Total Capitalization	Common Equity to Total Capitalization	Cash Flow Interest Coverage	Cash Flow for Construction	Cash Flow as a Percent of Debt Outstanding
A3	43.95%	8.56%	41.98%	2.72%	93.30%	13.51%
Baa1	46.55	6.17	40.42	2.64	140.52	12.94
Baa2	48.52	7.80	38.33	2.09	104.92	9.41
Baa3	57.84	4.34	29.34	2.61	200.48	11.39

Source: Moody's Investors Service.

assumptions behind them, however, are far too optimistic. Northeast has a poor position in a poor regulatory environment, is in an economically frail service territory, and has at-risk industrial customers. Furthermore, it apparently has several obstacles to overcome, such as the Dragon's Breath plant and the pending rate cases, and is not being realistic about what it faces. Northeast will probably have difficulty maintaining the kind of financial flexibility it needs in light of the risks it faces. Therefore, if this company is currently rated an A3, during the next few years, it will probably move down to a Baa category.

Evolution of the Mortgage Securities Market

Amy F. Lipton, CFA
Portfolio Manager
Aetna Life and Casualty

The mortgage-backed securities market has been growing enormously. As they turn to their balance sheets to fund their liquidity needs, financial institutions are securitizing loans, leases, and receivables of all kinds. The MBS market is thus large, liquid, and diverse enough to fit every investor's risk profile. Uncertainty defines the market, however, and analysts are struggling for accuracy in their MBS valuation models.

The large and liquid mortgage-backed securities (MBS) market serves a diversity of investors, including banks, insurance companies, and mutual funds. It provides them with an array of investment choices to satisfy their different liquidity preferences, risk profiles, and portfolio objectives.

Market History

Since its inception, the MBS market has grown dramatically in size and sophistication. The market has reached almost $2 trillion in fewer than 20 years and now represents a third of the taxable fixed-income market. Furthermore, the unique process for analyzing uncertainty in the market has evolved to match its complexity in a stunningly short period of time.

The MBS market began with a need for liquidity. In the 1970s, banks and savings and loan institutions could not meet the demand for residential lending because they had experienced a decline in reserves. This disintermediation, evidenced by the growth of money market funds, was caused by deregulation. The managers of savings institutions realized, however, that they could generate liquidity if they could sell the residential mortgage loans they had already made. As shown in **Figure 1**, even in the early 1970s, the sale of these assets provided ample funds to make more loans.

Bank managers combined the loans being sold into large pools for diversification. The U.S. government commissioned the Government National Mortgage Association (Ginnie Mae) to guarantee principal and interest on mortgage loans insured by the Federal Housing Administration (FHA) and Veterans Administration and the Federal National Mortgage Association (Fannie Mae) and the Federal Home Loan Mortgage Corporation (Freddie Mac) to guarantee conventional mortgage loans that conformed to specific guidelines with respect to size, loan-to-value ratio, and other parameters. The diversification, guarantee, and standardization increased market liquidity once the pools were securitized. Later, private conduits obtained outside credit enhancement through third-party guarantees, letters of credit, and credit tranching in order to sell pools of nonconforming loans.

Characteristics of Mortgage-Backed Securities

Because of the embedded prepayment option, mortgage securities are different from other types of fixed-income securities. The market developed conventions to describe the prepayment option and used them in analyzing the special characteristics that options give MBS with respect to duration and negative convexity.

Prepayment

Borrowers prepay their mortgages for two reasons. The first reason is demographic—death, divorce, and moving. As shown in **Figure 2**, this demographic turnover is relatively stable and easy to predict.

The second reason borrowers prepay is economic and arises when borrowers have the opportunity to refinance their mortgages. This aspect of the prepayment phenomenon is more difficult to predict than turnover. It is also more important to the ultimate value of the mortgage security. The amount of call protection investors have is an integral part of the value of an MBS. Because of points, fees, and documentation expenses related to the refinancing

Figure 1. Mortgage Debt Outstanding

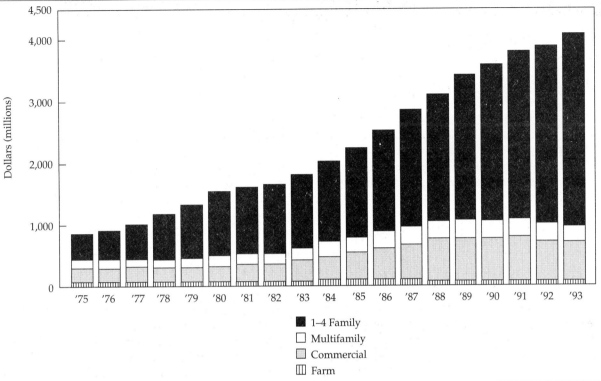

Source: Aetna Life and Casualty, based on data from the Federal Reserve Board.

process, the current mortgage rate had to fall 200 basis points (bps) below their current loan rates in order to induce borrowers to prepay, thereby calling the bonds from investors. This 200-bp cushion provided the call protection for investors.

In order to have a clear dialogue about the prepayment option, the market developed conventions for describing it. First, market participants assumed a 12-year life for MBS. They posited that all borrow-

Figure 2. Reasons for Prepayment

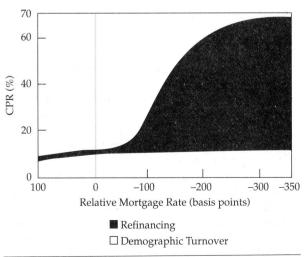

Source: Aetna Life and Casualty.

ers would pay only scheduled principal and interest in years 1 through 11 and would prepay the balance of their mortgage in year 12, at which time the security would be fully paid off. This assumption was simplistic.

To clarify what assumptions were appropriate for the prepayment option, the market next applied the prepayment history on FHA mortgage loans made during the 1970s. This study was not very robust because it considered only the age of a mortgage loan. Later, market participants used conditional prepayment rates, which described the percentage of the outstanding balance of the mortgage that would pay down either on a monthly basis (the single monthly mortality [SMM] rate) or on an annualized basis (the constant prepayment rate [CPR]).

In the 1980s, the Public Securities Association (PSA) developed a standard prepayment model to facilitate the analysis and trading of mortgage passthroughs and, ultimately, collateralized mortgage obligations. The model was a series of monthly CPRs, each of which corresponded with one month in the age of a mortgage. It assumed prepayments would increase linearly in each of months 1 through 30, then remain constant at a 6 percent CPR per month until payoff. The series was known as the PSA curve, and the relative prepayment of any MBS was measured as a multiple of the curve at 100 PSA.

In the early days, market participants often assumed one constant prepayment rate during the life of a mortgage. They could know the actual prepayment rate only *ex post*, of course, but to value the securities, they developed models to improve the accuracy of their *ex ante* prepayment predictions. They often used SMM, CPR, and the PSA measure to describe the output of the models. Investors have also used prepayment vectors, or multiple prepayment rates sequentially during the life of a mortgage, to generate better predictions of the various rates at which the securities will prepay during their lives.

Duration and Convexity

Accurate determination of prepayments is important because the prepayment option causes duration and convexity of a mortgage security to be different from those of a noncallable fixed-income security. The duration of fixed-income securities without embedded options will extend slightly in an interest rate rally and shorten slightly in a bear market, which improves the price performance of the security. This behavior reflects the positive convexity of a noncallable security. Borrowers are less likely to prepay their mortgages in a bear market, so MBS investors receive a loss of investment opportunity in a bear market because they have less cash flow to reinvest at the higher yield and because the mortgage security rolls up the yield curve (assuming the curve is positively sloped). In a bull market, interest rates fall, borrowers prepay, investors receive more cash flow to reinvest at lower rates, and as shown in **Figure 3**, the duration of an MBS shortens. Investors need to measure this negative convexity accurately to decide if they are sufficiently compensated for the risk in their MBS investments.

Figure 3. Duration of Fannie Mae 8 Percent MBS

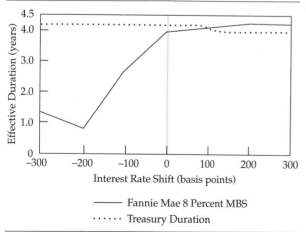

Source: Aetna Life and Casualty.

Analyzing Mortgage-Backed Securities

The analytical approach to MBS has evolved to match the complexity of the securities. To analyze the unique behavior of the MBS caused by its uncertain cash flows, investors often use the market convention of cash flow analysis, incorporating the prepayment assumptions from prepayment models. They project cash flows for the life of the security and then determine the absolute yield or yield spread between the MBS and a Treasury security of comparable average life that would discount the cash flows back to the current price. This valuation approach is relatively straightforward, but it requires numerous simplifying assumptions that may not be realized.

Investors now use an option-adjusted spread (OAS), which is a more robust way of analyzing mortgage securities than previous methods. In this process, investors use a prepayment model to project prepayments for a variety of interest rate scenarios. Then investors determine a spread that discounts the cash flows in such a way that the average price across all the scenarios equals the current price. The spread creating this average price is the OAS.

OAS can be useful as a measure of relative value among MBS with similar characteristics, but it is vulnerable to assumptions about prepayments, volatility, interest rates, and yield curves. These assumptions can make different OAS models yield different results, on both an absolute and a relative basis. Investors also use OAS in an applied fashion to perform expected-return analysis.

Another recent analytical development is the use of breakeven prepayment speeds, the speeds at which an MBS would break even with an investment in Treasuries or corporate bonds. Although MBS are difficult to value because of uncertain cash flows, if investors can determine prepayments correctly, they can earn superior total returns.

Collateralized Mortgage Obligations

Different types of investors tolerate different types of risks from a mortgage security. To satisfy different investors' objectives, Wall Street developed collateralized mortgage obligations (CMOs), which allocate the risks of the underlying collateral, particularly duration and convexity risks, by allocating the cash flows of the underlying pass-throughs. Although the CMO shifts the risks around, the aggregate risk remains the same.

Structures

As shown in **Figure 4**, the CMO market has grown to more than $300 billion in ten years. Like other MBS, the complexity of the CMO has evolved

Figure 4. CMO Issuance

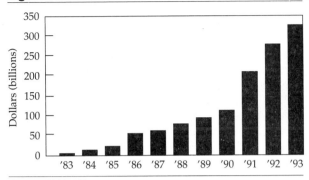

Source: CS First Boston.

in response to different investor desires. The first CMO structures appeared in 1983: sequential pay bonds, Z (accrual) bonds, and CMO residuals. Sequential pay bonds were structures in which the first class of investors received all of the principal payments until the bonds were paid down, then the second tranche received all of the principal payments, and so on. Introduced at approximately the same time, the Z bonds accrued interest at the stated rate so that their cash flows would pay down sequential tranches, and after those tranches were paid down, the accrual bonds were paid down. The residual was the "equity" interest in the CMO. The investor in the residual received all of the unallocated cash flow as the bonds were paid off.

In 1986, the interest-only (IO)/principal-only (PO) trust structure was created. In this relatively simple structure, one class of investors received all (or most) of the interest payments and one class of investors received all (or most) of the principal payments. This structure allowed different investors to act on different views about interest rates and prepayments and to do so explicitly with mortgage securities.

The floater/inverse-floater structure that appeared at about the same time allowed an investor to receive a floating rate instead of a fixed rate, either varying directly or inversely with market rates. This development introduced leverage into the MBS market because the floating-rate CMO investor could receive a multiple of the index rate on a smaller notional amount.

One of the most widely used CMO structures emerged in 1986, namely, a planned amortization class (PAC) companion structure. In this structure, the PAC bond received all of its principal paydown collateral according to a fixed sinking-fund schedule as long as prepayments fell within a specific range. At the same time, the support, or companion, bond acted as a shock absorber, allowing the PAC bond to maintain its duration. If rates were high and prepayments were slow, the companion bond received re-

duced cash flow and extended in duration. If rates were low and prepayments were faster than expected, the companion received increased cash flow and shortened in duration. Presumably, investors in companion bonds received additional compensation with respect to yield and potential total return for taking the risk of providing support for the stability of the sinking fund. The sinking-fund schedule was also used to provide investors with cash flow stability combined with some of the characteristics of IOs, POs, and accrual bonds.

Between 1987 and 1990, variations on the PAC structure were developed. PAC Zs were accrual bonds that exhibited more duration and average life stability when prepayments remained in the PAC range. PAC IOs were interest-only bonds stripped off PAC bonds. PAC POs were principal-only classes that paid to a sinking-fund schedule; often, they were backed by pools of trust POs. Very accurately defined maturity bonds (VADMs) were structured to pay off on a defined date; an accrual bond supporting them allowed them to mature as specified regardless of how slow prepayments might be. VADMs could shorten in duration, however, if prepayments were significantly faster than expected. The sinking-fund structure was also used in the targeted amortization class (TAC) and reverse-TAC bond structures to provide investors with prepayment stability in one direction.

Over time, more structure types have been introduced. Some are the Super PO, a principal-only support bond, and a Jump Z, a Z-bond that would "jump" to the first cash flow paydown priority if triggered by a specific prepayment or interest rate.

The CMO market has now almost come full circle. In 1993, cash flow (or "kitchen sink") bonds made their debut. These bonds took a number of complex CMO tranches, combined them, and reallocated their cash flows to investors willing to assume the different risks inherent in the new bonds. Again, these securities only reallocated the underlying risks; those risks could not be eliminated.

Risks

Investors in CMOs not only assume some of the risks of collateral, they assume some additional risks. Most notable is prepayment risk—the risk that prepayments will be faster or slower than expected. Furthermore, although the convexity characteristics of pass-throughs can be changed by using CMOs, investors retain some interest rate risk. CMOs also entail market risk—the risk that the CMO spreads will widen because of technical or liquidity reasons.

An important and unique feature of CMOs is whipsaw risk, which some investors experienced during the interest rate rally that began in 1992.

Some owners of PAC bonds found that, as rates fell sharply, prepayments speeded up significantly and the companion bonds underlying their PAC classes paid down. This phenomenon caused some PACs to shorten and begin to pay down. Since then, rates have risen significantly and prepayments have slowed significantly; because the support bonds are gone, PAC bonds may now extend through the other end of their prepayment band. The result would be securities that were much more negatively convex than investors had anticipated. When evaluating a CMO, investors should view the tranche in the context of the whole deal in order to understand how changing rates affect the way the classes interact.

Investors in floating-rate CMOs have basis and interest-rate-cap risk as with any other floating-rate bond, but in the case of CMOs, that risk is coupled with prepayment risk. CMO floater investors are also at risk in an environment of sharply changing interest rates. Their floaters may "cap out" and prepayments slow, leaving them with a fixed-rate bond that is longer in duration, and paying at a lower rate than the current market rate.

Methods of Analysis

CMOs must be analyzed dynamically. One way is scenario analysis—combining projected interest rates and projected prepayments to determine expected total returns. The aim is to identify how the bonds are expected to perform in a wide range of interest rate scenarios. Another method is to use OAS for expected-return analysis. OAS is sometimes useful as a relative measure, particularly for bonds backed by the same collateral, which eliminates the impact of different prepayment rates on the analysis.

Future of the Mortgage Securities Market

The prepayment paradigm has changed. Since about 1992, because of the magnitude and the severity of the interest rate rally, mortgage bankers have realized an additional cushion of profitability. The

bankers reduced the explicit costs of refinancing and built them into the refinancing rate, thus reducing the strike price of the embedded option from about 200 bps to about 50 bps. As shown in **Figure 5**, this reduction has made mortgage pass-through securities much more interest rate sensitive than previously. In a sense, mortgage securities have become even more uncertain than ever, which has led analysts to work hard to recalibrate their models.

Financial institutions now look to their balance sheets to meet their liquidity needs. Banks, finance

Figure 5. MBS Prepayment Models

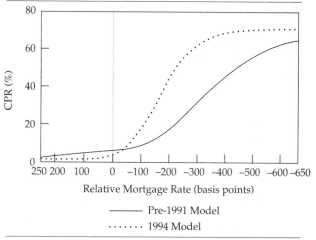

Source: Aetna Life and Casualty.

companies, insurance companies, and other lenders have realized that the MBS market is simply a matter of packaging and allocating cash flows and that they can securitize almost anything to help meet their liquidity needs. They are securitizing commercial loans, multifamily loans, car loans, boat loans, leases, and all types of receivables. This process will allow the MBS market to provide investors with a range of maturities and a breadth of credit exposures—something to fit every risk profile. Investors, in turn, will respond by trying to increase their accuracy in valuing uncertainty, because uncertainty is the only certainty in the mortgage securities market.

Prepayment Modeling in Mortgage-Backed Securities

Gregg N. Patruno
Vice President and Head of Mortgage Modeling
Goldman, Sachs & Company

Prepayment forecasting is a key factor in analyzing mortgage-backed securities, but such forecasting is difficult and complex. A useful approach is to view the elements that affect mortgage prepayments from the homeowner perspective. A complete prepayment forecasting model should include full information about the mortgages, current market information affecting homeowner decisions, past market information, seasonality, and when appropriate, the specific prepayment history of the mortgages in question. A realistic quantitative model is critical for projecting security cash flows, comparing relative value, and hedging portfolio risk.

The mortgage-backed securities (MBS) market has many complexities, and some aspects have tripped up fixed-income investors time and time again. Analysts agree on most of the valuation issues regarding MBS. They would not strongly debate, for example, the necessity of option-adjusted spreads or durations. The trouble is that these calculations require some fundamental assumptions about the likely cash flows of the securities. The cash flows, in turn, depend on prepayment forecasts, and prepayment forecasting has proved to be difficult for investors and analysts alike, particularly during the past two years.

The record mortgage refinancings of 1992 and 1993 led to widespread dissatisfaction with the performance of Wall Street prepayment models, and to a large extent, that dissatisfaction was justified. The old models were not accurate enough to be very useful in such an extreme prepayment environment. With so many of the old ground rules of the mortgage market changing, new approaches to the problem were clearly needed.

Building a new generation of prepayment forecasting models is enormously complicated because prepayment behavior is itself varied and complicated. Analysts must tackle prepayment behavior first, however, if they are to have any hope of analyzing the investment characteristics of MBS.

Goldman, Sachs has been working for many months on a comprehensive rebuilding of its prepayment models to incorporate the experience from the past few years. This presentation provides insights into the process of building—or rebuilding—prepayment forecasting models.

Incorporating History

The first step in predicting what will happen in prepayments is understanding what has happened. The largest refinancing wave in history occurred during the fourth quarter of 1993. Some two-thirds of all mortgages in the United States were originated within the past two years. The sheer magnitude of that wave was beyond anything in the market's past experience and understandably dominated the attention of mortgage investors.

In addition to what was reflected in the aggregate statistics, many distinct cross-currents were occurring in prepayment rate trends. These changes did not receive as much attention as they may have deserved, but they provide an enormous amount of information that must be incorporated in prepayment forecasting models.

For example, because the bulk of last year's rally occurred in the long end of the Treasury curve, prepayments of 30-year mortgages accelerated much more than those of shorter term mortgages. Whereas 30-year mortgages tend to track the 10-year Treasury, shorter term securities—5-year balloon mortgages, for instance—typically track 3-year Treasury movements with a lag of about two months. The most dramatic acceleration in prepayment rates occurred during the fall of 1993 when, as shown in **Figure 1**, the Freddie Mac (Federal Home Loan Mortgage Corporation) securities with 7.5 percent coupon rates (Freddie Mac 7.5s), which started off at about a 10 percent constant prepayment rate (CPR), accelerated by a factor of 4. This acceleration resulted from the 60-basis-point (bp) drop in 30-year mortgage rates, along with 10-year Treasury rates, that had occurred in the prior months. The prepayment rates of shorter term mortgages, such as seven- and five-year balloon mortgages, did not accelerate nearly as much. Starting from about a 12 percent CPR, the seven-year mortgages accelerated in prepayment terms by a factor of only about 3, and five-year mortgages by a factor of 2, because even though they are sensitive to interest rates, they are sensitive to a shorter part of the yield curve than long-term mortgages.

Figure 1. Recent Trends in Prepayment Rates

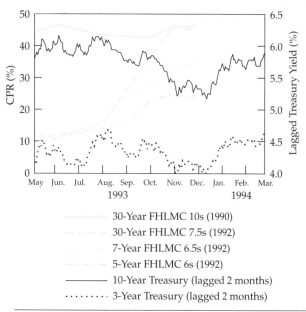

30-Year FHLMC 10s (1990)

30-Year FHLMC 7.5s (1992)

7-Year FHLMC 6.5s (1992)

5-Year FHLMC 6s (1992)

————— 10-Year Treasury (lagged 2 months)

·········· 3-Year Treasury (lagged 2 months)

Source: Goldman, Sachs & Co.

Premium securities, such as Freddie Mac 10s, behaved differently. Many of those mortgages, which were typically paying 10⅝–10¾ percent interest, are still outstanding, and even though they were prepaying at a healthy clip, they did not accelerate much with last fall's drop in interest rates. These mortgages had a 350-bp premium to current mortgage rates, and when the refinancing incentive is high enough, an extra 50 bps does not make much difference in their prepayment rates.

Different historical experiences explain the different trends for high and low coupons: The high coupons have been steadily refinanceable for two years, but the low coupons became refinanceable for

the first time only recently, and they accelerated dramatically with that first opportunity.

The history of mortgage rates is closely related to prepayment behavior. As shown in **Figure 2**, the decline of mortgage rates in January 1992, following years of double-digit rates, prompted five times today's volume of refinancing applications, even though rates are the same today as they were in January 1992. Many people are quick to take the first chance they have to refinance at lower rates, but after two years, refinancing loses some of its appeal; eventually, analysts can conclude that the people who have not yet refinanced probably will not. For investors in premium mortgages, this aspect of refinancing behavior is the most critical factor in the value of the securities. The refinancing boom has ended, and only a trickle of stragglers remains.

Figure 2. Mortgage Rates and Mortgage Application Volume

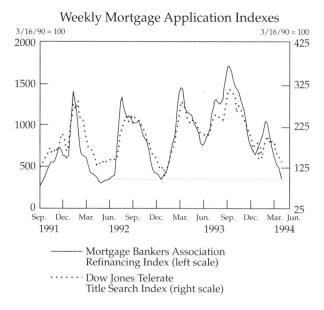

————— Mortgage Bankers Association
Refinancing Index (left scale)

········· Dow Jones Telerate
Title Search Index (right scale)

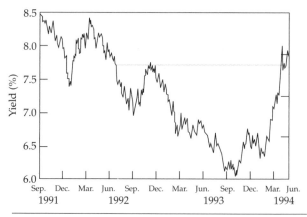

Source: Goldman, Sachs & Co., based on data from Mortgage Bankers Association and Dow Jones Telerate.

Historical Analogies

Given how different the past couple of years have been, the usefulness of historical prepayment analysis might be questioned. Is the world too different today for past patterns to provide any guidance?

Fortunately, historical analogies—if not direct parallels—to the recent environment can steer analysts with a reasonable amount of certainty toward predicting today's trends. One place to look for analogies is in the prepayment effect that the introduction of new mortgage types has. Most analysts agree that the balloon mortgages based on short-term interest rates have had a significant impact on refinancing incentives in the 1990s, especially with a steep yield curve. During the past couple of years, many people have refinanced out of 30-year mortgages into 5-year balloon mortgages simply to obtain the lower nominal interest rate. Although balloon mortgages had not existed before this period, the prepayment effect closely resembles that observed following the large-scale introduction of adjustable-rate mortgages (ARMs) in the 1980s. ARMs track the short end of the yield curve, and the yield curve has gone through several cycles since the early 1980s, ranging from very steep slopes to actual inversions. Therefore, the ARM experience can provide valuable guidance for understanding how balloon mortgages affect refinancing incentives today.

Another analogy can be found in the housing cycle. In 1990, national housing prices experienced their first outright decline in decades, but declines on the regional level occurred throughout the 1980s and can provide a learning experience for today. Indeed, the most recent national housing cycle—the downturn and the upturn—behaved quite consistently with those regional episodes, especially on an inflation-adjusted basis. Thus, historical regional patterns can help investors understand current national patterns in the real estate market as they relate to mortgage prepayment rates.

Although refinancing opportunities have never been sustained for as long a period of time for so many mortgagors as during the past two years, an analogous experience occurred in the 1980s for sizable groups of mortgagors who had resisted the refinancing pitches of mortgage originators for several years. As a result, the prepayment experience of those 12–13 percent mortgages can provide a fair amount of guidance as to how 10 percent mortgages will behave in today's environment.

Finally, the agency mortgage market (in which all loans conform to agency loan-size limits) contains enough of a variety of loan sizes for analysts to estimate the effect of today's jumbo loan sizes on prepayment rates, even though jumbo mortgages have become common in the market only in recent years. Very large mortgages are refinanceable even with only a small savings in interest rates because of the leverage of the dollar amounts of the loans, and prepayment speeds for premium jumbo mortgages are higher than anyone has ever seen before. Analysts can draw a useful analogy within the agency mortgage market, however, by comparing the prepayment behavior of recent $50,000–$100,000 agency mortgages with that of the agency mortgages that were packaged into securities 20 years ago—mortgages that were probably $30,000 at origination and are paid down to the $20,000 level today.

Analysts are justifiably concerned that the world is too different today to put much reliance on prepayment history. The complexity does complicate the modeling task considerably, but if analysts work at understanding the past patterns and applying what can be learned while also recognizing what aspects are different, they can carefully structure prepayment models to cope with the new developments.

Objectives of a Prepayment Model

A prepayment model can reasonably be expected to predict, compare, and hedge the values of mortgage securities. The "value" of a security in this sense is not necessarily the same as the market price; a prepayment model cannot predict what precise bid will be shown on a mortgage security next week. Instead, the value of a security is taken to be the risk-adjusted present value of its possible future cash flows—that is, the fundamental value of that bundle of cash flows. Analysts are trying to predict the cash flows of securities contingent upon what happens in the market environment (interest rates, real estate values, and so forth).

Prepayment models allow the comparison of the relative values of different securities. Does an investor want to invest in Ginnie Mae (Government National Mortgage Association) 9s, Fannie Mae (Federal National Mortgage Association) 9.5s, or Freddie Mac 10s? The value differences among securities are often driven by the prepayment differences among them, so tracking those differences consistently is important.

A prepayment model should also allow the investor to hedge the value of securities against changing circumstances. Investors want to be able to measure the potential valuation impact of changes in external market conditions—whether interest rates move to a new level or the yield-curve slope changes in an unexpected way or mortgage bankers become more efficient at soliciting refinancings—even without predicting those changes. This quantitative aspect of portfolio management derives fundamentally from the prepayment analysis.

The model must meet all of these objectives for actual, individual securities. That is, for investors who own specific pass-throughs or specific collateralized mortgage obligations (CMOs), prepayment models that fit well "on average" but miss by 50 percent on their specific securities do no good. Thus, analysts want a model that accurately fits the whole range of 50,000 CMO tranches in the mortgage market.

What all of these securities have in common is the behavior of the American homeowner. Thus, the key to constructing such a model is to understand the mechanisms underlying homeowner prepayments and to reflect those factors as closely as possible in the model equations.

Homeowner Prepayment Decisions

Homeowner prepayments generally consist of mortgage refinancings, housing resales, and partial prepayments of outstanding balance. Mortgage refinancings depend primarily on interest rates. Housing resales depend primarily on homeowner equity: Has a homeowner built up enough equity in the home to afford to trade up into the next higher priced house?

Homeowners can also make partial prepayments; they may not pay off their mortgages in one payment, but they may send extra cash monthly or yearly to pay down the balance ahead of schedule. As they occur, those partial prepayments are a negligible fraction of total prepayments (less than 1 percent), but they accumulate into major effects as the mortgages age, or "season."

Economic Incentives

Various economic considerations influence the homeowner refinancing decision. For example, homeowners evaluate all the relevant information about their existing mortgages (the interest rate, the outstanding balance, the payoff date, and so on). They also observe the terms on comparable mortgages in the current market: What would the down payment be; what would the monthly payment be? Goldman, Sachs combines these elements into an economic "refinancing incentive" variable—that is, the dollars each month after tax that a homeowner would save by refinancing today. Balanced against that future saving would be the transaction costs—the time and trouble, and in many cases, the up-front cash outlay required to complete a refinancing. The net result is the real dollar savings that homeowners would realize if they were to refinance their mortgages.

For the resale component of a prepayment model, analysts would also want to quantify the real

improvement in housing the homeowner could afford based on the homeowner's accumulated equity in the property.

These fundamental dollars-and-cents considerations drive the homeowner decision. Therefore, they are more appropriate factors in prepayment modeling than are sophisticated term structure models, abstract interest rate differentials, or theoretical option exercise rules. The behavior of millions of American homeowners may not be theoretically "rational," but analysts will find it consistent in key respects if they view it through the same variables as homeowners do. That consistent behavior of millions of homeowners over long periods gives a well-constructed statistical prepayment model its potential for success.

Mortgage Size

One aspect of the homeowner decision that analysts typically overlook is the effect of the loan size on the prepayment incentive. The prepayment pattern of groups of mortgages carrying the same interest rate can vary significantly depending on loan size. **Figure 3** depicts the prepayment patterns for three pools of agency mortgages (Fannie Mae 8.5s). The largest mortgages were the fastest prepaying of the three in 1993. The 1987 vintage, with a slightly lower loan size, lagged behind the 1991 mortgages, and the prepayments of the oldest (1977–79) securities accelerated slightly as interest rates continued to fall but not nearly as much as prepayments of the larger mortgages. Refinancing a 9 percent mortgage with $25,000 outstanding barely covers the trouble and expense of the transaction, so not many of those

Figure 3. Effects of Loan Balance on Agency Mortgages: Conventional 30-Year 8.5 Percent Pass-Throughs

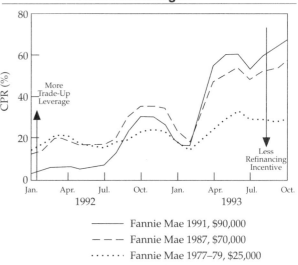

————— Fannie Mae 1991, $90,000
– – – Fannie Mae 1987, $70,000
· · · · · · Fannie Mae 1977–79, $25,000

Source: Goldman, Sachs & Co.

mortgage holders refinanced.

On the other hand, the loan-size effect sometimes works in a manner that is exactly the reverse of the pattern just described. In early 1992, for example, when Fannie Mae 8.5s were not refinanceable, the bulk of prepayments in these pools came from trade-up relocations. The 1970s' homeowners with the smaller mortgage balances had the most equity built up in their homes, so they were in the best position to afford a trade-up into larger homes, and their prepayments were the fastest of the three vintages. On the opposite extreme, the 1991 people had just taken out their mortgages; they had little equity built up in their homes, and as a consequence, their prepayment rates at that time were slow.

Thus, a small loan balance means that the homeowner is unlikely to be able to refinance but more likely to be able to move. By tracking those two effects separately and thinking about the relevant variables in the same terms as the homeowner, analysts can better capture this kind of behavior in their models.

The pattern of large loans refinancing the fastest extends through the whole spectrum of loan sizes. As **Figure 4** shows for nonagency mortgages, in 1993, even within the jumbo mortgage sector, the largest mortgages were the fastest to prepay and the smallest mortgages were the slowest. In October 1992, the $400,000 bracket was the only group of mortgages for which refinancing was strongly economical. In February 1993, the $300,000 mortgages started to be

heavily refinanced, and so on down the line until all of them were refinanceable, roughly in order of their loan sizes. The largest of those brackets, the $400,000 loans, experienced so much refinancing early in the process that they appear to have been the first to start running out of willing refinancers when interest rates began rising again in the fall of 1993.

Partial Prepayments

Discount mortgages may exhibit very different prepayment patterns from the pattern in Figures 3 and 4. The 20-year-old Fannie Mae securities shown in **Figure 5** have 6.5 percent pass-through rates, and their prepayments have been slow and relatively

Figure 5. The CPR Uptrend on Seasoned Discounts: Old Fannie Mae 6.5 Percent Pass-Throughs

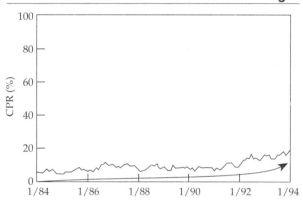

Source: Goldman, Sachs & Co.

steady during the past 10 years, but the trend has accelerated since 1992. Nothing fundamental in the housing market explains why those owners would be moving twice as often last year as the year before, and with their low mortgage rates, they certainly would not have been refinancing. The answer lies in another aspect of mortgage cash flow behavior, which can be understood by looking at the single mortgage pass-through shown in **Figure 6**.

The Figure 6 graph shows the same kind of upward trend for this pool as shown in Figure 5; the prepayments never fall below a smooth "baseline" in any month, even when not a single homeowner paid off the mortgage in that month. Yet, the standard prepayment calculation shows a substantial amount of unscheduled principal being returned. What is going on? The coupon is not high enough to have encouraged refinancing, and homeowners certainly were not moving at a 50 percent annual rate in 1992.

What is happening appears to be an indirect result of homeowners paying small amounts of extra principal early in the lives of their mortgages. By doing so, some of these homeowners dramatically

Figure 4. Effects of Loan Balance on Nonagency Mortgages: Conventional 30-Year 8.5 Percent Pass-Throughs

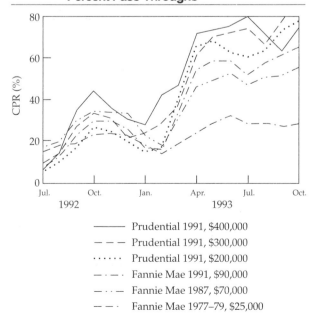

——— Prudential 1991, $400,000

– – – Prudential 1991, $300,000

· · · · · Prudential 1991, $200,000

— · — · Fannie Mae 1991, $90,000

— · · — Fannie Mae 1987, $70,000

— — · Fannie Mae 1977–79, $25,000

Source: Goldman, Sachs & Co.

Figure 6. Misspecified Amortization: Ginnie Mae Pool 1666 (5.5 Percent Pass-Through)

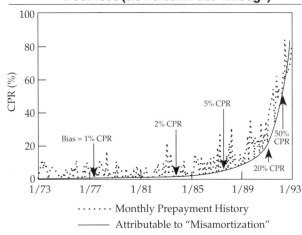

.... Monthly Prepayment History
———— Attributable to "Misamortization"

Source: Goldman, Sachs & Co.

Figure 7. Refinancing and Burnout "Layers" in Premium Fannie Mae Pass-Throughs

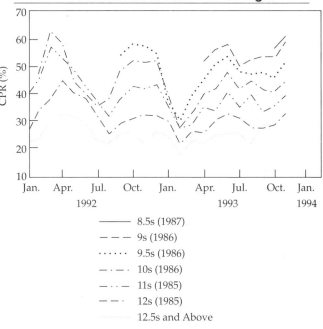

———— 8.5s (1987)
– – – 9s (1986)
· · · · · 9.5s (1986)
– · – · 10s (1986)
– · · – 11s (1985)
– – · 12s (1985)
12.5s and Above

Source: Goldman, Sachs & Co.

shortened the remaining terms of their mortgages. (Surprisingly few dollars are needed to shorten the term of 30-year mortgages to 27–29 years.) As the maturity of the pool approached, more and more mortgages ended up with principal balances being paid off ahead of schedule, and these exponentially accelerating paydowns appear in the data as unscheduled prepayments. To estimate the cash flows to the security holder as accurately as possible, analysts must incorporate this effect into their prepayment models.

Refinancing Burnout

Some aspects of prepayment behavior run counter to intuition. For example, one would generally expect that the higher the interest rate on existing mortgages, the more likely homeowners would be to refinance those mortgages. At year-end 1993, however, as **Figure 7** shows, exactly the reverse was true. The Fannie Mae 8.5s were the fastest to prepay. Each step up in coupon was accompanied by a step down in prepayment rates so that, in fact, the highest coupons were the slowest to prepay.

Another contrary pattern in Figure 7 is the trend over time. From 1992 through the end of 1993, mortgage rates declined dramatically—more than 200 bps. Yet, refinancings on Fannie Mae 10s were at their fastest at the beginning of 1992. Even as mortgage rates dropped, the 10s never regained their previous prepayment peak; in fact, at every stage of the two-year rally, each peak was lower than the previous one.

This phenomenon is the "refinancing burnout" effect—a gradual reduction in prepayment rates as the most efficient refinancers leave the pool. Homeowners who are most responsive to falling interest rates will be the first to refinance and leave the pool.

With only the less responsive homeowners left in the pool, at the next drop in interest rates, prepayment rates rise but not as high as they did previously. By year-end 1993, as shown in Figure 7, the 12.5s, which have been refinanceable for many years, show almost no sensitivity to further declines in interest rates. Their rate of refinancings remains slow and steady throughout the period.

Burnout is the most complicated aspect of prepayment behavior to model or forecast, and it has tripped up most mortgage investors during the past two years. As virtually the entire mortgage market fell into the refinanceable category by year-end 1993, burnout became the primary issue of mortgage prepayment analysis. Investors were aware of the phenomenon in general terms but were not sure if its effect was to produce a sharply declining trend in refinancing or a gradual trend that stretched out slowly. They did not know how much of a pickup in prepayment rates to expect for a coupon that had experienced, for instance, a year or two of refinancing. Would it accelerate or level off? If it accelerated, how fast would it get?

Because the burnout phenomenon arises from the changing composition of the homeowners in the mortgage pool over time, those changes must be incorporated into prepayment models. Goldman, Sachs tracks refinancing by looking at three dimensions of homeowner incentives. That is, for a mortgage to be refinanced in any given month, the homeowner must be "ready," "willing," and "able" to do the transaction.

We consider mortgage holders *willing* to refinance if the economic incentive is high enough to meet their requirements. Thus, when mortgage rates fall, a high number of mortgagors become willing to refinance. As mortgage rates rise, some cease to be willing.

Whether homeowners are *able* to refinance is a different question. It could be a question of credit situation or of resources, and ability is largely independent of interest rate levels. Do mortgage holders have the cash, the equity, or the time to do the transaction? Do homeowners think they will stay in their houses or be leaving them soon? (Refinancing a mortgage about to be paid off is pointless.) The able–unable classification can change over time as homeowners lose jobs, find jobs, and so forth. People constantly flow across the boundary of the able and unable categories, but making the distinction is important.

Finally, only a fraction of the mortgagors who are willing and able to refinance are *ready* to actually do so in any given month. The maximum prepayment rate of a diversified mortgage pool is 12–15 percent a month and is generally a question of timing. The homeowner might not prepay one particular month for reasons such as uncertainty about interest rates, procrastination, or being too busy to do it. Some homeowners will simply never prepay, no matter how much of an interest rate differential exists. Moreover, refinancing is not necessarily a question of sophistication; sometimes even the most sophisticated homeowners simply never get around to taking the refinancing step.

The Goldman, Sachs refinancing model tracks the entire distribution of homeowners across the ready, willing, and able dimensions from the time the pool is first originated as it evolves in reaction to the interest rates the homeowners see over time. From this tracking, we can estimate how many homeowners in any given pool are waiting to refinance if mortgage rates drop another, say, 50 bps.

Even relatively high coupon premium mortgages can have a substantial amount of interest rate sensitivity. **Figure 8** shows the prepayment experience of Fannie Mae 9.5 percent pass-throughs from January 1992 through late 1993 and their projected behavior through 1995. If mortgage rates stay at a fairly low level, the burnout phenomenon is expected to cause a steady trailing off in prepayment rates. When interest rates fall further, the slowdown takes longer to occur; when interest rates rise, especially to levels that have not been seen for several years, the prepayment rate falls sharply.

Figure 8. Prepayment Projections for High Premiums

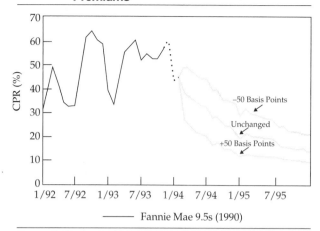

Source: Goldman, Sachs & Co.

Valuation

No single valuation measure can ever provide a complete picture of a security, but in combination, a variety of analytical measures can offer considerable information about the security's behavior. **Table 1** shows such a combination. The table depicts a typical mortgage-market quote sheet for January 1994, showing Fannie Mae pass-throughs with coupons ranging from 6 percent to 10 percent. The measures of price, static yield, average life, static spread, and 12-month CPR are static valuation measures; that is, they measure the security's characteristics assuming unchanged interest rates. Short- and long-term prepayment projections are used to predict how cash flows will behave, and these cash flows are then used to compute a yield and average life for the security. The static spread measure determines how many basis points above the Treasury yield curve would be necessary to discount the individual cash flows of the mortgage to match the market price.

The key with static measures is to get the cash flows right. Wrong cash flows cause everything else to be wrong in the analysis, and further analysis is then useless.

Once analysts are comfortable with their static prepayment forecasts in CPR and yield terms, then they can move to the next level of analysis. Option-adjusted spread (OAS) analysis is a more comprehensive way of viewing the valuation of a mortgage-backed security than static (unchanged or base-case) analysis, which does not take into account the risks of the MBS under changing market conditions. For true understanding of an MBS, analysts must simulate the distribution of future cash flows under hundreds of different interest rate assumptions, because the yield curve can vary in a volatile way and mortgage prepayments and cash flows vary

Table 1. Mortgage Valuation Summary

Fannie Mae Security Coupon Rate (percent)	WAC[a]	WAM[b]	Age	Settlement Date	Price	Static Yield	Average Life	Static Spread	CPR 12 Month	CPR Long-Term	Option-Adjusted Spread	Option-Adjusted Duration	Gain from Convexity	Volatility Sensitivity	Prepayment Sensitivity	Hedge Ratios 2 Year	Hedge Ratios 10 Year	12-month Rate of Return -200	12-month Rate of Return 0	12-month Rate of Return 200
6.0	6.65	358	2	2/14	97–08	6.45	9.6	56	3	7	44	6.3	0.04	-0.15	-0.34	0.00	0.84	15.17	6.70	-4.20
6.5	7.15	358	2	2/14	100–02	6.51	9.4	65	3	7	48	5.9	-0.08	-0.21	-0.22	0.08	0.79	12.39	6.75	-3.79
7.0	7.68	345	15	2/14	102–10	6.58	7.9	84	8	10	58	4.7	-0.48	-0.26	-0.09	0.21	0.60	8.70	6.63	-2.50
7.5	8.06	344	16	2/14	104–01	6.57	6.4	92	20	13	62	3.2	-0.75	-0.30	0.05	0.28	0.39	6.50	6.19	-1.26
8.0	8.55	341	19	2/14	105–10	6.34	4.6	85	32	19	62	1.9	-0.64	-0.27	0.23	0.32	0.20	5.55	5.48	0.22
8.5	9.13	331	29	2/14	105–24	5.75	2.8	63	45	31	58	1.3	-0.13	-0.17	0.41	0.41	0.09	5.96	4.73	1.77
9.0	9.57	329	31	2/14	106–25	5.73	2.7	67	44	31	68	1.4	-0.06	-0.14	0.52	0.47	0.09	6.31	4.77	2.19
9.5	10.09	317	43	2/15	108–20	5.56	2.8	51	41	30	57	1.7	0.06	-0.09	0.67	0.55	0.12	7.06	4.76	2.26
10.0	10.64	305	55	2/15	110–09	5.64	3.0	53	39	28	66	1.7	0.15	-0.09	0.77	0.56	0.12	7.43	4.86	2.31

Note: Pricing occurred January 13, 1994; analysis as of January 18, 1994.

[a]Weighted-average coupon (gross percent).

[b]Weighted-average maturity (months).

Source: Goldman, Sachs & Co.

correspondingly. OAS analysis takes these variations into account.

In considering the use of OAS analysis, analysts may debate what constitutes a realistic yield-curve simulation (is it a normal random walk or a lognormal random walk; is it single factor or multifactor; is it mean reverting or not?), but these are questions of detail. That the OAS measure is superior to any static measure receives little argument.

The sensitivity of the value of the security to a shift in the yield curve, assuming an unchanged OAS, is the option-adjusted duration—what the change in the value of a mortgage security would be for every 100 bps the yield curve is shifted, taking into account changes in the simulated yield curves and prepayment rates and cash flows. The results of that full simulation paint a very different picture from the static picture.

For example, the Fannie Mae 8 percent pass-through in Table 1 shows an average life of 4.6 years as of January 1994, but the duration of that security on an option-adjusted basis was, in fact, only 1.9 years. That 8 percent coupon was on the margin of refinanceability at the time, so a small increase in interest rates would have slowed down the cash flows substantially and a small decrease in interest rates would have accelerated the prepayments dramatically. A static analysis does not consider this variability and thus would have given a very misleading view of this security.

Interest rate sensitivity can severely hamper the performance of a security as interest rates diverge from the base case, and we can measure this effect by using the convexity of the security in Table 1. How much does the security underperform equivalent-duration Treasuries if interest rates move 100 bps in either direction? If investors did not adjust the duration of their hedge positions as interest rates made their big move in the first quarter of 1994, they found that portfolios with negative convexity substantially underperformed the Treasury market. Mortgage investors must monitor the Treasury market constantly because, with every move in interest rates, the durations of mortgage securities are changing and their hedges must be adjusted.

Sensitivity to volatility quantifies how much the value of the mortgage is likely to suffer if Treasury yield volatility increases by 10 percent. When investors suddenly start pricing in the risk of large interest rate changes, as they did in the first quarter of 1994, that development hurts the value of mortgage securities because adverse scenarios are more likely to occur. The premium securities in the middle-coupon range, such as those in the middle of Table 1, suffer the most.

An option-adjusted spread, even with all that goes into the calculation, still tells only part of the story. Investors should certainly use an option-adjusted spread as a foundation, but they should go a step further to consider which of the various assumptions in the OAS analysis could go wrong. What are the security's sensitivities to the risks not incorporated in the OAS framework? For example, the option-adjusted spread is calculated with the assumption that the prepayment model is permanently 100 percent accurate. Prepayment sensitivity tells the analyst what will happen if future prepayments are 10 percent slower than projected. It reveals the effect on the pass-through if analysts were to keep the same option-adjusted spread for the security but slow down their prepayment model by 10 percent. For the lowest coupons, slower prepayments hurt the value, and for the highest coupons, slower prepayments help the value. That kind of information shows up in the prepayment sensitivity measure.

Not all of these risks can be hedged, but some can. For example, the level and slope of the yield curve are two factors whose portfolio effects can be hedged. Investors can immunize themselves to small changes in either the level or the slope of the yield curve by offsetting their mortgage holdings with the amounts of two- and ten-year Treasuries indicated by the hedge ratios that emerge from the model's analysis.

Another important tool for assessing mortgage security behavior is scenario analysis. It can give analysts more insight into how the bond could behave than simply looking at a summary measure, such as option-adjusted spread or duration. In scenario analysis, questions include the following: If interest rates rise, what will the bond look like in a year? What is the actual return profile likely to be? Scenario analysis does not eliminate the reliance on assumptions, however; a terminal price assumption for the end of the holding period must still be made. This price is typically set by assuming the same option-adjusted spread as today, which comes down again to the model forecasting prepayments.

Table 2 provides an illustration of how dynamic the factors in mortgage analysis can be in a rapidly changing market by showing a quote sheet from six separate levels of the market sell-off through the past quarter. In January, the mortgage security trading at parity (the "current coupon") had a yield of 6.42 percent. Analysis of the 30-year Fannie Mae sector indicates that durations were as short as 1.3 years on 8.5s. As the market sold off through the spring and yield levels continued to rise, durations changed dramatically. In April, the duration on those same 8.5s had almost tripled, to just under 4 years. Mortgage pass-throughs almost always extend in dura-

Table 2. Mortgage Valuation at Six Stages of the 1994 Market Sell-Off

Fannie Mae Coupon	Option-Adjusted Spread	Duration	12-Month CPR	Long-Term CPR
Thursday, January 13 (current coupon mortgage yield = 6.42 percent)				
6.0	44	6.3	3	7
6.5	48	5.9	3	7
7.0	58	4.7	8	10
7.5	62	3.2	20	13
8.0	62	1.9	32	19
8.5	58	1.3	45	31
9.0	68	1.4	44	31
9.5	57	1.7	41	30
10.0	66	1.7	39	28
Wednesday, February 23 (current coupon mortgage yield = 6.85 percent)				
6.0	44	6.3	3	7
6.5	47	6.1	3	7
7.0	51	5.6	3	8
7.5	51	4.4	4	9
8.0	54	3.1	17	12
8.5	42	1.7	34	21
9.0	50	1.7	35	23
9.5	56	1.9	33	23
10.0	57	1.9	33	24
Wednesday, March 2 (current coupon mortgage yield = 7.01 percent)				
6.0	46	6.3	3	7
6.5	49	6.1	3	7
7.0	51	5.7	3	7
7.5	50	4.7	4	8
8.0	52	3.5	12	11
8.5	37	2.0	31	19
9.0	43	1.9	33	22
9.5	46	2.0	32	22
10.0	43	2.0	32	23
Friday, March 11 (current coupon mortgage yield = 7.25 percent)				
6.0	54	6.4	3	7
6.5	53	6.2	3	7
7.0	55	5.8	3	7
7.5	55	5.1	4	8
8.0	61	4.1	7	9
8.5	55	2.5	23	15
9.0	60	2.3	29	19
9.5	59	2.2	29	20
10.0	51	2.0	29	21
Monday, March 28 (current coupon mortgage yield = 7.45 percent)				
6.0	60	6.4	3	7
6.5	61	6.2	3	7
7.0	63	5.9	3	7
7.5	66	5.2	4	7
8.0	72	4.4	5	8
8.5	68	3.0	17	12
9.0	70	2.6	25	16
9.5	69	2.5	26	18
10.0	60	2.2	26	19
Friday, April 8 (current coupon mortgage yield = 7.75 percent)				
6.0	63	6.3	3	7
6.5	62	6.2	3	7
7.0	62	5.9	3	7
7.5	63	5.4	4	7
8.0	66	4.8	5	8
8.5	66	3.6	9	10
9.0	69	3.0	20	14
9.5	68	2.8	23	16
10.0	66	2.6	24	18

Source: Goldman, Sachs & Co.

tion during a market sell-off, so their prices will tend to underperform Treasuries. In a rallying market, mortgages will shorten and, again, their prices will tend to underperform Treasuries. When Treasuries move sharply in either direction, the mortgage market is almost guaranteed to underperform on a price basis, and that risk is built into the extra yield cushion of mortgage securities.

At each level of the market sell-off, the option-adjusted spreads were fairly uniform across all of the coupons shown in Table 2. The mortgage pass-through market is not 3-bp efficient the way Treasury trading would be, but things are not widely out of line, primarily because of the accuracy of the prepayment forecast behind these option-adjusted spreads. Many models will show a bias. If the model is too slow on prepayment rates, for example, it will chronically show the highest coupons with the highest option-adjusted spreads. In effect, it will always recommend buying premium mortgages because it underpredicts how quickly they will be prepaying. Many analysts have used this bias as an excuse to discard OAS analysis as irrelevant. If the prepayment rates and cash flows are accurate from the beginning, however, the results will be much more realistic. Appropriately calculated option-adjusted spreads make the mortgage pass-through market look substantially more efficient than other approaches do, and the resulting duration calculations are much more in line with the way the securities actually trade.

In summary, model inputs should include mortgage information (type, coupon, origination date, loan size), current market information affecting the homeowner decision (mortgage rates, transaction costs, home appreciation rates, tax rates, regulations), past market information (prior refinancing opportunities), seasonality (for both resales and refinancings), and as an optional input, the specific prepayment history of the mortgage in question. This last information is important because, even after accounting for mortgage rate, loan size, and so forth, not all MBS will behave like the average mortgage. **Figure 9** provides a sense of the magnitude of these differences.

All the MBS in Figure 9 are high-premium Fannie Mae pass-throughs with 10 percent coupons. All five groups are recent originations, with essentially the same mortgage rate, are nationally diversified, and are about the same in average loan size. Yet, between one mortgage originator and another, the prepayment difference can be more than a factor of 2. This difference can translate into enormous performance differences; the prepayment difference between the pass-throughs of issuers A and B, for example, amounted to a difference in rate of return

Figure 9. Quarterly Prepayment Rates on Fannie Mae 10 Percent Pass-Throughs

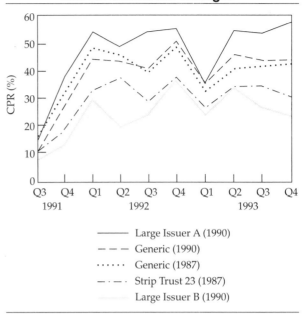

Source: Goldman, Sachs & Co.

of more than 200 bps during the two-year period. Nothing in the data on the securities could have explained why. Perhaps one issuer has a different sort of clientele for mortgage originations; perhaps one solicits refinancings more aggressively when it goes into the servicing phase. Regardless of the reason, when analysts see such prepayment differentials, they should search for appropriate ways to build them into the valuation analysis.

When comparing different mortgage securities, investors may find the prepayment patterns to be fairly similar, as shown in **Figure 10**; when those

Figure 10. Relative-Value Dependency on Relative Prepayment Rates

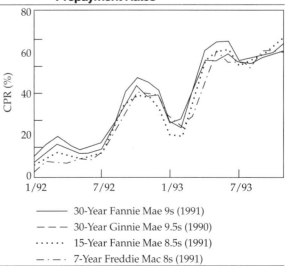

Source: Goldman, Sachs & Co.

similarities are faithfully captured within the prepayment model, investors can make intelligent choices among those securities. Investors should make sure, however, that they are not trying to value an atypical security in a generic way. They should compare the prepayment history of a mortgage security with the average prepayment behavior of similar securities to determine whether they have a "normal" mortgage security or an outlier.

Various aspects of risk analysis that investors should perform on their mortgage securities are illustrated in **Figure 11**. As with the analysis of interest rate risk for fixed-income securities, MBS investors should not settle for a one-factor measure of prepayment risk. Although yield curves can

Figure 11. Multiple Dimensions of Risk Analysis

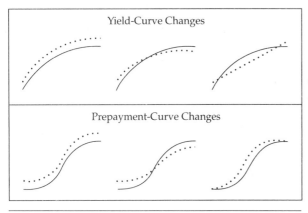

Source: Goldman, Sachs & Co.

move in parallel, they often do not. Investors cannot say they have no interest rate risk in a portfolio if it passes the test of a parallel yield-curve shift but fails the test of a flattening yield curve.

Similarly, astute mortgage investors should take into account the separate aspects of prepayment risk. They can speed up or slow down the entire range of prepayment activity by a factor of 10 percent, as shown in the lower left sketch of Figure 11, and see how that affects value.

They should also consider what would happen if relocations were to speed up prepayments for the lower coupons and the refinancing were actually to slow down prepayments for the higher coupons, as

shown in the lower middle sketch of Figure 11.

Additionally, investors should consider scenarios, along the lines of the past two years, during which the prepayment curve shifted a bit toward the lower coupons, as shown in the lower right sketch of Figure 11. As transaction costs came down, the homeowner costs that figure into the refinancing incentive diminished; the refinancing incentive for a given coupon level rose. The slowest and fastest prepayment rates stayed roughly the same, but investors owning coupons in the middle, where the shift of the prepayment curve had the greatest impact, might not have predicted that refinancing costs would decrease as much as they did and, therefore, might have misestimated their cash flows. To assess their exposure to a prepayment shift of this type, they could have run simulated experiments on the value of their holdings. This kind of quantitative risk management is critical when security valuations are contingent on changes in today's dynamic mortgage industry.

Summary

For a complete prepayment forecasting model, analysts must consider much more than the simple interest rate differential. The model must take into account the size of the mortgages and the various real dollar incentives affecting the various homeowner prepayment decisions.

Looking at the elements that affect mortgage prepayments from the homeowner perspective can give analysts considerable insight into why prepayments have behaved the way they have—not only for the past two years but for the past two decades. Moreover, tracking the composition of mortgage pools as to whether homeowners are ready, willing, and able to refinance can enhance the analyst's understanding of how mortgage refinancing actually takes place.

Finally, by analyzing all of their securities on a consistent basis and monitoring the impact of changing assumptions, investors can perform the most appropriate valuation analysis, scenario analysis, and risk analysis on the full complement of mortgage securities in their portfolios.

Question and Answer Session

Gregg N. Patruno

Question: Given the current profile of the MBS market, if rates continue to rise, will we experience unprecedented extensions that are not captured by current models?

Patruno: In the Fannie Mae and Freddie Mac sectors, most of the extension that can happen has already happened. People could have refinanced at today's mortgage rates two years ago. If they have not already done so, they probably will not; so, the market is experiencing close to the slowest prepayment rates possible. The next 100 bps in potential interest rate rise would have a much less dramatic effect than the last 100 bps.

The Ginnie Mae mortgage sector has some unusual extension potential: The underlying mortgages are assumable by the buyer if the homes are sold. If a current homeowner locked in a 6.5 percent mortgage rate last fall, that house could change hands four times during the next ten years. That same original mortgage might be passed on from one buyer to the next like a treasured heirloom because that 6.5 percent is looking like the mortgage rate of a lifetime. So, these mortgages have the unique ability to prepay even more slowly than the rate at which people are selling their homes. Therefore, the Ginnie Mae sector is where most of any further extension would come from in the mortgage market.

Question: Please comment on the usefulness of the Public Securities Association (PSA) curve; will it be adjusted in any particular way?

Patruno: The PSA curve was introduced in the mid-1980s as a simplified yardstick for how prepayment rates behave for current coupon mortgages. If interest rates never move, the PSA curve says the prepayment rate would start at zero, rise gradually for 2.5 years, and then stay at a steady 6 percent annual rate thereafter. The PSA curve was intended for current coupon securities, so last year when the whole market was at a premium, the PSA curve was of limited usefulness. When premium mortgages are refinanceable, homeowners certainly do not wait 2.5 years to act; the time frame is much shorter. Now that premium refinancing is dwindling in importance, the PSA curve should become much more useful than it was at the height of the refinancing wave.

Question: Did the 1985–86 mortgage pool of homeowners overpay for their homes and thus could not come up with the big principal payments needed for refinancing?

Patruno: The homeowners who had the most trouble refinancing were the ones who bought their homes at the peak of the most overpriced real estate markets in about 1989, especially in California and in the Northeast. The reason was not that they didn't have enough cash; in many cases, they didn't have enough equity to qualify for refinancing. This factor is precisely the sort of thing we are trying to capture with the able–unable component of the refinancing model.

Question: Should investors depend on Wall Street prepayment models, or should we put more emphasis on independent analysis?

Patruno: Independent analysis is a nice idea, but it is very, very difficult to put into practice. Five or ten years ago, buy-side firms commonly maintained their own in-house prepayment models, but as the market became increasingly complex and the data became more difficult to manage and expensive to maintain, more and more consolidation seems to have occurred in the prepayment-modeling business.

Even those firms that do maintain their own data on an efficient basis can benefit from checking with sell-side dealers and comparing the results of several independent models. Any particular model is subject to drifting out of calibration and may be subject to its own biases on one particular coupon or another. If an investor gets substantially different forecasts from different dealers, he or she should take a close look at what is built into those prepayment forecasts and judge how sensible the analyses are, how well the models have tracked prepayments in the past, and how realistically they seem to capture the factors relevant to the market today. This sort of examination will help an investor decide how much weight to put on which forecasts—and which ones to ignore entirely.

We are all doing the best we can on these forecasts. The best models reflect many years of work by large teams of market experts and statistical professionals. None of the models is perfect, but they can definitely outguess the marginal investor, which is what's necessary in order to outperform.

Credit Analysis of Mortgage-Backed Securities

Andrew B. Jones
Group Vice President
Duff & Phelps Credit Rating Company

Investors and rating agencies can use a variety of quantitative and qualitative analytical tools to evaluate mortgage-backed securities. The most important empirical information is data on delinquencies and foreclosures, housing prices, and local economic conditions. Sophisticated models use the data to characterize a base pool of securities, which analysts can vary according to changing assumptions. Loan structures, particularly senior/subordinate structures, present special analytical challenges today.

Investors in rated securities can benefit from understanding the methods rating agencies use to assign credit ratings. This overview of an agency's credit analysis for mortgage-backed securities discusses both quantitative and qualitative analytical tools. The overview highlights the data that state-of-the-art credit analysis incorporates—particularly loan-level delinquency data and regional housing price series. Finally, the overview points out special considerations rating agencies must give to senior/subordinate structures in evaluating the creditworthiness of mortgage securities.

Some investors rely entirely on ratings for credit analysis; for them, this overview offers a chance to understand the methodology supporting a rating. Other investors rely on ratings primarily for regulatory purposes and conduct their own credit research. These investors will benefit from this discussion of the tools the agencies have developed because investors also can use these tools in credit research. Some investors are active participants in buying unrated mortgage pools but do not buy rated securities; the techniques for performing credit analyses that are discussed here should be of particular interest to these investors.

The Role of Rating Agencies

Rating agencies perform several functions that are valuable to investors in mortgage-backed securities (MBS). First, rating agencies judge credit quality. The types of MBS that typically receive ratings are private-label MBS, sometimes called pass-throughs or collateralized mortgage obligations (CMOs). The term "private label" in this context means transac-

tions not connected to Fannie Mae (the Federal National Mortgage Association), Freddie Mac (the Federal Home Loan Mortgage Corporation), or Ginnie Mae (the Government National Mortgage Association). Originally, the term "CMO" referred solely to debt structures of the pre-REMIC (real estate mortgage investment conduit) form, but today "CMO" refers to almost any multiclass structure, even a pass-through security. This presentation addresses only "whole loan" MBS, which are MBS backed directly by mortgages rather than those backed by certificates that are, in turn, backed by mortgages.

Rating agencies do not simply examine a transaction and then assign a credit rating to the mortgages backing the security. An issuer will request a specific rating and provide the rating agencies information on the particular mortgage pool. The rating agencies then use analytical models to determine the amount of protection against credit losses that will allow the MBS to achieve the rating requested by the issuer. This protection is termed "credit enhancement."

Investors should be aware that ratings carry slightly different meanings for different securities. A rating on a mortgage pass-through, for example, will typically address timely payment of interest and eventual return of principal but will not address return of principal according to any particular schedule. In the case of certain types of subordinate certificates, those on which interest payments may be delayed in order to provide liquidity for other classes, the rating may "carve out" or exclude the timeliness of interest (discussed in detail later in the presentation). A rating agency will allow carve outs only to the extent that investors appear willing to take on the risk. Another aspect excluded from the ratings of MBS is interest payment shortfalls arising from prepayments on the mortgages.

A second function of rating agencies is monitoring rated transactions' performance. For MBS, the trustee provides monthly reports on delinquencies on the mortgages backing an MBS, which the rating agencies evaluate in order to affirm, downgrade, or upgrade the MBS rating.

Third, rating agencies conduct and disseminate research. This research is the foundation for the quantitative analysis of mortgages. Research, especially regarding trends in mortgage performance, is also important for accurately monitoring transactions. The dissemination of the rating agencies' research is important in helping investors understand the credit considerations related to the securities they buy.

Quantitative and Qualitative Analysis

Rating agencies assign ratings based on qualitative as well as quantitative analysis. The quantitative analysis of the mortgage collateral takes into consideration what the expected losses on the pool of mortgage loans would be under different levels of economic stress. Rating agencies do much more than analyze collateral, however. For example, the manner in which transactions are structured from a legal perspective and with respect to payment priorities has significant rating implications. Also, the quality of the underwriting and the diligence of the servicing are important factors in assessing the likely performance of the group of loans backing an MBS.

Analytical Models

Duff & Phelps Credit Rating Company (D&P) grounds its analyses in empirical research. D&P examines mortgage performance data by applying statistical techniques to assess credit quality. The agency incorporates conclusions from this research into its analytical models.

The purpose of D&P's computer models is to estimate the behavior of a pool of mortgage loans. The model incorporates the levels of protection required for a base pool (a sample pool of mortgages with identical characteristics) under stresses corresponding to each rating. The model adapts these levels to a particular pool so that the numerous characteristics (more than 20) of the mortgage loans can be factored in. The model accomplishes this adaptation by assigning a multiplier to the degree to which each characteristic of the mortgage will increase or decrease loss, as compared with the base pool. The output of the model is the credit-enhancement level

needed for each desired rating.

The most important data for these models are delinquency data, both current and historical. Also useful are data to estimate the losses on defaulted loans—in particular, housing prices and liquidation costs. Other data include general economic data in order to correlate defaults and losses with economic conditions.

Delinquency Data

The determination of mortgage default rates is based on the evaluation of the actual delinquency and foreclosure experience of mortgages. Traditionally, rating agencies analyzed delinquency data on a national level. Numerous sources produce such data; the Mortgage Bankers Association (MBA) is an example. The MBA also produces statistics on a state-by-state basis, which allows greater regional specificity. Mortgages in different localities may behave differently, however, even if they are in the same state. Delinquencies on mortgages in Los Angeles will differ from those in San Francisco or in San Diego, for example, although all three localities are in California. Similarly, default frequencies in Rochester, New York, might be expected to have a strong correlation with those in New York City, but historically, the two cities' economies have behaved differently, and as a result, mortgage delinquencies differ as well. The fact that mortgage performance is sensitive to location means that a rating agency must choose the appropriate level of geographical specificity for evaluating delinquency rates.

Much of the information used by D&P is sorted by metropolitan statistical area (MSA), which is a city and its surrounding areas. One source of MSA information is the Mortgage Information Corporation (MIC), a private data-base provider with a loan-by-loan data base of several million securitized transactions. The MIC receives information from servicers of a substantial portion of MBS.

The MIC's information is useful in analyzing mortgage portfolios in order to understand whether, for example, a particular group of loans has high delinquencies relative to the national average. If a particular pool with high delinquencies is located in an area where all mortgages are experiencing high delinquency rates, then the pool may be performing consistently with its economic environment. If a mortgage pool with high delinquencies is located in an MSA where delinquency rates are generally low, a credit analyst should be concerned about the credit quality of the loans.

Delinquency information on an MSA level is vital in building a model to analyze mortgages. For example, although the MBS marketplace has focused on the supposedly poor performance of mortgages and the economy in California for the past few years, many MSAs in California have delinquency and foreclosure rates only slightly above average. The following MSA data from the MIC show that the New York City MSA and areas of New Jersey and Connecticut have foreclosure and delinquency rates (rates are for mortgages 60+ days delinquent as of March 1994) as high as or higher than California rates (all the MSAs listed here are above the national rate of 1.84):

Monmouth–Ocean, N.J.	4.79
New York, N.Y.	4.78
Los Angeles, Calif.	4.74
Orange, N.Y.	4.55
Nassau–Suffolk, N.Y.	4.53
Bergen–Passaic, N.J.	4.17
Newark, N.J.	3.57
Scranton, Penn.	3.09
New Haven, Conn.	3.07
Middlesex, N.J.	2.88
Riverside, Calif.	2.86
Santa Barbara/Ventura, Calif.	2.31
Hartford, Conn.	2.27
Allentown, Penn.	2.26
Boston, Mass.	2.13
Providence, R.I.	2.06
Fairfield, Conn.	2.05
Philadelphia, Penn.	2.04
Worcester, Mass.	1.87
Anaheim, Calif.	1.86

When comparing delinquency data, an analyst cannot simply look at serious delinquencies and foreclosures and start drawing conclusions immediately from those numbers. A significant characteristic of the data provided by the MBA, the MIC, and others is that the data typically reflect rates of delinquencies on an entire mortgage portfolio, thus mortgages originated over several years. In contrast, an MBS typically includes loans originated over a short period of time prior to issuance, and after issuance, the pool rarely acquires any new mortgages. Thus, MBS pools are said to be fixed or "static." Using portfolio statistics to judge static-pool performance can lead to erroneous results. For example, in the case of a portfolio that has grown rapidly in the past few years, the delinquency rates on the portfolio are probably lower than what they would be for a seasoned static pool because the new mortgages generally have not had a chance to become seriously delinquent. If more than 50 percent of a portfolio is less than two years old and the remainder of the pool is three-to-five years old (the peak years of default), the former portion of the pool might have very low delinquencies while the latter portion might have very high delinquencies. Therefore, the average delinquency rate on the portfolio would overstate the delinquencies on new loans and understate the delinquencies on older loans.

In order to use foreclosure rates for constructing a static pool for analysis—to isolate a group of mortgage loans and to track them over time—the agency must interpret the data and make systematic adjustments. Occasionally, large issuers will have static-pool information and will have already segregated the information by groups of mortgages of particular years of origination. Often, however, these data are hard to obtain. (The presentation will turn to techniques to simulate a static pool later in this section.)

When studying foreclosure rates, the credit analyst must also remember that foreclosure is a legal process determined by state laws. The foreclosure rate on a portfolio is based on the percentage of loans in the foreclosure process at a fixed point in time, but the periods of foreclosure vary by state. In Georgia, for example, the foreclosure period is one month. Other states' foreclosure procedures could result in foreclosure periods of as much as two years. Rating agencies are not concerned with the amount of loans in the foreclosure process at a fixed point in time but, rather, with the number of loans entering the foreclosure process during a fixed interval. Therefore, the different foreclosure periods must be taken into account in analyzing foreclosure rates.

In order to understand the importance of this aspect, consider a state with a one-month foreclosure period, such as Georgia, as compared with one, such as California, with a four-month period. If the same number of loans is going through a liquidation process in Georgia and California, one would expect the foreclosure rate in Georgia to be one-fourth the rate in California—because only one-month-old loans are counted in Georgia, whereas the foreclosure statistics in California include one-month-old loans, two-month-old loans, and so on. The manner in which loans are repeatedly counted will overstate the rate of foreclosure relative to the rate at which loans enter foreclosure. Thus, the foreclosure statistics of a portfolio must be viewed in light of state-by-state distinctions.

The first step in transforming delinquency and foreclosure data into a static-pool format is to determine an annual default rate for mortgages of different years of origination. For a rating agency's analysis, the term "default" carries a specific meaning. It refers only to those loans that do not reinstate ("cure") and that result in the liquidation of the underlying property. On a national level, based on a sample of several million loans, D&P has concluded that about 90 percent of loans in foreclosure status will still be in foreclosure in the following month. Of the 10 percent that move out of foreclosure status, about 4 percent will cure and 6 percent will enter into the "real estate owned" (REO) category. REO refers to property that a servicer has acquired at the property's foreclosure proceeding. A property may be sold by the owner during the foreclosure process, at an amount either sufficient or insufficient to pay the mortgage (termed a "short sale"). A property may also be sold at the foreclosure proceeding to an unrelated third party (but only if the buyer bids an amount greater than the mortgage).

Because some loans cure or are sold at short sale at a price sufficient to pay indebtedness, foreclosure rates may overstate the percentage of loans that actually go through liquidation to result in a loss. The following equation thus expresses the default rate as a rating agency would define it, namely, a product of the foreclosure rate and the inverse of the foreclosure rate, adjusted by the cure rate:

$$\text{Default rate} = \text{Foreclosure rate} - \frac{12}{\text{Foreclosure period}} \times (1 - \text{Cure rate}).$$

The cure rate is the percentage of foreclosed mortgages paid in full by the mortgagor prior to liquidation (which could include short sales) or liquidated at no loss.

The next step in constructing a static pool from delinquency data is to group the loans by age, or year of origination. The resulting delinquency information will reveal the behavior of loans that are one year old, two years old, and so on. Grouping the loans by age, subject to adjustments to be described, simulates a static pool. Note that, between the time the loans are originated and the period of data collection, some of the original mortgagors may have prepaid their mortgages in full. Therefore, when calculating delinquencies as a percentage of the original balance of a simulated static pool, the balance today of a group of loans of a particular origination year must be adjusted upward to reflect loans that have prepaid.

The adjustment for prepayments assumes that the bad credits, the loans expected to default, will probably not prepay—a generally safe assumption. In recent years, however, mortgages were prepaying rapidly, so the data from these years may contain data on bad credits that have also prepaid. Some of the loans expected to default may have prepaid before their period of deterioration, which is the opposite of conventional thought. In scenarios for times of extremely high prepayments, current delinquencies could understate static-pool delinquencies because the defaulting loans have been removed prior to their peak years of credit loss. In evaluating delinquencies, an analyst must be careful when drawing conclusions based on performance data in abnormal prepayment environments.

Loans grouped by age and adjusted for prepayment effects correspond to the static pool. The sum of the annual default rates for each year of origination is the cumulative default rate on the static pool—that is, the percentage of loans expected to become liquidating loans. The relative levels of default rates over time form a pattern called the "default curve" or "loss curve." Generally, defaults are low in early years, highest in the third through fifth years of the pool, and decline thereafter.

With this information on the timing and level of cumulative defaults, credit analysts can determine cumulative rates of default in the data sample under the economic conditions corresponding to each rating. A rating of AAA assumes the security will withstand extremely onerous economic conditions—depression scenarios. At each step down the scale from AAA to CCC, the assumed ability to withstand economic stresses decreases. That is, a security rated AA is judged able to withstand less stress (recessionary rather than depression stresses) before experiencing losses than the AAA-rated security can withstand.

Data on loan-by-loan mortgage characteristics and default patterns in a depression-case scenario do not exist. Credit analysts can isolate mortgage performance in particular localities, however, that have experienced conditions commensurate with ratings of A to BBB—that is, economic-stress scenarios slightly less extreme than depression. Many MSAs on the northeastern seaboard, including Boston in the late 1980s, suffered through an economic scenario approaching A–BB conditions.

After the appropriate data have been gathered and the static pool has been identified, the next step in building a model is to use regression analysis to understand how the different mortgage characteristics affect defaults. D&P first isolates the appropriate characteristics and assures that the data are broken down accordingly. From these data, we have been able to obtain loan "cohorts" (groups of loans sharing identical characteristics) for various combinations of more than 20 mortgage characteristics. The result is about 400,000 cohorts, which we have examined through our statistical software.

We were seeking to identify which mortgage characteristics are most important—that is, which have the most meaning in terms of predicting mortgage defaults. Generally, our research confirmed what much of the market understands: Loan-to-value ratios are the most significant factor in predicting mortgage defaults.

The loan-to-value (LTV) figure is the ratio of the mortgage balance to the value of the property, measured as the lesser of the purchase price or appraised value. LTV is thus the measure of the amount by which a property is leveraged. The higher the LTV, the greater the leverage and the smaller the homeowner's equity in the property. The mortgagor's equity is initially represented by the down payment, and it may increase or decrease as the loan amortizes and as the property value changes. If the value of the property falls, the equity in the home will decline—in some cases, to a negative level.

D&P next sought to understand the relative impact of the other significant risk factors on default rates. In analyzing loan type, for example, one of the most significant model factors, we compared the risks of a 15-year fixed-rate mortgage with those of a 30-year fixed-rate mortgage. Investors are well aware that 15-year collateral is much less risky than 30-year from a credit perspective, but we found the risk reduction to be much greater than rating agencies had previously recognized in their models.

Several reasons account for the superior performance of 15-year mortgages. A 15-year mortgage generally involves a more sophisticated borrower who is willing to make higher monthly payments than a 30-year borrower. The 15-year loan amortizes faster, so at any given time, the mortgagor of this property has more equity in the property (in case of the need for liquidation) than the 30-year mortgagor. Finally, if a 15-year borrower has economic difficulties, he or she has the option of refinancing to a 30-year mortgage rather than risking a foreclosure or liquidation.

Housing Price Data

As discussed earlier, the LTV ratio, a measure of the mortgage debt to the value of the collateral, is a key determinant of default. The changing value of residential homes affects the LTV ratio, and therefore, housing price data are important elements of credit analysis.

The availability of data on housing prices has allowed credit-rating models to improve analysis of (1) how the change in LTV over time affects frequency of loss and (2) what part of the loss on a liquidated mortgage is attributable to price changes. With respect to the latter analysis, dramatic housing price declines between the periods of origination and liquidation will increase the size of losses. From the frequency perspective, declining housing prices cause deterioration in equity, and in many different parts of the country, declines in housing values have caused borrowers to reconsider whether to continue their mortgage payments. Typically, people do not default solely because of negative equity, but the presence of negative equity in combination with financial hardship increases default frequencies.

The National Association of Realtors (NAR) provides median housing price data on an MSA-by-MSA basis. A problem with median sales price data, however, is that they do not distinguish among the different types of transactions in the market. Housing markets include homes of different tiers of housing. A median price at a fixed point in time describes the median value of the houses selling at that point.

Therefore, rather than reflecting changes in the fundamental value of existing homes, a median price index describes the changing makeup of the particular types of property that happen to be selling from time to time. For example, an analysis of the Atlanta, Georgia, area in several quarters in the mid-1980s, indicated a plateau of prices. Prices rose, stayed constant, and then fell. During this period, however, the transaction mix was apparently biased toward new housing in the upper-middle tier, which inflated the median price even though the value of existing homes had not changed. Repeat sales data are more meaningful to MBS investors because repeat data describe changes in the value of existing housing without the distortions created by new housing stock.

Another problem with the NAR data is that NAR does not have information on housing price tiers, and the high-price tier of housing generally is the most volatile in price. The performance of the median tier in a particular area does not give an agency or investor the full picture of what is happening in the market. Many MBS are backed by jumbo or super-jumbo mortgages that may be secured by these high-tier properties and, as a result, may be riskier than the median tier of mortgages.

Because of these deficiencies in the NAR data, D&P has turned to new sources. One particularly useful set of data is found in repeat sales indexes, such as the indexes developed by Case Shiller Weiss. These indexes are based on thousands of samples consisting of the current sales prices of particular properties as recorded in the deeds in local county courthouses together with previous sales price(s) for the same properties. Thus, the data track the changes in the values of existing houses. This type of information reflects changes in existing loan values more accurately than NAR data. In addition, the index data can be broken down by price tier.

The California market provides about 60 percent of the mortgages backing private-label MBS. Thus, the recent decline of the California economy and the corresponding decline in housing prices have been of particular interest to MBS investors. As shown in **Figure 1**, housing prices in the Los Angeles area increased dramatically in the late 1980s. Since 1990, the prices have fallen, on average, about 25 percent.

A pattern found in this market and in other MSAs is that the high-price tier fell first, as **Figure 2** indicates. Perhaps the purchasers of high-tier housing are financially sophisticated, and when they see an economic downturn approaching, they scale down the prices they will pay for housing. Rather than buying a $1 million house, such a buyer may purchase an $800,000 house; the potential buyer of an $800,000 house may purchase a $600,000 house;

Figure 1. Los Angeles Repeat Sales Index: Single-Family Market

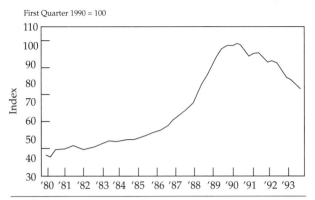

Source: Case Shiller Weiss.

and so forth. The high tier experiences unalleviated declines in demand, whereas the demand in other sectors is actually propped up (initially) by shifting buyers. In addition, the high-price tier typically falls the farthest, as also shown in **Figure 2.**

The low-price tier tends to experience a delayed reaction (in part, as a result of the impact of trading down); when it ultimately does decline, it declines somewhat less than other tiers. The only exception to this rule occurs when, in the period before the economic decline, a disproportionate increase in the price of low-tier housing has occurred in the association with a rapid increase in construction or rehabilitation of new low-tier housing (the Boston experience). In this case, the low tier may experience declines as great as or greater than the high tier decline.

D&P uses the information on housing price changes in several different ways. First, in the formulation of credit-enhancement levels, D&P as-

Figure 2. Los Angeles Repeat Sales Index: Single-Family Index by Price Tier

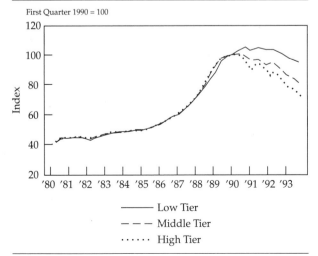

Source: Case Shiller Weiss.

sesses historical defaults in the context of economic factors, including housing prices. For example, if the secured properties are in an area in which housing prices have recently risen, the portfolio may show no losses. That result does not necessarily mean that the loans were creditworthy; it probably means that the housing price increases were so dramatic that liquidation of the defaulted loans caused little or no loss.

Another area in which D&P incorporates housing prices into its models is in the analysis of seasoned portfolios with mortgages located in areas where housing prices have changed. In assessments of the LTV over time, the loan amount must, of course, reflect the new balance. More significantly, D&P adjusts the "value" portions of the LTV ratios for housing price changes on a loan-by-loan basis. D&P matches the particular loan with the amount of housing price decline in the mortgaged property's MSA in the period between origination of the loan and the time of issuance, and the model adjusts the ratio accordingly. A loan that had positive equity a few years ago could have zero equity today. In California, for example, a loan originated in 1990 at an LTV of 75 might have an adjusted LTV of 90. The adjustment to LTV ratios allows the model to reflect the increased riskiness of those loans with deteriorated equity.

D&P also uses housing prices to understand the riskiness of various housing markets. In 1992, D&P developed a housing-price volatility index, which provides a factor for every MSA based on the riskiness of that area. D&P is particularly concerned about areas that appear to be experiencing a speculative cycle. Rapidly rising housing prices do not necessarily mean an area is becoming economically stronger; it may indicate that the housing market is becoming economically riskier through speculation.

Credit analysts need to study a variety of underlying economic indicators and determine whether they justify the degree of housing price increase. In the Seattle, Washington, area, for example, housing price increases were extremely steep in 1992. The high home prices were justified somewhat by demographics, but D&P analysts were wary of the price rise because of the concentration of aeronautics and computer software industries in the area. Indeed, some downward adjustment has occurred in housing prices since 1992.

With respect to high-value homes with large loans, the concern is not the size of a loan but the property that secures the loan; large loans are not particularly risky simply because of their size. They are risky to the extent that they are secured by high-price homes, which tend to be the most volatile category in price. Consequently, D&P analyzes the value of the mortgaged properties relative to the median value in their MSAs on a loan-by-loan basis to determine relative risk in light of local markets. Regional analysis is important because housing prices vary so dramatically in different parts of the country that the cutoff between price tiers will be different for each MSA.

Finally, D&P considers housing prices when analyzing B-quality and C-quality mortgage loans—loans to borrowers with impaired credit histories. These mortgages have high frequencies of default and also tend to be originated with low LTV ratios. Many B and C issuers, however, are focusing on mortgages secured by properties in the low- and medium-price tiers and are thus less vulnerable to housing price downturns than some A-quality lenders, who are lending on high-value homes.

Other Economic Data

Rating agencies look at a variety of economic data nationally, regionally, and by MSA. For example, a current concern is the effect of military base closings. Analyzing California on a state level does not provide a clear picture of what effect military base closings will have on particular mortgage pools. Some pools might be concentrated in the San Francisco and Oakland MSAs; others in Los Angeles and Anaheim. As **Figure 3** shows, the impact of the base closings depends on where the mortgaged properties are located. The impact is likely to be significant

in the Oakland MSA, less significant in San Francisco, and of little significance in Los Angeles.

The important point is that the credit analyst must consider the effect of economic factors on a highly localized level. Some analysts try to divide California by an arbitrary north/south line, but this simplification does not reflect economic realities. For example, the closure of military bases will negatively affect some areas in southern California, such as Riverside, whereas other areas in southern California—namely, San Diego—will actually gain jobs from the military bases being closed elsewhere because bases are going to be consolidated in the areas. Thus, not only will statewide analysis lead to inaccurate conclusions, so also will approaches that make arbitrary divisions, such as north/south, rather than divisions based on actual variation in local conditions.

Special Considerations in Evaluating Senior/ Subordinate Structures

Rating agencies examine more than issues of collateral; they must also analyze the structures of MBS, including the senior/subordinate structure. Many transactions have multiple classes, or tranches, rated from AAA down to CCC, as depicted in **Figure 4**. The effect is to concentrate much of the risk of losses (to "leverage" losses) in the lower-rated classes. The

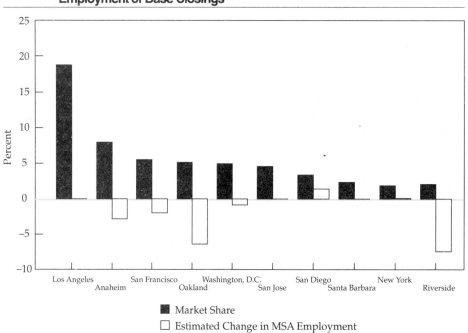

Figure 3. Selected MSAs' Shares of the Private-Label MBS Market and Effect on Employment of Base Closings

■ Market Share
□ Estimated Change in MSA Employment

Note: Market share measured by dollar amounts.

Source: Andrew B. Jones, based on data from MIC and Regional Financial Associates.

Figure 4. Example Senior/Subordinate Structures

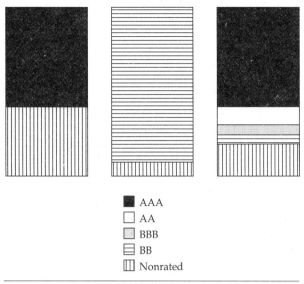

- ■ AAA
- □ AA
- ▨ BBB
- ▤ BB
- ▥ Nonrated

Source: Andrew B. Jones.

graph on the left of Figure 4 is a simple two-class structure consisting of a AAA class supported by a large nonrated class; this structure needs a set amount of credit enhancement to achieve its AAA rating. The next graph shows a BB class supported by a small nonrated class; the BB rating would require less credit enhancement than the AAA rating. Some part of that nonrated class in the first graph must be AA in quality, and some part A or BBB. Thus, the third graph in Figure 4 represents how these transactions are structured from AAA down, with the top class being supported by the aggregate subordination of the lower classes. The issue illustrated in this example is that, in D&P's opinion, the unrated class in the right graph of Figure 4 must be larger than the unrated class in the middle graph, even though they are both supporting BBs.

Rating agencies have different opinions on this issue. D&P's view is that the losses are highly leveraged into the BB class in the right graph, which adds risk. In the absence of leveraging, a BB amount of credit enhancement (e.g., 1 percent subordination) will protect the pool under different assumptions appropriate to a BB rating. Because the economy could worsen, some variance exists between the BB required protection and actual losses. If the losses are structured as they are in the middle graph, any loss that exceeds the amount of the nonrated class would be spread throughout the transaction. In that case, a buyer of $1 of the top class in the middle graph might suffer only 1/99 of any excess losses. In the graph on the right, however, under a leveraged structure, the holder of $1 of that BB class could potentially be wiped out. To equate those risks, D&P analysts require additional subordination for the risk

of leverage. This additional credit enhancement covers some of the variance of actual losses and reduces the chance of that variance occurring. Not all rating agencies cover this leveraging risk.

Another important rating issue in the senior/subordinate context is the presence of two fundamentally different methods of allocating cash flow between senior and subordinate classes. These allocation methods were mentioned earlier in reference to the meaning of ratings. In some transactions, interest on the subordinate classes is not available to cover current losses of principal to senior classes; in other structures, the subordinate class's interest is available, which results in a potential delay of interest payments. This practice is characteristic of several transactions by major issuers and is referred to as "the subordination of interest" structure. In these cases, D&P's rating addresses ultimate receipt of interest but not its timely payment.

The distinction between these two allocation methods arises in the manner in which mortgage losses are allocated. Assume that a $100 loan is foreclosed and the property is liquidated in such a way that the recoveries are $90 and losses are $10. Theoretically, the subordination structure protects the senior holder from the loss by allocating that loss to the subordinate class. Typically, transactions are structured so that senior holders receive their share of the recoveries on the loan ($90) up front, but the transaction may be structured so that the senior holders receive their share of the unpaid principal balance ($100) up front.

These two structures have profoundly different effects under the subordination-of-interest method of allocating payments, in which the senior class's principal rights are paid before the junior's entitlements to interest are paid. If the structure is to pay the senior share of the entire loan amount ($100), the senior class must be paid its share of recoveries ($90) and the difference between the recoveries and the loan amount ($10, which is equal to the loss). The unique characteristic of this structure is that the difference ($10) is paid immediately with funds borrowed from the subordinate class's interest cash flows in that month. Mathematically, the interest on the subordinate class is often sufficient to cover the amount of the loss. When it is not sufficient, the remainder of the loss is charged to the subordinate class.

The effect for the senior class of this structure is that, as the pool deteriorates and as losses are experienced, the senior class is paid faster. It receives the credit-enhanced loss amount up front.

This provision was required to make transactions attractive to purchasers of the senior classes. Some investors in senior classes prefer subordination-of-interest structures because they view them as providing added credit support. If a senior holder is protected by a 10 percent subordinate class in a transaction that has this feature, the holder is getting more than 10 percent subordination. He or she is getting 10 percent plus the interest cash flows of the subordinate class. Determining its value is difficult because the value depends on how losses are grouped—whether they are bundled together or spread out over time. The more spread out they are, the more likely a senior holder is to obtain the benefit of the subordination of the subordinate class's interest.

The effect on the subordinate class is a subject of controversy among investors. Investors in subordinate securities typically have years of experience investing in MBS. Many have entered the MBS market by purchasing agency pass-throughs, then proceeded to private-label MBS (but only the most senior tranches), and subsequently purchased highly rated mezzanines. They may explore lower-rated subordinate classes only years later. As a result, some of the investors owning subordinate classes may be the same investors who, two or three years earlier, had wanted the subordination-of-interest structure to strengthen their position as senior holders. Nonetheless, whether these investors factored their knowledge of the structure into the pricing of the subordinate classes is not entirely clear.

The chief effect of the subordination-of-interest structure is a reduction in yield on the subordinate classes. Under the terms of the securities, these structures provide that the right to the reallocated interest does not disappear; instead, an interest shortfall account is created. Under the terms of the transaction, however, the interest shortfalls do not accrue interest. Mathematically, the interest owed to this account will be available later. In effect, it will come out of cash flows on the unrated class or other, more junior, classes in the transaction. The problem is that, if the pool suffers a period of constant losses, the interest might not be available for several months or years. The result may be a reduction in yield because no interest accrues on the shortfall account.

Because of the interest-delay feature, the subordination-of-interest structure is fundamentally different from structures that do not subordinate interest to senior-class principal. As a result, rating agencies face the dilemma of whether they can rate the transaction and be comfortable that investors understand the terms of the transaction or whether they should not rate the transaction because it is not structured to provide interest on the interest shortfall. D&P currently takes the former position, allowing investors to have access to rated securities of either structure. (D&P, in effect, rates the security according to its terms.) Nonetheless, the issue is becoming moot for most new issuances as investor preference moves issuers toward structures that do not have the subordination-of-interest feature.

Rating agencies have different opinions about credit issues involving mortgage credit and structural factors. Therefore, investors in MBS need to understand the agencies' methodologies and the scope and definition of the rating on the security in which they are interested in order to make an informed purchasing decision. Seasoned investors are often well aware of the subtleties of these securities; indeed, they may have played a part in the development of some of the unusual features. The role of the rating agencies, therefore, is to communicate appropriate credit analysis so that the complex features of credit can be understood by all investors in the market.

Question and Answer Session

Andrew B. Jones

Question: In the case of a natural disaster, what amount of "walk away" risk does an investor have on a whole-loan MBS?

Jones: Rating agencies call this risk a "special hazard risk." It primarily applies to earthquakes, which are especially significant because of the large percentage of California properties in MBS. A danger does exist that a borrower will walk away from a mortgage after an earthquake, but the important factor for the rating is the loan-to-value ratio. The fact that the house might be destroyed does not necessarily mean the property has no value. In California, land values as a proportion of total property values are about 55 percent in some MSAs and property values are the highest in the country. Therefore, even if a California house is completely destroyed, the borrower will not necessarily walk away from that property, especially if his or her equity in the property is substantial. Of course, the risk will vary from loan to loan.

In a senior/subordinate transaction, special-hazard risk is covered by subordination. The subordinate security is usually available to cover special-hazard losses, at least up to a certain dollar amount. In transactions that do not cover these losses, D&P requires a separate reserve fund or separate policy to cover special-hazard risks.

Asset-Backed Securities

Tracy L. van Eck
Director, Fixed Income Research
CS First Boston Corporation

Securities backed by consumer loans or trade receivables have recently returned to popularity. Credit analysis of asset-backed securities explains some of their appeal: high ratings, generally low loss experiences, a history of few downgrades, and gratifying return performance. Changes propelling future growth of the market include increasing bank participation, mark-to-market accounting requirements, and the introduction of credit card use in grocery stores, health care facilities, and fast food restaurants.

Asset-backed securities are similar to mortgage-backed securities, in that they are backed by a pool of loans, but they are also different, in that the loans are typically consumer loans, or sometimes even trade receivables, instead of mortgages. In late 1990, the offering spreads for asset-backed securities were generally 100 basis points (bps) or more above Treasury notes of comparable maturities. Consumer loans were not particularly popular because of the recession, so finding investors for asset-backed securities was difficult.

Today, everyone wants to buy asset-backed securities and is wondering what happened to the spreads, which have halved in size. Now, investors are enthusiastic about a spread of 50 bps over comparable Treasuries.

Since the inception of the asset-backed securities (ABS) market, cumulative issuance has been about $280 billion; the outstanding issues as of spring 1994, because of paydowns and maturing transactions, are about $168 billion. Automobile loans and credit card debt account for the largest shares of the market, as shown in **Table 1**. Although auto loans represent 37 percent of issuance, they compose only about 18 percent of outstandings because of their monthly amortization. Credit card ABS, which typically resemble corporate bonds and have bullet maturities, remain outstanding for a longer period of time than auto loans. They represent approximately 37 percent of cumulative issuance but about 62 percent of current outstandings.

Market Participants

To determine what types of investors buy asset-backed securities, CS First Boston Corporation studied more than 6,600 transactions on some 750 different accounts during the past two years (1992 through 1993). As shown in **Table 2**, investment advisors' 40 percent share of the market in 1992 dropped to 25 percent in 1993. One reason for this considerable drop is that investment advisors are typically, for better or for worse, the most aggressive investors. Investment advisors tend to buy when spreads are wide and to lose market share when spreads narrow. At that point, more conservative investors jump into the market.

CS First Boston also studied which types of investors bought B-pieces—subordinated security classes that turn ABS into AAA-rated (the rating for most ABS) securities—which represent a smaller part of the market than ABS. Typically, ABS make up a pool of credit card loans of not even investment grade. To achieve an AAA rating, the ABS need some form of credit enhancement. One way to get it is for the offerer to put up extra collateral or a subordinated class.

The buyers of B-pieces are aggressive investors willing to take first-loss positions. Of course, they are compensated in spread. The B-pieces are typically rated A and have some credit enhancement of their own. As shown in **Table 3**, investment advisors in 1993 were taking about a 42 percent share of the B-piece market. In 1992, when spreads were wider, investment advisors' share represented 60 percent.

Another interesting difference in B-pieces between 1992 and 1993 is the new account types that have appeared. This change indicates a rising interest in the riskier classes of ABS.

One megatrend in the ABS market is an increase

Table 1. Distribution of ABS Issuance and Outstandings as of First Quarter 1994

Loan Type	Issuance	Outstandings
Total amount (billions)	$279.8	$167.8
Auto, retail	36.9%	17.9%
Auto, wholesale	2.8	3.4
Credit card	37.1	62.0
Home equity, floating	6.1	3.1
Home equity, fixed	6.0	4.1
Manufactured housing[a]	3.9	4.4
Agriculture	1.3	—
Computer lease	1.1	—
Equipment lease	—	1.8
Trade receivables	—	1.2
Other	4.8	2.1
Total	100.0%	100.0%

[a]Mobile homes.

Source: CS First Boston Corp.

Table 2. Distribution of ABS Investors
(percent of market value)

Investor Types	1992	1993
Investment advisor, general	39.1%	24.9%
Non-U.S. accounts	14.4	16.4
Bank trust	7.4	15.4
Life insurance	4.7	8.2
Bank portfolio	7.2	6.8
Insurance money management	4.9	5.7
In-house pension	2.3	4.8
Security lending	2.4	2.6
Government agency	3.2	2.6
Property and casualty	1.6	2.0
Mutual fund, general	—	1.4
Credit union	1.1	1.4
Public pension	2.1	1.3
Hedge fund	1.1	0.9
Corporation	3.3	0.8
Advisor, money market	—	0.8
High-net-worth individuals	—	0.8
Other	5.1	3.0
Total	100.0%	100.0%

Note: Percentages may not total 100 because of rounding.

Source: CS First Boston Corp.

in floating-rate issuance and buyers; as the market consensus turned bearish, buying floaters looked like a good move. In 1993, about 33 percent of issuance had floating-rate coupons, an increase from 8 percent in 1991. Buyers of floaters in 1993 were as follows:

Investor Profile	Market Share
Bank trust	29.3%
In-house pension	11.5
Investment advisor, general	10.8
European bank portfolio	5.5
Insurance money management	5.2
Life insurance	5.1
Government agency	4.5
Security lending	4.0
European capital	3.7
Bank portfolio	3.5
Sovereign	2.9
Asian bank portfolio	2.5
Credit union	1.8
Mutual fund, general	1.6
European insurance money management	1.3
Corporation	1.0
Other	5.6

The number of buyers involved in ABS is surprising considering that ABS are a relatively new and small market compared with, for example, the $1.5 trillion mortgage market. ABS constitute only about 1 percent of the common aggregate indexes.

Five new types of buyers were added to the ABS market in 1993, and recent deals have been structured in order to provide something for everyone. For example, new classes of securities backing ABS now meet eligibility requirements for money market funds that are restricted by the legal finals of 397 days.

Second, ABS have attracted security lending operations as a new-buyer category. Security lending operations are accounts with large Treasury portfolios that put up collateral to borrow money at sub-LIBOR rates. They then find a floating-rate asset yielding an above-LIBOR rate to lock in the spread.

Because the ABS market contains many new floaters, it has attracted numerous security lending operations of this type with deep pockets (the top 35 security lending operations have about $10 billion each).

The third change in the market is increased participation from Europe. The acceptance of ABS in general is growing in Europe, but the increase in floaters is a particular draw to Europeans. European investors are typically more LIBOR funded than U.S.

Table 3. Distribution of ABS Investors in B-Pieces
(percent of market value)

Investor	1992	1993
Investment advisor, general	62.8%	41.6%
Life insurance	8.2	16.2
Insurance money management	11.9	11.9
Mutual fund, general	—	6.1
Property and casualty	—	5.9
Sovereign	—	4.2
European bank portfolio	—	2.5
Insurance advisor	—	2.3
European insurance money management	—	2.1
European corporation	—	1.6
Security lending	—	1.6
Bank trust	—	1.4
Bank portfolio	—	1.3
European advisor, insurance	—	0.7
Mutual fund, money market	—	0.6
Public pension	8.1	—
Asian bank portfolio	4.0	—
Government agency	1.7	—
Asian corporation	1.0	—
Other	2.2	—
Total	100.0%	100.0%

Note: Percentages may not total 100 because of rounding.

Source: CS First Boston Corp.

investors, so they are looking for the floaters.

The fourth change is an increase in participation from domestic banks. By the end of 1994, risk weights for ABS are expected to drop from 100 percent to 20 percent, so domestic banks should be showing even more interest than at present.

Finally, Japanese investors have entered the market. In 1993, the Japanese Ministry of Finance defined ABS as securities, which made ABS eligible for investment by Japan's investors.

Credit Analysis

Credit analysis of asset-backed securities explains why they have become so popular and creditworthy and how they reach their AAA ratings. **Table 4** shows a comparison of senior classes and subordinate classes for four types of bonds. The bonds listed are backed by auto loans (Chrysler), credit card debt (Citibank), home equity loans (Fleet), and manufactured housing loans (Green Tree Financial Corporation). As indicated, each bond except Green Tree has an Aaa/AAA rating. Also shown are the B-class ratings, which will generally achieve A ratings.

An important aspect to note is the loss rate these securities can sustain before an investor loses $1 in principal. Premier's recent loss experience on an annualized basis, for example, was reported as 63 bps. Losses would have to increase instantaneously to 8.04 percent (also an annualized number) and remain there for the life of the deal before investors would lose principal. Therefore, the senior class can sustain more than 12 times current losses. In the credit card class, losses are fairly high, close to 4.5 percent, but these structures can withstand loss rates

of 31 percent in the A class and 24 percent in the B class. Investors have concluded that, if they take the senior class, they can obviously take the subordinated; by giving up minimal credit quality, they pick up an extra 15–20 bps in spread.

Since the beginning of the ABS market, A-rated corporate bonds have been more popular investments than ABS even though historical performance indicates that ABS are the better investment. Since 1985 when the first ABS deal was made, Standard & Poor's has made more than 1,000 downgrades for corporates rated A or better, whereas no downgrades for collateral performance have been made in the ABS market. A few deals were downgraded because they had letters of guarantee from Aaa/AAA entities and those Aaa/AAA entities were downgraded. The lack of downgrades in the ABS market is even more impressive considering that the United States has been in a recession and consumer loan losses have increased significantly.

In summary, asset-backed securities are and tend to remain Aaa/AAA-rated securities. One reason is that the rating agencies' approach to ABS is somewhat different from their approach to corporate bonds. With corporates, the agencies apparently operate under the premise that they can tell investors a bond is Aaa/AAA today but not project into the future. With ABS, they analyze the bond under several depression-like scenarios and perform stress tests. Then they can say, "Under all these scenarios, we expect the bond to maintain a Aaa/AAA rating."

The home equity and manufactured housing classes' maximum allowable loss rates given in Table 4 are rather skimpy in light of recent experience. The rates are somewhat misleading, however, because

Table 4. Senior Classes versus Subordinate Classes

Issue	Credit Enhancements	Excess Servicing	Moody's/S&P Ratings		Maximum Allowable Instantaneous Loss		Record Loss Experience
			Class A	Class B	Class A	Class B	
Premier Auto Trust, 1994-1	3.75% subordination 2.00% reserve Turbo	4.74%	Aaa/AAA	A2/A	8.04%	5.89%	0.63%[a]
Standard Credit Card Master Trust I, Series 1994-2	6.00% subordination 7.00% shared cash collateral	1.58	Aaa/AAA	A2/A	31.30	24.00	4.46[b]
Fleet Home Equity Trust Loan, 1993-1	22.25% subordination 13.00% reserve	7.13	Aaa/AAA	A3/A	17.47	8.82	1.34[c]
Green Tree Financial Corporation, 1993–94	11.00% subordination 0.50% reserve	3.67	Aa2/AA	Baa3/A–	5.27	4.30 (B – 1)	0.92[a]

[a]Year end December 31, 1993.
[b]February 1994.
[c]December 1993 (0.40 percent at year end 1993).

Source: CS First Boston Corp.

some of these structures work in such a way that the credit enhancement grows over time. As **Table 5** shows, from day 1 to the end of the term for the Fleet home equity bond, an investor could withstand a

with short durations is presented in **Table 6**. The portfolio contains 20 percent auto loans, 20 percent home equities, 40 percent credit cards, and 20 percent credit card floaters. In the "Unchanged" scenario,

Table 5. Fleet Home Equity Trust Loan, 1993-1: Maximum Allowable Defaults

Period of Net Loss Rate	Scenario 1	Scenario 2	Scenario 3
Class A senior certificates			
First 12 months	1.34%	1.34%	17.47%
Second 12 months	1.34	27.85	17.47
After month 24	49.35	27.85	17.47
Class B subordinate certificates			
First 12 months	1.34	1.34	8.82
Second 12 months	1.34	11.63	8.82
After month 24	14.56	11.63	8.82

Source: CS First Boston Corp.

17.47 percent annual loss rate and still not lose $1 in principal. On the other hand, if reported losses for the first year are only 1.34 percent, investors can withstand a 27 percent annual loss rate for the remaining life of the deal. Furthermore, if losses hold steady at 1.34 percent for the second year, investors can withstand a loss rate of 50 percent for the remaining life of the deal.

Over time, credit enhancement builds because the class A piece is paying down while the subordinated class remains fully outstanding and continues to grow as a percentage of the deal. Moreover, the reserve funds are building up over time—typically, through excess servicing, which is the difference between the coupon on the underlying loans and the coupon on the bond. In a home equity loan, for example, if the coupon is 10 percent on the underlying loan and the coupon on the bond is 7 percent (6 percent for the coupon, plus a servicing fee of 1 percent), then the remaining 3 percent is called excess servicing. The excess servicing often goes toward building reserve funds.

Relative Value

Cash should outperform bonds in an environment of rising interest rates. Historically, in the first year following a tightening by the Federal Reserve, cash has outperformed bonds five out of the last six times. An investor who is a buyer of cash or a holder of Fed funds should consider investing in a portfolio of short-duration asset-backed securities, however, in order to limit exposure to rising interest rates. By following this strategy, investors can even beat cash. As shown in **Figure 1**, a short-duration ABS portfolio will beat cash in several scenarios, with Fed funds ranging from an unchanged 3.5 percent to 6.0 percent.

The performance of a generic portfolio of ABS

the one-year returns of Fed funds would be 3.5 percent and the ABS portfolio would have returned 5.42 percent. In the "One-Year Returns, Scenario 1" column, which assumes that Fed funds increase to 5 percent, the ABS portfolio still outperforms the Fed funds. In short, an actual investor in Fed funds would probably receive a return somewhere between 3.5 and 5 percent; the ABS portfolio return of 5.13 percent would have substantially outperformed the Fed funds.

Figure 1. Short-Duration ABS Portfolio versus Fed Funds

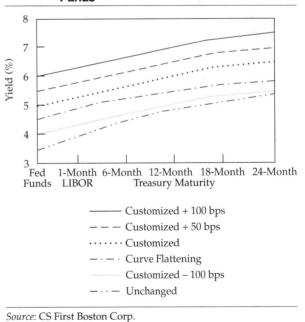

Source: CS First Boston Corp.

Bullet versus Current-Pay Structure

In bear markets, many portfolio managers wrestle

Table 6. Short-Duration ABS Portfolio versus Fed Funds

Holding	Current Face Value	Current Offering	Maturity	Price 4/8/94	Average Life (years)	Effective Duration (years)	One-Year Returns						Market Value[a] (4/8/9; millions)
							Unchanged	Scenario 1	Scenario 2	Scenario 3	Scenario 4	Scenario 5	
Fed funds	10,000	—	—	—	—	—	3.50%	5.00%	5.50%	6.00%	4.00%	4.50%	$10.0
ABS portfolio	10,000	—	12/01/96	101.556	1.62	1.09	5.42	5.13	5.02	4.91	5.35	5.22	10.2
HOND94A[b]	2,000	+45 bps	04/15/97 9/95	99.078	1.45	1.34	5.64	5.16	4.99	4.81	5.53	5.35	2.0
FHE911[c]	2,000	+80 bps	10/15/97 7/95	103.578	1.42	1.29	5.75	5.35	5.19	5.05	5.67	5.51	2.1
HCC911[d]	4,000	+30 bps	03/15/96 9/95	102.578	1.46	1.35	5.83	5.29	5.10	4.91	5.68	5.44	4.1
MBNA932[e]	2,000	Floating rate[f]	02/15/97	99.969	2.29	0.10	4.03	4.52	4.70	4.88	4.17	4.32	2.0

[a]Including accumulated interest.
[b]Auto ABS.
[c]Home equity ABS.
[d]Credit card ABS.
[e]Floating credit card ABS.
[f]One-month LIBOR +17 bps.

Source: CS First Boston Corp.

with choosing between bullets and current-pay structures. A bullet is simply a security with a single payment of principal; bullet securities are similar to corporate bonds. According to conventional wisdom, in a bear market, investors try to shorten durations; so they would rather have a current-pay structure, such as amortized assets that pay monthly, than a bullet in order to reinvest the principal cash flows at higher rates. The Treasuries of shorter maturities yield less, however, so the choice is always a trade-off.

Bullets do have advantages even in a bear market. If the yield curve has a positive slope, the bullets can realize roll-down value. Roll-down value results because a two-year credit card ABS with a bullet maturity will, at the end of one year, have a new average life of one year. The average life decays day for day with the passage of time. If an investor starts with a two-year bond today, a year later, the investor will have a one-year bond. An amortizing security that pays current principal with a two-year average life however, such as an auto ABS, may have a 1.6-year average life a year from now. Thus, a bullet security will have a shorter duration at the end of the total time period, when total returns are computed, and the shorter duration will result in a smaller price decline because rates are rising.

Another advantage bullets have in a bear market is that a bullet will be repriced off a shorter maturity Treasury. If the curve has any steepness, a new benchmark Treasury will have a lower yield than the bullet, and that lower yield will produce a higher price.

An analysis of yield curves under various assumptions can help explain the advantages a bullet structure has over current-pay structures. **Figure 2** shows three yield curves under different assumptions for Fed funds out to seven years. One curve is today's (April 10, 1994) yield curve; curve A is

slightly flatter; and curve B assumes today's yield curve plus a parallel shift.

Keeping these yield curves in mind, look at the credit card (a bullet security) and the home equity loan (an amortizing security) in **Table 7**. The credit card ABS is offered at 35 bps over and the home equity is offered at 90 bps over the three-year Treasury note. Typically, investors want to buy the one that is offered at 90 bps off the three-year Treasury. The returns, however, indicate that the credit card, based on the April 10, 1994, curve, outperforms the home equity by 9 bps. Because it rolls down the yield curve, the credit card ABS reprices off the shorter maturity Treasury, and it suffers a smaller price decline during rising interest rates.

Managers should not be fooled by the initial or incremental spreads. As shown in Table 7, if investors had bought the home equity at 100 bps off the Treasury initially, they would have had the same total return as the credit card offered at 35 bps off the Treasury, which is not what one would expect intuitively.

The same thing happens for credit cards and auto loans. As shown in **Table 8**, although the credit card debt is offered at 32 bps off Treasuries and the auto loan is offered at 50 bps off, the credit card will outperform the auto, which is an amortizing asset. Furthermore, the credit card will outperform the auto loan in all three cases—that is, under all three curve assumptions. The auto breakeven spreads of 79, 60, and 65 bps indicate that auto loan is rich.

Trends in Home Equity Loans

The appeal of home equity asset-backed securities depends a great deal on the prepayment trends in home equity loans compared with trends in the first mortgage market. As shown in the **Table 9**, home equity loans, which are typically second mortgages, were originally priced at a prepayment speed of 18–20 percent constant prepayment rate (CPR). The first mortgages, in contrast, were typically priced at 8.5 percent CPR.

Prepayments are not stable, however, and prepayments in the mortgage market have recently accelerated. Table 9 indicates a peak CPR for ADVANTA 91-1 of about 57 percent, which is a considerably faster rate than when this issue was priced. The peak CPR was 217 percent greater than at new issue.

The situation for first mortgages was far more extreme than for home equity ABS. Table 9 shows the peak CPRs for first mortgages, which are typically priced at 8 and 9 percent CPR, to be off by approximately 650 percent. First mortgages prepay at exactly the worst time for the investor: When rates

Figure 2. Yield-Curve Assumptions

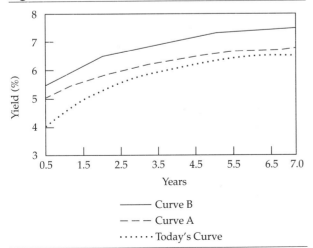

Years

——— Curve B

– – – Curve A

······· Today's Curve

Source: CS First Boston Corp.

Table 7. Bullet versus Current-Pay Security: 3-Year Average-Life Securities

Panel A. Description of securities

	Principal Window	Average Life			Prepay	4/10/94 Price	Coupon Pays
		Start	End	Decay			
Credit card	1 month	3.06	2.06	1.00	NA	+35/3-year Treasury	Semiannually
Home equity	128 months	3.05	2.91	0.14	22 CPR[a]	+90/3-year Treasury	Monthly

Panel B. Breakeven analysis[b]

	One-Year Actual Returns		Difference (bps)	Breakeven Spread Required Initially for Home Equity
	Credit Card +35/3-Year Treasury	Home Equity +90/3-Year Treasury		
4/10/94 curve	6.95%	6.86%	+9	+100/3-year Treasury
Curve A	6.38	6.41	−3	+87/3-year Treasury
Curve B	5.20	5.29	−9	+80/3-year Treasury

NA = not applicable.

[a]Constant prepayment rate.

[b]Reinvested at 3-year Treasury rate.

Source: CS First Boston Corp.

are rising, they extend, and when rates are falling, they shorten. Quantifying negative convexity accurately in first mortgages is important in order for the investor to receive compensation up front in spread. The negative convexity of first mortgages explains why home equities, even though they are second mortgages and the percentage changes in their peaks may initially look unappealing, are much more attractive than first mortgages.

Home equities originated by banks are different from those originated by finance companies. Typically, the more creditworthy borrowers go to banks

and tend to be more aggressive in refinancing their loans; so, the bank-originated home equities show greater sensitivity to interest rate movements. A regression analysis of interest rate changes and prepayments illustrates the differences. As **Table 10** indicates, prepayments for the 15-year first mortgages had a correlation (R^2) of about 52 percent, the bank home equities had an R^2 of about 38 percent, and the finance home equities had an R^2 of about 28 percent. Interest rates were dropping during the entire time this analysis was performed, and the X-coefficients indicate an increase in pass-throughs

Table 8. Bullet versus Current-Pay Security: 1.5-Year Average-Life Securities

Panel A. Description

	Principal Window	Average Life			Prepay	4/10/94 Price	Coupon Pays
		Start	End	Decay			
Credit card	1 month	1.50	0.50	1.00	NA	+32/1.5-year Treasury	Semiannually
Auto	55 months	1.51	1.17	0.34	1.5 ABS	+50/1.5-year Treasury	Monthly

Panel B. Breakeven analysis[a]

	One-Year Actual Returns		Difference (bps)	Breakeven Spread Required Initially for Auto
	Credit Card +32/1.5-Year Treasury	Auto +50/1.5-Year Treasury		
4/10/94 curve	6.04%	5.82%	+22	+79/1.5-year Treasury
Curve A	5.64	5.57	+7	+60/1.5-year Treasury
Curve B	5.46	5.35	+11	+65/1.5-year Treasury

NA = not applicable.

[a]Reinvested at 1.5-year Treasury rate.

Source: CS First Boston Corp.

Table 9. Home Equity Prepayments

Issue	Rate Type	Origination Year	Weighted-Average Coupon	Pricing Prepayment Speed	Peak CPR	Percent Change from Pricing Speed	Latest CPR
Home equities							
ADVANTA 91-1	Fixed	1990	13.45%	18.00%	57.07%	217.06%	57.07%
ADVANTA 91-2	Fixed	1990	13.61	20.00	46.93	134.65	46.93
American Financial 91-1	Fixed	1990	14.69	20.00	35.82	79.10	24.52
BW Home Equity 90-1	Fixed	1989	11.30	20.00	75.44	277.20	66.49
Equicon 92-7	Fixed	1992	13.81	21.00	38.25	82.14	32.25
Chevy Chase 90-1	Floating	1989	11.50	25.00	51.43	105.72	36.07
Chevy Chase 91-1	Floating	1989	9.00	22.00	55.27	151.23	31.17
FICAL 90-A	Fixed	1989–90	11.57	20.00	62.66	213.30	40.07
Fleet 90-1	Fixed	1990	15.91	23.00	30.12	30.96	24.10
Fleet 91-1	Fixed	1990	15.65	23.00	30.45	32.39	26.51
Home Equity 90-1 (HFC)	Floating	1990	12.00	26.00	39.38	51.46	26.29
Home Equity 90-2 (HFC)	Floating	1990	13.50	26.00	33.21	27.73	22.37
Oldstone 92-1	Fixed	1991	11.84	21.00	39.79	89.48	20.86
Oldstone 92-2 A1	Fixed	1992	12.44	25.00	46.22	84.88	28.13
Oldstone 92-2 A2	Fixed	1992	12.78	25.00	44.27	77.08	32.08
Security Pacific 91-A	Fixed	1990	14.86	23.00	42.05	82.83	32.08
SPBN 91-1	Fixed	1990	11.75	20.00	60.31	201.55	31.66
First mortgages							
FNMA 15-year, 8%, 1992		1992	8.75	8.50	63.76	650.12	34.38
FNMA 15-year, 9%, 1990		1990	9.75	8.50	65.06	665.41	43.74

Source: CS First Boston Corp.

every time interest rates dropped 100 bps. Conventional 15-year pass-throughs were off 140 percent from their pricing speeds for every 100-bp move, and finance companies were off about 6 percent.

The Future

Several changes or emerging trends will have positive impacts on the asset-backed securities market. First, investors can expect increased bank participation in ABS because of changes in risk weights. Risk weights for U.S. banks define required levels of capital for different investments. A proposal being spearheaded by the Federal Financial Institutions Examination Council would calibrate risk according to credit ratings. For example, a AAA-rated ABS would have its risk weighting reduced from 100 percent to 20 percent. That risk weight would be in line with conventional mortgages, so from a capital standpoint, banks would be indifferent between ABS and first mortgages. If ABS were yielding more than conventional mortgages, banks would have an incentive to purchase ABS.

Another trend will be the growth in credit card ABS. Many people wonder how the credit card market can possibly grow; after all, everyone already has a credit card, even many credit cards. Nevertheless, this market is expected to grow a great deal because three areas that have not traditionally accepted credit cards are now generating billions of dollars in credit: supermarkets, about $330 billion annually; health care outlets, about $162 billion; and fast food restaurants, about $65 billion estimated by CS First Boston. Outstandings in credit cards should increase 5–8 percent annually. Cumulative outstandings of credit card ABS, about $400 billion today, are expected to grow to about $880 billion by the year 2000, as shown in **Figure 3**. Charge volume is expected to increase 11–12 percent annually.

Figure 3. Projected Cumulative Average Growth Rate: Credit Card Industry

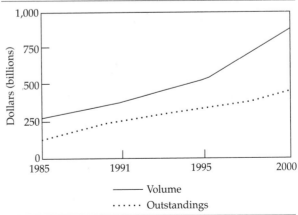

Source: The Nilson Report, Oxnard, Calif.

Table 10. Home Equity Prepayments and Interest Rate Changes

Type	Average R^2	Average X-Coefficient	Percent Change in Prepayments
Conventional 15-year pass-throughs	51.93%	13.9%	140.31%
Bank home equities	38.29	5.1	20.56
Finance home equities	27.94	1.5	6.34

Source: CS First Boston Corp.

Question and Answer Session

Tracy L. van Eck

Question: Do all types of asset-backed securities have negative convexity? Shouldn't auto loans and credit card debt have less refinancing risk than some other types? Are they interest rate sensitive?

van Eck: ABS that show sensitivity to interest rates are securities backed by home equity loans that are second mortgages and the ABS backed by manufactured (mobile home) housing loans. Auto and credit card ABS do not have nearly the negative convexity that first mortgages have, and because of their structures, some of them even have positive convexity.

Auto loan asset-backed securities are not interest rate sensitive. Suppose you have a 10 percent auto loan, for example, and because rates have dropped 300 bps, you go to refinance the auto loan. The car is a used car now, so you are charged a couple of percentage points more in refinancing and you incur another fee. Thus, achieving any savings from refinancing a car turns out to be economically impossible. The only time you want to prepay an auto loan is when you wreck the car or when you want a new car, and that moment does not necessarily correlate with interest rates. A study of prepayments at General Motors Acceptance Corporation indicated that sometimes auto loans actually have inverse relationships to interest rates.

Question: Why are securities backed by manufactured housing considered asset-backed securities instead of mortgage-backed securities?

van Eck: The main reason is that manufactured housing has historically shown less interest rate sensitivity than first mortgages.

Question: Given that asset-backed securities have been structured to meet certain institutional demands, particularly regulatory demands, are they overvalued generally for the unconstrained investor?

van Eck: No, they are not overvalued for the unconstrained investor. ABS outperformed everything in 1993 and in the first quarter of 1994 because they tightened in spread. The spreads on alternative sectors widened. Because ABS have reached historically tight spreads, they may no longer be home-run trades, but I would categorize them as defensive assets. The spreads will not widen. Remember, the ABS market is so tiny that, if one big investor group comes in to buy securities, spreads can tighten immediately.

The market will never let ABS spreads become too wide; ABS are too valuable as core assets. Other sectors are more vulnerable to widening spreads. The mortgage market and the corporate market today are particularly vulnerable. That is why asset-backed securities will be superior performers relative to alternative investments.

Question: What is the liquidity in the secondary market?

van Eck: Typically, credit card and auto ABS have secondary markets of 1–2 bps; the others might have something like 5–bp markets.

Question: The ABS market seems to be well seasoned and straightforward; did the recession have any effect on it?

van Eck: An increase in loss rates on the underlying collateral occurred, but none of the ABS was adversely affected.

Question: How has your analysis changed since 1990 in terms of reviewing the structure of credit card and home equity deals?

van Eck: I used to worry about creditworthiness and potential loss of principal. It turns out, however, that not only has no investor ever lost a single dollar in ABS, neither has any credit enhancer. No entity that has provided cash collateral or a reserve fund as a first-loss position has ever lost a dollar. Now, therefore, I am more concerned about the timing of cash flows and such aspects as negative convexity. I am interested in the structures and what kind of implications the structures have.

Question: For comparing prepayments of asset-backed securities with prepayments of underlying mortgages, how useful are the home-equity-loan prepayment models?

van Eck: I would be suspicious of any home-equity-loan model. Consider the following example: A homeowner has a $60,000 first mortgage outstanding and a $20,000 second mortgage outstanding. It looks like she can refinance her first mortgage now because rates have dropped, so she goes to the bank. The bank suggests, as banks typically do, that if she is going to refinance her first mortgage, she might as well throw in her second. She agrees, and the bank ends up refinancing her mortgages as an $80,000 first mortgage. In effect, the first mortgage drove her to prepay her home equity loan even though that loan had nothing to do with the first mortgage. Because of such circumstances, no one can build an accurate prepayment model; to do it would require knowing the underlying rate on the first mortgage, and that information is not available.

The evidence suggests that home equity ABS have less negative convexity and that they react less to interest rates than first mortgages. The uncertainty lies in why. One reason is the much smaller loan balances of the ABS. The average loan balance is $25,000, whereas the average loan balance for first mortgages is $150,000. With small loan balances, refinancing incentives require a much larger rate drop than when loan balances are large.

Municipal Bonds

Jerome J. Jacobs, CFA
Vice President
The Vanguard Group of Investment Companies

> Opportunity abounds in the municipal bond market, but the complexity in the market places a premium on sophisticated analysis. An important part of valuation is to study the nuances and trends in buying and selling. Municipal bond derivative securities can provide definite advantages to certain portfolios but only if they are used properly.

The municipal market can be described in two words: complexity and opportunity. The complexity stems from the broad array of asset classes in the market. Unlike investment managers in the taxable market, in which the segments are highly specialized and highly divided, municipal market participants cover a variety of assets, and in consequence, they are usually generalists. The municipal market has almost every type of security found in the taxable market, such as government bonds, corporate bonds, mortgages, and high-yield bonds. It also has some assets that are dissimilar to the taxable market.

The opportunity arises because some of the highly sophisticated quantitative techniques that have been developed for the taxable market are not yet being fully exploited in the municipal market. Therefore, a wealth of opportunity awaits those astute managers who are using the techniques.

This presentation discusses the structure of the municipal bond market, including who the issuers and buyers are and the trends. It also explores new analytical techniques applicable to municipal bonds, such as option-adjusted duration and yield-curve analysis. The discussion then turns to derivative securities, credit analysis, and finally, portfolio construction.

Market Structure

The municipal bond market consists of two broad categories. The first is general obligation bonds, which can be described as the plain vanilla investments backed by the full faith and credit of various governments. General obligation bonds currently represent about one-third of the total municipal market, with the categories as shown in **Figure 1**. Up until 15 years ago, these bonds represented more than two-thirds of total municipal market issuance. The bonds in this category have much more volatility in their ratings than investors might expect. A recent example is the Commonwealth of Massachusetts bonds; they declined from an AA to a BBB rating within several years.

The other category in the municipal market can be broadly called revenue bonds. Revenue bonds, as broken down in **Figure 2**, accounted for about two-thirds of the total issuance in 1993. These securities are much more complex in structure than general obligation bonds; investment bankers are ingenious in developing ways to meet the specific needs of issuers through complicated securities structures.

The major issuers of revenue bonds are in the fields of electric power, health care, and housing. Electric power issuers are joint-action agencies, collectives of municipal entities that purchase power, and municipal entities themselves. The large health care sector includes hospitals, for which the bond ratings range from AA down to nonrated, nursing homes, and some other issuers. Bonds in the housing category, which applies to multifamily and single-family housing, are roughly akin to securities in the mortgage-backed markets. Currently, this sector is small, primarily because of restrictive provisions in the most recent tax acts that toughened issuance guidelines. This sector represents a larger overall weight, however, than Figure 2 indicates because of higher levels of issuance in prior years. The "Other" category encompasses several types of special-situation bonds that look like corporate-backed bonds, such as airline bonds and financings for investor-owned utilities. The sector also includes unusual revenue bond financings for such projects as prisons, racetracks, stadiums, and aquariums.

An important simplifying aspect of the munici-

Figure 1. Municipal Bond Issuance by Sector: General Obligation Bonds, 1993

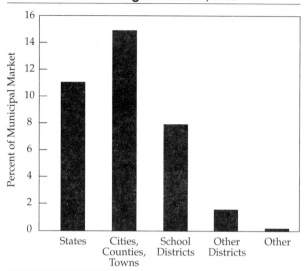

Source: The Bond Buyer 1993 Yearbook, The Vanguard Group, based on data from Securities Data Corp.

pal bond market is municipal bond insurance. As shown in **Figure 3**, municipal bond insurance grew from about 15 percent of the total market in 1983 to nearly 40 percent of the market in 1993. Two primary reasons explain this rapid growth. One is the liquidity and cost-effectiveness that result, particularly for small issuers, from paying a municipal insurer to re-rate bonds AAA at an efficient price. The other reason is that the complexity in the market has caused some individual investors to give up trying to analyze specific risk features of municipal securi-

ties, particularly in the case of the more complex structures.

In 1993, the size of the municipal bond market was almost $300 billion in total long-term new issuance. This amount is clearly a record in the market, as **Figure 4** shows. When historical trends of issuance are examined, two periods of significance are the 1985–86 and the 1991–93 periods. The bloat in issuance in the 1985–86 period was inspired by the tax code restrictions on numerous types of municipal issuance that were to go into effect in 1986. Issuers rushed to the market in 1985 to beat the tax changes. Re-funding issuance because of low interest rates further increased total supply. The second period that stands out in Figure 4 is the 1991–93 explosion in total municipal bond issuance. This explosion was exclusively driven by record levels of re-funding activity. In fact, "new money" issuance grew only at a modest clip.

Predicting future issuance has both easy and difficult aspects. The easy part, new-money issuance, is illustrated in **Figure 5**. The historical pattern initially looks somewhat bumpy; the 1985–86 period shows accelerated issuance prior to enactment of the Tax Reform Act of 1986 . Smoothing out the accelerated issuance of 1985 and 1986 to issuance from 1987 through 1989 provides an idea of what historical issuance might have been without the 1986 act. This "normalized" new-money market is roughly $100 billion in annual issuance and growing at approximately the rate of inflation.

The portion that is tough to predict is re-funding issuance. As demonstrated in **Figure 6**, this portion

Figure 2. Municipal Bond Issuance by Sector: Revenue Bonds, 1993

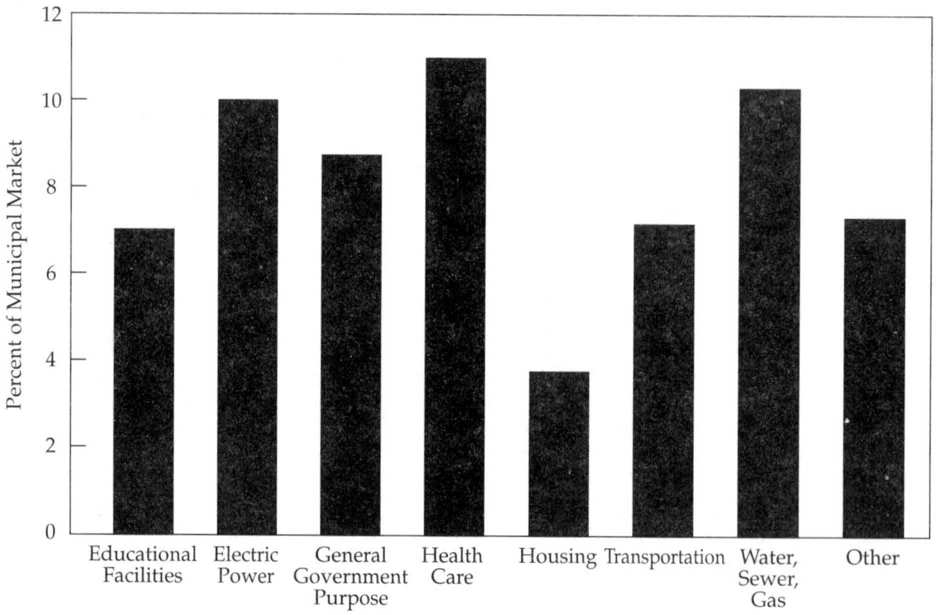

Source: The Bond Buyer 1993 Yearbook, The Vanguard Group, based on data from Securities Data Corp.

Figure 3. Municipal Bond Insurance

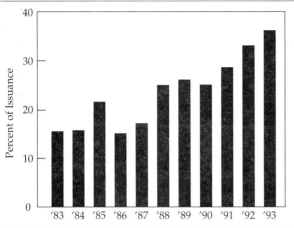

Source: The Bond Buyer 1993 Yearbook, The Vanguard Group, based on data from Securities Data Corp.

has been extremely unstable, particularly from 1990 through 1993. The municipal market, like the mortgage-backed securities market, had its greatest number of refinancings in history in 1992 and 1993, when almost half the municipal market was refinanced.

One unique feature of the municipal market is that municipal issuers, unlike their corporate brethren, leave their issues outstanding in the market when they refinance. This practice has a powerful effect on the level of total municipal debt outstanding because the "old issue" and "new issue" remain outstanding simultaneously. Advance re-funding, or pre-re-funding, makes the market complex to analyze because investors must consider not only interest rates in general but also the clustering of coupons in the market, transactional efficiency, and issuer behavior—all patterns that are tough to predict.

The municipal market attracts four broad types of buyers: individual investors, bond funds, property and casualty (P&C) companies, and commercial banks. The mix of buyers has been changing dra-

Figure 4. Long-Term New Issuance

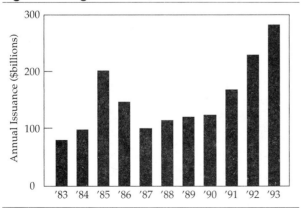

Source: The Bond Buyer 1993 Yearbook, The Vanguard Group, based on data from Securities Data Corp.

Figure 5. New-Money Issuance

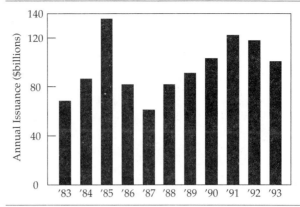

Source: The Bond Buyer 1993 Yearbook, The Vanguard Group, based on data from Securities Data Corp.

matically, and the changes affect all types of valuation analyses—of yield curves, quality, and sector spreads. As shown in the upper panel of **Figure 7**, the market had considerable balance in 1983. Commercial banks and households each held about a third of the bonds. The relatively small, infant, mutual fund industry held slightly less than 6 percent of the total, divided into about 2.65 percent in the hands of mutual funds and 3.32 percent in money market funds. P&C companies accounted for about a fifth of the municipal market.

Figure 6. Re-Funding Issuance

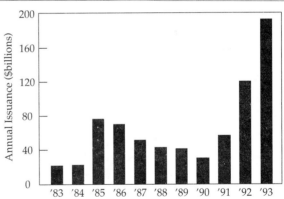

Source: The Bond Buyer 1993 Yearbook, The Vanguard Group, based on data from Securities Data Corp.

The balance of municipal debt holders has tilted away from institutions, as shown in the lower panel of Figure 7. The household, mutual fund, and money market fund categories, which are essentially either direct individual investments or conduits for individuals' investments, total an alarming 64 percent of the market. Commercial banks have virtually disappeared from the municipal market, which relates to the 1986 tax code's elimination of the ability of commercial banks to deduct the interest of carrying tax-

Figure 7. Breakdown of Municipal Debt Holders

1983

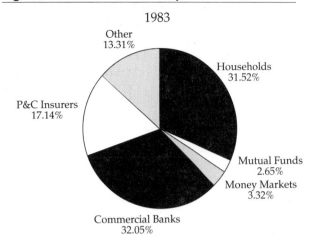

Other 13.31%
Households 31.52%
P&C Insurers 17.14%
Mutual Funds 2.65%
Money Markets 3.32%
Commercial Banks 32.05%

1993

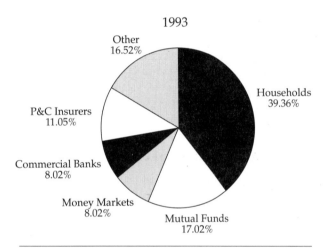

Other 16.52%
Households 39.36%
P&C Insurers 11.05%
Commercial Banks 8.02%
Money Markets 8.02%
Mutual Funds 17.02%

Source: The Bond Buyer 1993 Yearbook, The Vanguard Group, based on data from the Federal Reserve Board, Flow of Funds Accounts.

Figure 8. Closed-End Funds, Mutual Funds, and Money Market Funds: Share of Tax-Exempt Debt
(percent of total outstanding)

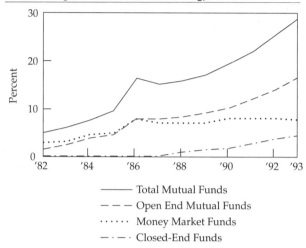

—— Total Mutual Funds
– – – Open End Mutual Funds
· · · · · Money Market Funds
– · – · Closed-End Funds

Source: The Bond Buyer 1993 Yearbook, The Vanguard Group, based on data from the Federal Reserve Board, Flow of Funds Accounts.

exempt bonds. P&C companies' share of holdings fell to 11 percent. This situation explains how, for example, a municipal bond contract could have declined 17 points from January 28 to April 4, 1994—about 5 points more than the Treasury bond contracted during the same time. Many aspects of these developments relate to the lack of balance in today's municipal market. Mass redemptions by individual investors and bond funds cause serious imbalances in the market.

The rate of growth in the mutual fund sector is astonishing, as can be seen in **Figure 8**. The growth from about 6 percent of all bonds in the tax-exempt market in 1983 to almost 30 percent in 1993 amounts to a fivefold increase in a decade. On a net basis (issuance minus calls, redemptions, and maturities), the trend is even more astonishing: The mutual fund sector in 1993 had accumulated more than the total growth of the market. In other words, on a net basis, all other sectors in 1993 were net redeemers in the

tax-exempt market. This trend is alarming, and it helps explain the recent meltdown, which is similar to that of 1987, when redemption activity caused mutual fund portfolio managers to sell securities into a rapidly declining market.

The growth in the mutual fund sector is clearly coming at the expense of other sectors, as illustrated in **Figure 9**. The sharp decline for commercial banks from 1986 to 1993 occurred as their large tax-exempt portfolios matured; the banks retained the tax-exempt advantage that was grandfathered and simply let those maturities occur over time.

Figure 9. Households, Commercial Banks, and P&C Insurers: Share of Tax-Exempt Debt
(percent of total outstanding)

—— Households
– – – Commercial Banks
· · · · · P&C Insurers

Source: The Bond Buyer 1993 Yearbook, The Vanguard Group, based on data from the Federal Reserve Board, Flow of Funds Accounts.

Initially, after the 1986 tax code eliminated the banks from the market, individual investors picked up some of the slack. Then, starting about 1991, their share of the market also began declining. This decline was probably attributable to the growing popularity of the bond funds. Their increasing specialization and customization offer convenience and attractive returns. An astonishing number of funds is available; among them, they cater to virtually every need of the individual investor. Offerings include state-specific funds, a vast array of short-term and intermediate-term offerings, and funds composed of all mixes of credit quality.

The P&C company decline in Figure 9 appears straightforward and uninteresting at first glance, but it is more significant than it looks. The 1986 tax code changed the environment for P&C companies by establishing a minimum tax provision that required complex analysis. Additionally, the cyclical nature of P&C company profitability has strongly influenced buying behavior. Although not evident yet in Figure 9, the trend of this sector's significant decline from 1987 to about 1993 is now strongly reversing. The P&C companies have recently found some advantages to increasing the weight of tax-exempt securities in their portfolios. Moreover, parent and individual P&C companies are becoming much more profitable, and consequently, they are once again buying aggressively.

In summary, the municipal bond market is a complex one made up of several types of securities with many individual characteristics. The most important considerations in valuation in this market are the nuances in buying and selling activities; trends in buying and selling affect every type of valuation analysis.

New Techniques for Analysis

Much of the excitement in the municipal market today is related to analytical techniques that have become available, most of which have been adapted from those used in the taxable market. Not all fund managers in the tax-exempt market have warmly embraced the evolving quantitative techniques. In fact, a certain amount of fear and trepidation has been evident as the tax-exempt market was forced to follow the quantitative techniques that have been developed. This section covers techniques for assessing market risk, including analyzing option-adjusted duration, and yield-curve measurement and analysis.

Assessing Market Risk

To demonstrate how assessing market risk in a portfolio has evolved over time, this section will use a state-specific portfolio, chosen because this portfo-

lio has much of the optionality that is difficult to price in the market. In other words, the portfolio contains several long bonds, with calls, sinking funds, and other complicated provisions.

About ten years ago, the "effective maturity to worst" technique shown in **Figure 10** was prevalent for assessing the behavior of a tax-exempt portfolio. It is a crude calculation, and the technique has many obvious flaws and drawbacks. For example, relatively small changes in interest rates generate a large amount of variation in effective maturity, from slightly more than 9 years (–100 basis points in yield) to almost 15 years (+100 basis points in yield). Most importantly, however, this kind of analysis does not accurately predict the "true" market sensitivity of a portfolio. It tends to understate the downside potential of this particular portfolio in environments of low interest rates and to overstate the upside potential in times of sharp rises in interest rates.

The next step in the evolution was the technique called "modified duration to worst," which is what analysts were using five or six years ago. This technique appears to be a great improvement, in that the amplitude in the graph is much more manageable than in the earlier technique and the changes are more continuous over time. The technique nevertheless has many drawbacks; for instance, the changes in modified duration are still too large. Most importantly, this technique only crudely captures a portfolio's volatility over time.

Today's analysis, "option-adjusted modified duration," includes all the optionality that a tax-exempt portfolio has within it. The optionality consists of call options, sinking funds, and advance re-funding

Figure 10. Three Methods of Assessing Market Risk: Data as of February 28, 1994

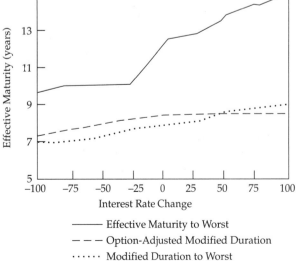

Source: The Vanguard Group.

effects, which are particularly important in the tax-exempt market. This technique is a "friendly" way to manage a portfolio; the changes in price sensitivity over time are smooth and continuous, and more significantly, they capture the way the portfolio is behaving more accurately than the early methods. Disadvantages to the technique are that it requires analysts to know their models and be comfortable with the assumptions that go into the calculations, particularly volatility assumptions and advance re-funding analysis. In addition, updating the model components as information is received is important. If analysts are not comfortable with the techniques and tools used in the model or do not understand how the model works, or if the assumptions are erroneous, the result will be incorrect output.

The "advance re-funding option" is the great positive option in the tax-exempt market; thus, understanding this option and knowing how to calculate it are very important. Using a model that does not capture the advance re-funding effect over time, such as a model for analyzing corporate bonds, and trying to crunch municipal securities into that model is particularly dangerous. **Figure 11** demonstrates how advance re-funding works for an A-rated 30-year municipal bond with a standard 10-year call protection. As can be seen in the top line, the bond was yielding slightly under 7 percent in 1992. By late 1993, the environment had changed, and as the figure shows, the curve had shifted downward; the bond was yielding about 5.75 percent. Then, the A-rated bond, which started out as a garden variety bond with standard call provisions, was pre-re-funded, and three very good things happened to the bondholder.

First, the bond received an upgrade. The municipal issuer pre-re-funded the bond. As noted, the original bond stayed outstanding, but now it was backed (in almost all cases) by Treasury securities; thus, it was re-rated to AAA. In this example, the upgrade effect on the original bond was about 60 basis points (bps).

Second, the bondholder was repositioned along the yield curve. Pre-re-funding has such an effect in any positively sloped yield-curve environment.

Third, all of the original optionality of the bond disappeared. Essentially, the bondholder now has a nine-year bond rated AAA with all the characteristics of a nine-year bullet security. Rather than declining approximately 125 bps in yield, this particular security has declined about 250 bps in yield. The commensurate price appreciation is about 14 points—roughly double what a corporate bond might have experienced in the same environment.

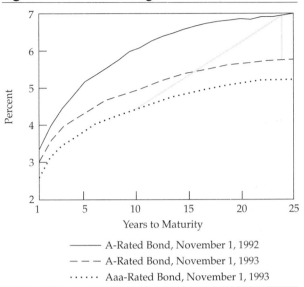

Figure 11. Pre-Re-Funding Effect: A-Rated Bond

——— A-Rated Bond, November 1, 1992
– – – A-Rated Bond, November 1, 1993
· · · · · Aaa-Rated Bond, November 1, 1993

Source: The Vanguard Group.

Yield-Curve Analysis

To illustrate how to use yield-curve analysis to measure and assess municipal bonds, this section will use a portfolio of long, tax-exempt bonds. The portfolio also holds cash portfolios in various regions, as well as important futures and options offsets that are both in the taxable and tax-exempt markets. **Table 1** provides a breakdown of everything in the portfolio and how each element is positioned within sectors along the yield curve. The table is organized by duration contribution by sector, and everything in the portfolio is measured against a Vanguard Group internal benchmark. Negative numbers—as in the case of "Electric revenue" bonds with a duration of more than ten years—indicate an underweighting against the benchmark.

This kind of analysis has evolved from much more complicated systems; a key purpose is to put analysis in the most understandable format possible. The focus of this approach to managing a long-bond portfolio is on measuring risk along the yield curve, measuring its contribution, and trying to add some value as the yield curve changes.

Although this tool is fine for a long-bond portfolio, some of the tools for managing in intermediate-bond regions of the market will be much more sophisticated and complex. The intermediate regions require optimization techniques and modeling in order to optimize the roll down the yield curve and yield per unit of duration, with the ultimate aim of optimizing total return within a portfolio's objectives.

Table 1. Portfolio versus Benchmark: Duration Contribution by Sector

Sector	Duration					Total
	0–2	2–4	4–7	7–10	10+	
General obligation	—	—	—	0.50	−0.45	0.05
Electric revenue	—	—	—	−0.58	−0.72	−1.30
Hospital	—	—	−0.19	0.01	−0.41	−0.59
Housing	0.01	—	—	−0.19	−0.53	−0.71
Pollution	—	0.04	—	−0.16	0.06	−0.06
Insured	—	—	0.01	0.23	0.98	1.22
Local general obligation	—	—	—	0.44	0.35	0.79
Lease fee	—	—	—	0.20	0.71	0.91
Pre-re-funded	0.01	0.03	−0.60	0.05	0.25	−0.26
Transportation	—	—	—	—	−0.64	−0.64
University	—	—	—	0.32	−0.54	−0.22
Water	—	—	—	0.27	0.72	0.99
Reserves	0.19	—	—	—	—	0.19
Futures/options	—	—	−0.23	−0.82	−0.64	−1.69
Other	—	—	—	−0.10	0.15	0.05
Total	0.21	0.07	−1.01	0.17	−0.71	−1.27

Source: The Vanguard Group.

Derivative Securities

Municipal derivatives have received much attention recently in the press. Indeed, considerable confusion—even hysteria—attends the use of derivatives in the markets in general, not only in the tax-exempt market. An example of the basis for the hysteria is the following story from an April 15, 1994, *Wall Street Journal* article. The *Journal* reported that a municipal bond fund agreed to settle out of court with New York's attorney general for allegedly failing to disclose the risk it took by investing 40 percent of its portfolio in exotic derivative securities.[1] These securities were inverse floating-rate instruments, and they caused the fund to decline an alarmingly large amount in comparison with its competitors.

Derivatives are a tool, and in this case, the tool was used improperly. To take a portfolio described in one way (a tax-exempt portfolio) and create an altogether different type of price sensitivity in it is not only improper and unethical; it borders on being criminal.

In *Barron's*, columnist Alan Abelson wrote, "Stocks and bonds are investment instruments. Derivatives are instruments of the devil, that even he does not always understand." He noted, "Procter & Gamble took a bath when it sought to offset the risk of interest rate swings. It is a well-known fact in the detergent business that every eighth of a point change in interest rates causes consumers to stampede in and out of detergents."[2]

Again, derivatives are a tool. Derivatives are a prudent and proper tool to use if investment managers are using them in a way that is consistent with the behavior of their fund or the behavior of their company. In the case of Procter & Gamble, the managers who were using derivatives were not engaged in company-related business.

Derivatives are created from host bonds in which risk and return characteristics of fixed-income securities have been embedded. Derivatives carry the same risk and return aspects investment managers have always analyzed, such as duration, convexity, sector bets, credit-specific wagers, and cross-market activities. Two common structures for the municipal market are inverse floating-rate instruments and embedded interest rate caps. Since 1992, when municipal participants first accessed the inverse floating-rate instrument (which had been around the taxable market for awhile but was a brand-new instrument in the municipal market), the market for this instrument has grown to $15–$20 billion in total size. The largest use of inverse floaters has been in open-end bond funds. These funds are buying the inverse floaters for their yield and dividend effects and to avoid capital gains on the underlying portfolio.

The embedded interest rate caps are the exact opposite of inverse floaters: Interest rate caps receive additional coupons when short-term interest rates rise. Investors have used interest rate caps less frequently than the inverse floaters. Considering that the Federal Reserve has raised short-term rates three times since February 4, 1994, some investors may wish they had considered interest rate caps a little more seriously.

Advantages and Disadvantages

Derivatives can provide a tax-exempt portfolio

---

[1]Robert McGough, "Bond Fund Sets Disclosure Pact on Derivatives," *Wall Street Journal* (April 15, 1994).

[2]Both quotations from Alan Abelson, "Up and Down Wall Street: Sore Loser," *Barron's* (April 17, 1994).

numerous advantages, and a few disadvantages. The first advantage is efficient customization. Suppose, for example, a policy decision is made that requires a broad change in a portfolio's positioning—in both duration and position along the yield curve. The portfolio manager has two choices: One alternative is to turn over a large amount of bonds in the portfolio. This approach creates a potpourri of problems. For instance, transactions are expensive, and the manager may not be able to find the desired securities in the appropriate sizes and positions. The alternative is to use derivatives to take a small amount of bonds and efficiently embed in them all the characteristics the manager is now seeking. Derivatives allow a manager to pick exactly the desired characteristics—such as positions along the yield curve, duration, and convexity profiles—and to make specific credit and sector wagers.

The second advantage is speed. A broad change in portfolio positioning for a large portfolio could require turning over 25 percent of the securities, and that task would take considerable time. A manager can accomplish the repositioning quickly, however, with the right kind of derivative instrument.

Derivatives also provide two significant tax advantages in the tax-exempt market. First, these instruments allow capital gains in the underlying portfolio to be avoided. Capital gains taxes have been a particularly difficult problem in the 1991–93 period. Through derivatives, investment managers can make necessary portfolio changes without incurring the tax liability that turning over underlying bonds creates. Second, investors can convert profits from a derivatives transaction into tax-exempt "step-up" coupons. This conversion of capital to tax-exempt income is a powerful advantage.

Use of derivatives has significant disadvantages, however. The first is fees; issuers, investment bankers, and others will not provide customization for free. The fees come in all forms—structuring fees to create the exotic instrument, certain types of auction fees, reset fees, reconstitution fees, and so on.

Illiquidity is the second disadvantage. Many of these securities have not been tested in difficult market conditions. The municipal derivatives market is not large, so maneuvering can be difficult if an investor desires to liquidate the instrument. Third, these derivatives involve significant regulatory and disclosure issues. Explaining such complex securities is no simple task, particularly in an open-end fund because of the many shareholders involved. On the regulatory side, the SEC has been known to audit bond and money market funds for proper derivatives use. The commission is particularly interested in how each portfolio's derivatives work and in finding out whether the fund managers understand the complex features, can explain them, and have modeled their behavior out over time.

A simple test can be applied for deciding on the use of derivatives in a portfolio: If the behavior of the overall portfolio with the derivatives will be consistent with the fund's objective, and if the fund's objective is reasonable and prudent, then the use of derivatives is reasonable and prudent. If the overall behavior of the portfolio that includes derivatives is not consistent with the fund's objective, the use of derivatives poses problems.

Valuation of Derivative Securities

This section offers several tips on how to define the complex features of derivatives, model them, and present them in a simple way. The initial format the Vanguard Group uses for analysis is a payoff matrix that expresses all packages of securities in a risk-neutral way. We include in the analysis all the transactions costs and all the tax implications of the particular set of transactions.

The result is a total return matrix like that illustrated in **Table 2** showing change in long rates on one axis and change in short rates on the other. Thus, a manager has a payoff matrix indicating positive and negative numbers. Table 2 shows the matrix for a package of securities consisting of an inverse floating-rate instrument plus the pre-re-funded bond. This combination is a popular package that the open-end bond funds have been using to avoid the capital gains on pre-re-funded bonds.

Table 2. Total Return: 20-Year Inverse Floater plus 7-Year Pre-Re-Funding Issue less 20-Year Noncall
(duration neutralized)

Change in Long Rates	Change in Short Rates					Equal-Weighted Expected Returns
	−2.00%	−1.00%	0.00%	1.00%	2.00%	
−2.00%	−1.697%	−1.520%	−1.347%	−1.176%	−1.008%	−1.350%
−1.00	0.492	0.613	0.732	0.848	0.961	0.729
0.00	0.874	0.949	1.021	1.091	1.159	1.019
1.00	−0.170	−0.135	−0.102	−0.071	−0.041	−0.104
2.00	−1.085	−1.084	−1.083	−1.085	−1.088	−1.085
Average	−0.317	−0.235	−0.156	−0.079	−0.003	−0.158

Source: The Vanguard Group.

When a matrix like that shown in Table 2 is completed, the analysis is simple: What is the forecast for this scenario? What is the expected total return? What happens if the expectations are wrong? To the extent that they are wrong, what are the concomitant negative payoffs? We are interested in what kind of symmetry those negative payoffs have, in what regions they occur, and what kind of probabilities we attach to those scenarios.

The important aspect of this analytical approach to complex securities is not so much the numbers presented as the thought process that goes into the analysis. Almost all complex securities can be formatted this way, and although the modeling is complex, the presentation format can be simple.

Credit Analysis

The payoffs and penalties of municipal credit decisions may surprise some taxable market participants. We have made both successful and unsuccessful decisions. First, a successful decision: In 1991, we purchased a lease-obligation bond from the city of Philadelphia at an 8.85 percent yield. About two years later, we sold it at a 4.3 percent yield. The bond had been pre-re-funded. The positive credit effect and the pre-re-funding effect had turned our non-rated security into what was then an 8-year AAA-rated security. The result was a 455-bp decline in yield and a 33-point appreciation in price. During the same period, the Treasury market rallied about 200 bps.

Some unsuccessful credit decisions, particularly in high-yield analysis, can be alarming and significant. Some of the life-care obligations are selling at about 50 cents on the dollar. We are trying to work them out by bidding with other co-holders.

Credit analysis can be quantified. We use several tools to try to simplify the complex process so as to facilitate decision making. We look at four areas: the analyst's rating, the trend analysis of that rating, the degree of conviction that the analyst has when predicting a change in credit rating, and the time horizon. We measure and quantify successes or failures. Improving the bets made on credit decisions is important, and we use backtesting to measure how we have done. Also, when we get into nonrated situations or low-grade situations, we are disciplined about asking our analysts for both the probability of default and how that probability changes over time.

Current Trends

This section focuses on some specific current trends in three sectors: hospitals, electric utilities, and general obligation bonds.

The regulatory environment surrounding hospitals is undergoing a great deal of change, which is prompting a great deal of opportunity and risk. Hospital bonds are a "buyer beware" sector where analysis counts and can add value.

With respect to electric utilities, the municipal market is pricing their bonds like general obligation bonds today, which is why we have sharply underweighted them. The market has not fully acknowledged that this industry is operating under a great deal of additional cost and competitive pressure; thus, this sector will probably underperform.

In the general obligation bond area, several important and significant regional trends are emerging. Some of the regional economies, particularly in the Northeast, are showing strong, positive credit trends, and we are overweighting many of those sectors. The West Coast has had some well-publicized negative trends, and we have been underweighting that sector for several years.

A simple way to take several pages of output for a particular bond and determine both the probability of its default and its time-weighted expectancy is to construct a breakeven line like that shown in **Figure 12**. This method allows an analyst to look at a bond's price and, in some rational way, convert the analyst's expectation for that bond to the price in the market.

Portfolio Construction

The process of portfolio construction at Vanguard has three important components. The first is choosing a benchmark consistent with the objectives of the portfolio. The second, because we are a top-down organization, is the macroeconomic forecast. Everything that we do, all valuation decisions, stem (at least in part) from that forecast of the overall envi-

Figure 12. Example of a Market-Implied Cumulative Probability of Incurring a Default

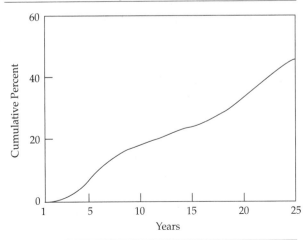

Source: The Vanguard Group.

ronment. The third component is to drop down into valuation techniques. Given the overall environment, what kinds of things do we see happening? What do those phenomena mean for the components we are examining? What do they mean for the various yield-curve components, sector components, and so forth?

The process of benchmarking in the tax-exempt market was growing even before the SEC required all mutual funds to choose a benchmark and include it in their semiannual and annual literature, but the SEC requirement has greatly accelerated the process. Our bogey for the high-yield portfolio is the Lehman Brothers Municipal Bond Index, which we consider the most accurate and most consistent index in measuring the broad market.

The forecast for our sample portfolio was based on the beliefs of the director of Vanguard's fixed-income activities. He believed that economic growth was accelerating beyond current market expectations. The Fed had just begun raising interest rates, but he had expected them to do so; thus, we were in a good position.

We included in our portfolio construction an expectation for a cyclical bear market for bonds. We expected the yield curve to flatten (and it is somewhat perplexing that, up to this point, it has not). The yield-curve flattening meant several important things to us. First, the worth of the pre-re-funding option would decline. Second, the value of the convexity should rise. Third, certain lower rated credits would benefit from stronger growth even though quality spreads would widen generally.

Finally, the portfolio was constructed around the expectation that the cash flows of open-end bond funds would be weak (as they have been). We also expected municipal supply to be low, considering the dropping off of re-funding activity.

Conclusion

The municipal bond market is a complex one made up of several types of securities with many individual characteristics. This market carries a fair amount of opportunity, particularly if a manager is on the cutting edge of quantitative analysis and is able to investigate and manipulate these complex features to add value. Municipal derivatives are a useful tool when properly used.

One of the most important elements of valuation in this market is a study of the nuances and trends in buying and selling activities. Understanding pre-re-funding analysis is extremely important for option-adjusted analysis, option-adjusted duration, calculations, and valuation.

Question and Answer Session

Jerome J. Jacobs, CFA

Question: Please comment on the growth of municipal insurance and how much value there is in insurance.

Jacobs: With respect to municipal bond insurance, I'll make two points. First, issuers tend to insure the smaller deals. It is cost-effective for a $25 million issuer to pay an insurer to have its bond trade generically and at an appropriate price. That small issuer saves costs. As a bond fund manager, I try to avoid municipal bond insurance unless the sector becomes attractive. I pick the credits I think have better value. Default ratios have been low, so the securities that have been picked have been quite profitable.

Question: How much risk is in pre-re-funded structures? Can these structures be unwound even though the original deal is not extinguished?

Jacobs: For the most part, the structures of pre-re-funding issues are pretty tight. The defeasance is generally irrevocable. The securities have been bought in the Treasury market. They fully defease the obligation and ensure that no loopholes exist to wiggle out of that obligation.

There are some exceptions—technically called economic defeasances—in which some complexities exist. Analysts must examine the escrow documents for them. These exceptions are pretty rare and unusual, however.

Question: Given the illiquidity

in the market when shareholders are selling, should no-load tax-exempt mutual funds have exit fees?

Jacobs: I would feel more comfortable if the industry were balanced between structures that had exit fees and structures that did not. For the whole industry to be in a no-exit-fee position would exacerbate the illiquidity that is already building. An improvement would be for some of the closed-end products to increase market share in other products, such as unit investment trusts, that are not as easy to exit.

Question: What are the best ways to take advantage of what looks like an undervalued tax-exempt market?

Jacobs: If you are going to get involved, you should be a student of the underlying bonds in the municipal bond contract, their pricing, and their characteristics. Do not go blindly into the municipal futures contract as a long or short position without performing analysis on the underlying components and their relative values.

If you think the tax-exempt market is underpriced, then the most secure move is to buy the long municipal bond, in which you can identify the characteristics precisely—the duration, convexity, and other statistics—and precisely measure them against your hedge vehicle in the Treasury market. If you plan to do this, you should probably pick

something that is liquid and generic. An insured bond is good, as is a commodity that does not require much analysis to understand. Some of the higher quality general obligation bonds would also be good.

Question: Please comment on bank-qualified issuance. Are banks coming back into this market?

Jacobs: To my knowledge, the bank-qualified limit (i.e., the limit at which banks are permitted the deduction for carrying that bond) is $10 million, so you are dealing with a small component of the tax-exempt market, tiny issues that tend to originate in specific regions of the country.

As far as I know, no trend is under way to return the exemption that banks held in 1986 and earlier. That would be doubtful, given the significant revenue loss it would entail.

Question: What do you think about soft-dollar use in the municipals market?

Jacobs: The distinction lies with whether soft-dollar use enhances shareholder value. If the soft dollars are not improving the broker's fees but, instead, are enhancing the benefit to the shareholder, that is an ethical, appropriate, and prudent thing to do. If the soft dollars are used to improve the fee of an organization or an individual, that is an improper and unethical use.

Managing Risk and Capturing Opportunities with Derivative Securities

Carl O. Bautista
Capital Markets Group
Bankers Trust Company

Kris Mahabir
Director of Derivative Strategy
Fidelity Management and Research Company

Derivative securities can provide investors flexibility to pursue high current or future income, diversification, tools for risk management, new opportunities, and liquidity. Derivatives can be of great use in adjusting portfolios, but their use requires careful risk analysis and comparisons among investment possibilities. A productive approach is to start with country and sector research, develop conclusions about relative yield curves, analyze how derivatives can be used, and make asset and trade choices. The use of derivatives puts a premium on internal control, compliance with the firm's policies and regulations, and portfolio monitoring.

The popularity of derivatives in today's markets is unquestionable. Derivative securities allow investors to unbundle risks that are packaged into underlying cash securities, customize desired risk and return characteristics into an investment, and hedge a portfolio from shifts in the market without the need to sell or buy the underlying securities. The first part of this presentation defines derivative securities and discusses their major uses. The second part of the presentation explores the benefits of using derivatives, provides examples of derivative use, and outlines a framework for incorporating derivative securities in fixed-income portfolios.

A Primer on Derivative Securities (Carl O. Bautista)

Derivatives are financial instruments or contracts with values that are linked to or derived from underlying financial assets or physical commodities. Examples include swaps, forward contracts, options, and futures. Derivatives are quoted on a variety of underlying assets and are traded on exchanges and over the counter.

Exchange-Traded Derivatives

In the United States, the most commonly used exchange-traded derivative is the Eurodollar (ED) futures contract. ED futures settle against three-month LIBOR, which is the rate at which banks rated AA or higher lend money for three months in the Euro-interbank market. ED futures are actively traded in the International Money Market of the Chicago Mercantile Exchange.

Exchange-rated derivatives also include futures and options on Treasury bonds and notes, which are available on the Chicago Board of Trade. As their name implies, these derivatives are linked to the value of U.S. T-bonds or T-notes. Futures and options on foreign interest rates and bonds are also available in such foreign exchanges as the London International Financial Futures Exchange and Le Marché à Terme International de France.

Exchange-traded futures and options are standardized in order to facilitate trading. For example, ED futures contracts have a notional amount of $1 million, they expire every third Wednesday in March, June, September, and December, and 1 tick is defined to be worth $25 (which is essentially 1 basis point of $1 million for 90 out of 360 days).

OTC Derivatives

The primary advantages of OTC derivatives are customization and flexibility. In the OTC market, swaps, forwards, and options (and hybrids of these forms) on a wide variety of assets can be tailored to specific needs.

OTC derivatives have no central market for trading; the counterparties simply agree to the terms of the contract. Investors should note that derivatives typically involve an exchange of cash flows, so credit is an important issue in OTC trades. That is, traders need to confirm that a counterparty can honor the contract.

The basic building blocks of the OTC derivative market are interest rate swaps, forward contracts, and options on underlying assets.

▪ *Interest rate swaps.* In its plainest form, the interest rate swap is an agreement between two parties to exchange coupon cash flows—one fixed, one floating. Theoretically, both cash flows have net present values of zero. Hence, each counterparty is indifferent to exchanging these flows because the flows are worth the same. In a frictionless market, the swap rate is a fixed interest rate that one counterparty is willing to pay or receive instead of receiving or paying floating LIBOR. In reality, market makers pay and receive at different rates to make a spread for themselves. In the United States, the bid–ask spread for swaps is normally 4 basis points (bps).

Swaps are typically quoted as a spread to Treasury yields. For example, ten-year swaps may be quoted as T+40–T+36, which means that the counterparty is willing to receive a fixed rate for ten years at the current ten-year Treasury yield plus 40 bps or to pay a fixed rate for ten years at the ten-year Treasury yield plus 36 bps against paying/receiving the floating three-month LIBOR. The spread to Treasuries reflects market supply and demand for swaps. If heavy demand exists to receive fixed cash flows, spreads will narrow to Treasuries, and vice versa.

The swap spreads are also a function of corporate credit spreads. For example, a corporation that wants to raise fixed-rate debt for five years may go directly to the market and find that it would cost T+50. Demand for floating-rate debt may be such, however, that the corporation could issue floating-rate bonds at LIBOR plus 5 bps. At the same time, a dealer may be willing to receive a fixed rate of T+40 against LIBOR flat. Then, the corporation can issue floating-rate debt and enter into a swap to pay T+40 instead of receiving LIBOR, thereby achieving fixed-rate financing at essentially T+45 and saving 5 bps. If a growing number of corporations use this strategy, spreads will eventually move out to eliminate the advantage of issuing floating-rate bonds and swapping back to fixed rates.

Dealers typically use arbitrage pricing models to value swaps. Because swaps are quoted against three-month LIBOR, market makers will use the Eurodollar futures contracts to find the no-arbitrage level of an interest rate swap. **Table 1** provides an illustration of how the process works. Assume the spot rate for three-month LIBOR is 4 percent and the June, September, and December contracts imply three-month LIBOR of 4.5 percent, 5 percent, and 5.5 percent, respectively. If investors could reinvest a dollar at these rates, they would have $1.0483 at the end of one year. For no arbitrage to exist, the one-year swap rate should be 4.83 percent.

If market swap rates are different from those implied by ED futures, then an arbitrage opportunity exists. In this example, if the one-year swap is 5 percent, an investor would want to receive 5 percent and agree to pay floating LIBOR. At the same time, the investor would short the Eurodollar futures contract to hedge the floating-rate risk. For example, assume that LIBOR moves up to 5 percent in the second quarter. The investor must then pay 5 percent for that quarter (or $12,500 per million dollars of notional value) instead of the assumed 4.5 percent (or $11,250 per million dollars of notional value). In short, the investor paid $1,250 more than was originally assumed would be payable. Because the investor also shorted the June ED futures at a price of 9550, however, the investor would have made 50 ticks on the hedge—because LIBOR in June would be 5 percent, the futures contract would be 9500—or $1,250 per contract ($0.125 per $100).

As **Table 2** shows, an investor would have gained approximately 25 bps from the futures contract, plus 5 percent on the fixed position, for a total receipt of 5.25 percent (or $5.25 per $100). The inves-

Table 1. Arbitrage Pricing Valuation

	Price	Implied Three-Month Spot Rate	Value of $1 Reinvested
Three-month LIBOR spot rate	—	4.0	1.0100
June 1994	9550	4.5	1.0214
September 1994	9500	5.0	1.0341
December 1994	9450	5.5	1.0483

Source: Bankers Trust Co.

Table 2. Illustration of Arbitrage

Quarter	Floating Rate	Floating-Rate Payments per $100	Gain or Loss on Futures Contract	Gain or Loss on Futures per $100
First	4.0%	$1.000	—	—
Second	5.0	1.250	50	$0.125
Third	5.5	1.375	50	0.125
Fourth	5.5	1.375	0	0.000
Total		$5.000		$0.250

Note: Notional value for each quarter is $1 million.

Source: Bankers Trust Co.

tor would have paid 5 percent on the floating-rate obligation and thus would have arbitraged the market and gained the 25 bps. (More accurate counting and compounding would put the gain at about 17 bps.)

■ *Forwards.* Another basic building block in the derivatives market is the forward contract, or forward agreement, which is an agreement between two parties to buy or sell a certain asset at some future time at a prespecified price. The party assuming the long position must buy the asset at that price, and the party assuming the short position must sell it at that price. Forwards are similar to futures contracts, but the terms are negotiated rather than standardized.

■ *Options.* The third basic form of derivatives is options, which are contracts offering the right—but not the obligation—to buy or sell an underlying asset at a predetermined price. Option buyers pay a premium for an option. Option owners may exercise the right to buy or sell the underlying asset, but they will do so only if it is in their favor. If not, they will let the option expire worthless. Sellers gain the option premium if the option expires worthless.

Options in the fixed-income market include swaptions, caps or floors, and bond options. Swaptions are the right to receive (call) or the right to pay (put) at a certain predetermined fixed rate (the strike price) for a specific term starting at some future time. For example, an investor can buy an option to enter into a swap one year from now for two years. That rate is agreed upon today, and the option buyer will pay a premium for it. Assume an investor buys the right to receive at some rate—say, 6 percent for two years. If in one year's time two-year swaps are at 5 percent, then the investor will be "in the money"; that is, the investor will benefit by exercising the option.

Caps and floors are periodic options on some floating interest rate. These forms are available on LIBOR, the Cost of Funds Index, constant-maturity Treasuries, constant-maturity swaps, and other assets. Caps benefit the investor if the floating rate is higher than the cap strike price. For example, a

two-year cap on three-month LIBOR struck at 6 percent will benefit the cap owner if three-month LIBOR is greater than 6 percent. The floating rate is determined at the beginning of each quarterly period. Therefore, the investor essentially owns eight options or caplets (four quarters for two years). Floors are similar to caps, but they benefit the investor when rates are lower than the strike price. The benefit is equal to the difference between the rate set and the strike price.

Another type of option is bond options, which are asset specific or bond specific. An investor buys the right to call (purchase) a specific bond or the right to put (sell) a specific bond at a predetermined price on or before some expiration date.

Factors that affect option valuations include the price of the underlying asset, the agreed strike price, the time to expiration, volatility, and interest rate levels. Volatility is the driving force in option valuation: The higher the volatility (or the implied volatility) in the market, the higher the underlying price of the option, and vice versa.

Using Derivatives (Kris Mahabir)

The use of derivatives has grown as rapidly as it has because derivatives provide certain definite benefits to investors. After exploring those benefits, this part of the presentation will discuss the use of interest rate swaps for different portfolio purposes.

Benefits of Derivative Use

Among the benefits derivatives can provide are the flexibility to seek high current income, diversification, risk management, new opportunities, liquidity, and favorable treatment by the National Association of Insurance Commissioners (NAIC).

■ *Income flexibility.* If investors have a view on the market, they may want the flexibility to benefit if their view is correct in the form of current income (coupons) or principal repayment (redemption). Derivatives offer a way of structuring securities so that investors can benefit in whatever way is most advantageous to them.

For example, an investor can make certain plays that, by the way they are constructed, affect primarily, or exclusively, the coupon. If an investor believes rates are declining, he or she might choose to receive on a swap, embed on a note, and create an inverse floater, which is a coupon-linked security. If the investor's view is correct, the investor will receive an above-market coupon; if it is incorrect, the investor will receive a below-market coupon or, perhaps, no coupon at all.

Many investors find this flexibility useful because many markets have upward-sloping yield curves. With an inverse-floater in such a market, for example, investors benefit from receiving fixed rates naturally in an above-market coupon, and then as they roll down the curve, as long as rates do not increase as fast as the forward curve is implying, the investors keep that above-market coupon. If investors' views about the market are wrong and rates increase, they can close out the instrument. They will probably do so at a loss, but the loss will be less than the benefit they received from rolling down the yield curve.

■ *Diversification.* In the context of derivatives use, diversification is meant to move a portfolio away from credit risk. In an environment in which spreads have tightened considerably, many investors benefit from having a portfolio that spreads the risk away from pure credit risk. Investors who use structured notes can tie the bets embedded in those securities to AA- and AAA-rated bank and corporate bonds. Thus, if spreads tighten, the investors can avoid having to eliminate a security if the issuer is downgraded and liquidity in the underlying instrument decreases.

■ *Risk management.* Managing risk consists of identifying the well-priced risks in the market and removing the ones not worth taking. For example, placing outright duration bets has proved to be very dangerous for many international investors. The market has been choppy since about February, and many people are expecting steepening yield curves. However, if investors want to place a yield-curve-steepening bet through a security without exposure to outright duration or currency risk, they can use derivatives to construct a security that pays off if they bet right.

■ *New opportunities.* The rate of innovation in derivatives is unparalleled in any other area of finance, and that pace will likely be maintained. Investors should learn about derivatives because, some time in the future, some innovation will emerge and be part of the solution to some issue affecting their portfolios. Understanding derivatives allows investors to have a complete set of useful strategies at their disposal.

■ *Liquidity.* In many foreign markets, most of the flow occurs in the swap market and the swap market is actually more liquid than the cash market. So, in many cases, structured notes offer investors a vehicle in which to get out of tight bid–ask spreads with greater liquidity than they might find in the cash market.

Liquidity is demonstrated by the growth in interest rate swaps. The liquidity has been very high in this market and has not diminished substantially despite the reversals in several global markets. Moreover, no slowdown in the growth of interest rate swaps is expected.

■ *Favorable NAIC treatment.* Favorable treatment by the NAIC is primarily a benefit for insurance companies that want to diversify away from credit risk. Many securities and trades have interest rate risk but little to no credit risk and thus receive a favorable interpretation by the NAIC. Therefore, use of those strategies will probably increase in the future.

Portfolio Construction with Derivatives

Managers interested in incorporating derivatives into portfolios must address the method in which these instruments will be treated as compared with the treatment of cash market securities. One approach for derivatives is to start with a fundamental or a quantitative view that makes sense in a portfolio and then think about the best way to benefit if that view is right on a risk-adjusted basis. Fidelity Management and Research Company starts with fundamental research conducted by country analysts or sector analysts who are responsible for understanding all the nuances and details of the markets on which they focus. They develop a view about the yield curve in a particular country and then ask themselves, "Based on this view, does more opportunity lie at the long end of the curve or at the short end? Where are the largest discrepancies?"

When we talk about discrepancies, we are referring to what is discounted in the market on a forward basis. Recall the Eurodollar futures curve, which indicates what the implied three-month rates are in the United States at different times during a calendar year. To make money in any of these securities, investors have to bet against the forward curve, and their view has to be correct with respect to that curve. In the French market, for instance, the front end of the curve is currently inverted, which implies that interest rates will drop; investors will not make money by betting that interest rates will fall, therefore, unless the rates fall more than the forward rates already imply.

The next step is to determine the risk objectives of the various portfolios and evaluate the different opportunities in light of those objectives—determine how much risk the different funds can take. Then, for the portfolio under consideration, the opportunities in the derivatives market are compared, on a risk-adjusted basis, with those in the cash market. For example, suppose the analyst thinks interest rates will fall primarily on the front end of the curve, as they did in 1993 when many central banks were in a credit-easing mode. According to this view, the long end would rally, but not nearly as much as short-term interest rates would fall. In the cash market, however, no securities would pay if short-term interest rates fell in a meaningful way because the duration of the short-term securities is very small. Derivatives, however, provide a way of increasing exposure at the front end of the yield curve and thus benefiting the investor if this view is correct.

Comparing derivatives with cash market securities must be done on an apples-to-apples basis to determine how much risk in the securities is linked to the short end. Then, the analyst should determine whether the portfolio will make more money if the analyst's view about the short end of the curve pans out than it will, after adjusting for the comparable risk, in the long end of the curve. When this analysis is complete and derivatives have been compared with cash market securities on a country-by-country, sector-by-sector, and market-by-market basis, the analyst can develop recommendations on best trades for each segment of the market.

The next decision is asset allocation. The different derivative trades that emerged from the analysis should be marked to market historically to obtain historical standard deviations for the trades—that is, historical covariance between those trades and any other trades a manager might be considering in the portfolio. The analyst can then use some type of asset allocation routine, a simple form or a quadratic program, to allocate among the different trades.

Using Derivatives

Our whole business is taking risks and figuring out where Fidelity's investors will benefit most from the risks we take based on the views we have. We do trades based on fundamental analysis and pricing various scenarios and risks. We design the trades to ensure that we do not incorporate risks into the portfolio that are not well priced. In most cases, we buy cash market trades, but in certain cases, purchasing a structured note offers a clear advantage.

The first trade discussed in this section, the index-amortizing note, illustrates the use of derivatives in the investment manager's job of taking risk and managing it—finding the best return in the market per unit of risk. Such a trade requires a considerable time investment.

■ *Taking and managing risk.* In the summer of 1993, Fidelity identified an opportunity in Japan that appeared to be attractive in the front end of the yield curve. We analyzed the difference between Fidelity's forecast and the implied forward curve. Based on the belief that a greater rally would occur in the front end, we determined the volatility of the three-year point on the curve and then determined the volatility of a comparable cash market instrument. Based on that comparison, we could determine whether we would make more money by having exposure in the three-year part of the curve or by having it in the back of the curve. As a result, we purchased an inverse floater with a 10 percent coupon.

A comparison of the marked-to-market figures of that trade with three-year yen interest rates during that period shows they moved almost exactly in tandem in opposite directions: When three-year rates were declining, the security was appreciating; when three-year rates bottomed out and started to increase, the security dropped in price. If we had purchased a 20-year bond in Japan on the same day, we would have received a lower return. The inverse floater worked because we had exposure in the part of the curve that rallied the most.

This derivative security was extremely transparent and extremely liquid. When we were buying the inverse floater and when we were selling it, we could determine by looking at quote screens exactly where it should be priced. Every day that we owned it and received the marked-to-market figures, we could determine whether we were correct. In summary, the transparency of derivatives provides the ability to know exactly where an investor should be able to buy and sell and what the price should be every day in between. Managers can pull up a quotation screen at their workstations and see exactly where a trade should be. They can work their orders and confirm that they are not moving the market.

In addition to transparency, another important aspect of this trade was its liquidity. In the course of two trading sessions in Japan, we purchased approximately $1 billion in three-year swaps. We were then able to unwind that entire position over the course of two evening sessions. (We took two days because we did not want to have any impact on the market. If we had not cared about price, we could have exited immediately.)

■ *Disaggregating risks.* Derivatives also allow investors to disaggregate interest rate risk and credit risk. In 1993, the U.S. market experienced a large exodus of capital into foreign markets to take advantage of extremely strong foreign fundamentals. This year, with the Federal Reserve tightening, is a good time for defensive trades in the United States. Such trades will provide protection to portfolios as interest rates rise, but they will not cost much if interest rates stay low.

Another example of derivatives use involves one of the top-selling structured notes last year, an index-amortizing rate swap or index-amortizing note. In such a trade, investors receive a fixed coupon; the only question is how long to receive it. These securities resemble mortgage-backed securities because MBS investors buy a fixed-rate coupon but do not know whether the mortgage will prepay or extend. Because of this similarity, investors who have analyzed the whole class of structured notes and have a good background in MBS and collateralized mortgage obligations can easily relate to an index-amortizing swap.

Index-amortizing notes have a minimum maturity and a maximum maturity with a cleanup provision. They do not have any of the tailing effects that sometimes occur with MBS. All exposure is based on LIBOR, so the issue is a short-term interest rate versus a ten-year rate that requires assumptions about demographics and the link between the ten-year rate and prepayments. An MBS purchaser is betting against the implied forward curve at the back end of the curve; a purchaser of an index-amortizing note is betting against the forward LIBOR curve at the front end of the curve. An investor who does not have particularly strong views about where the implied forwards are most in error may be wise to diversify exposure across the curve instead of concentrating at the back end.

Fidelity's experience has taught us that, when the Fed tightens, it tends to tighten faster than what is implied in the forward curve. Therefore, investors in index-amortizing notes need to exit the trades as soon as they see the Fed tighten. If they do not, the next question is how to protect the portfolio with the index-amortizing note in it in the future.

Perhaps the most intuitive protection is to bet on the spread between two-year and ten-year Treasury notes. If the spread compresses, the trade will pay out some amount that will protect the losses on the rest of the portfolio. The problem with that idea is that, as in the example discussed earlier, the investor would have to bet against the implied forward curve, not the current curve. The current spread is about 150 bps, but the forward curve implies that the spread will flatten by 40 bps during the next six months and by about 70 bps during the next nine months. For investors to make any money on such a trade, the yield curve has to flatten faster than that.

Other ways exist to get around the negative cost of carry. One way relates to swap spreads in the United States. Many U.S. corporate treasurers during the past two or three years actually had locked in

swaps in which they were paying floating rates and receiving fixed rates. They were booking that carry between the three-month rate and, say, the seven-year rate. In the process, they forced swap spreads narrower. Since January 1990, swap spreads have tightened because dealers had considerable customer flow coming one way: Everyone wanted to receive fixed and pay floating rates. The swaps were executed at successively tighter and tighter spreads to Treasuries.

Interest rates have now started to rise, and corporate treasurers do not want to miss the opportunity to lock in and fix their liabilities at possibly the lowest interest rates of their careers. They do not want to have to explain to their boards of directors why they did not lock in these rates, so they have reversed their transactions. The flow is still predominantly one way, but now it is in the opposite direction. These treasurers want to pay fixed and receive floating rates. The dealers will naturally demand fixed rates at wider and wider spreads over Treasuries.

One alternative for an investor is to bet that the curve will flatten. This alternative has a huge cost of carry, and if the curve does not flatten, the investor will end up paying a lot of money without receiving the desired protection. The alternative is to bet that swap spreads will stay close to where they are. In this strategy, the investor does not have the negative carry, and if the curve does not flatten, the swap does not cost much. The risk is that it will not prove to be a good hedge. Investors have to decide, based on an analysis like this one and an understanding of the flows, whether they think it is a good risk to take.

Managing the Process

Incorporating derivatives into portfolios involves significant issues of internal control and compliance with the firm's policies and regulations. Fidelity begins the process with a Global Research Group to develop fundamental views on the market and a Derivatives Strategy Group to identify the best opportunities in light of those fundamental views. Then, the Credit Research Group, which knows what the most attractive credit is at any given time, evaluates the potential issuers that we can access that day and determines the best credit. Meanwhile, the Legal and Compliance Group checks all of the details of each potential trade. Most of the trades we make are boiler plate trades that have already cleared the approval process, but all trades are reverified to confirm that they are consistent with the prospectus disclosures and mandate and with any Commodity Futures Trading Commission or SEC regulations that apply.

The Tax and Accounting Group ensures that the

tax treatment of the derivative securities is consistent with the method used to evaluate the tax treatment of all the cash market trades in the portfolio. This group needs to agree completely with how the interest will be accrued and, if applicable, how the trade will affect the yield of the fund.

The final step in the process is feedback. Over time, an investment management firm will accumulate a portfolio of these individual structured notes.

Thus, a process to check the credit of the portfolio with the credit group in some frequent and regular fashion is extremely important. This process will ensure that the high credit quality of each structured-note portfolio is maintained. Also important is regular and frequent checking with the fundamental research group to make sure that, when its views change, the portfolio of trades remains the most efficient way of capitalizing on those views.

Question and Answer Session

Carl O. Bautista
Kris Mahabir

Question: How do investors get out of a structured note? How expensive is it? What are the risks?

Bautista: When you buy a structured note, the seller must show you mark-to-market each day, which should be the best indication of the unwind value of the structured note. Any market moves will be reflected in the mark-to-market, and if the markets are functioning normally, you should be able to get out at or close to where you were marked for that day.

The liquidity of the structure will be a function of the liquidity of the underlying market. For example, if an investor were to purchase a structured note linked to one-year swap rates at maturity ten times leveraged, then the bid–ask spread on the structured note would be at least ten times the bid–ask spread of the one-year swap rate. So, if the bid–ask spread on one-year swaps is 4 bps, the bid–ask price of the structured note will be 99.6–100.0 percent.

Question: Although the swap market is extremely liquid, the deals seem to be specific, not generic, so a deal attractive to one investor may not be attractive to somebody else. How liquid is the swap market in actuality with respect to both primary and secondary issues?

Mahabir: The only way you will know that your trades are liquid and will perform the way you expect is if you come up with the ideas yourself. If you base your trades on the dealer term sheets, you will lose money.

If you want to be active in this business, you need more than the fundamental view. You have to evaluate a whole set of different trades based on real-time swap curves from a data service, and then you have to determine how much money you will make or lose on each of those trades and what the risk, or volatility, of each is so that you can adjust accordingly. You have to adjust for transaction costs on all the trades, the hedging if there is any currency exposure that you do not want, and the interest rate caps that will limit your downside risk to whatever level you deem acceptable. When you are ready to trade, you prepare a term sheet that has the exact terms of the trade you want and you give it to someone on your trading desk to fax, with a note that they have 15 minutes to bid on the business, to the three best dealers. You have to initiate the process and be in control.

The derivatives part of your business should resemble the way you do business in any other sector. No one waits for a dealer to call up with a recommendation on a particular corporate credit. Most likely, you have a fundamental credit research department responsible for knowing the entire story behind that name, and it has a view on what will happen to the spread. The approach is the same in the derivatives market, but in some cases, your own research is even more important because of the many variables to control.

Although many different structures are available, you should start out with only the most liquid structures. You can see on a Telerate or Bloomberg screen where the rates are at any given moment, and you can understand the pricing and transparencies of those trades. As users of the product, you have the responsibility to consider only trades that belong to the extremely liquid set. Don't believe all the marketing material about different trades that are interesting and unique and exploit all the arbitrages and inefficiencies in the market. Start with the liquid trades and determine which ones will give you the best risk-adjusted return if your view is right. Then, approach the best dealers in that particular market and have them bid on the business.

Bautista: The investor should be familiar with the liquidity of the underlying market before buying a structured note. The investor should be able to obtain that information from the dealer who is selling the trade. Simple questions to ask are what the bid–offer spread of the structured note is and what could happen to cause liquidity to dry up.

Question: If the top two or three dealers were taken out of the market, would liquidity still be available?

Bautista: Yes. A variety of markets have more than two or three big dealers. In Germany, if you took out the top two or three, a good amount of liquidity would remain among other dealers. In the United States, if you took out even the top five, liquidity in the swap market would remain good. In the small countries, eliminating the top two or three dealers might cause liquidity to diminish in terms of the volume you can do, in which case you would make the decision to accept that situation when you entered the market. Before you enter a market, you need to know how much liquidity is traded in the market, how much swap volume is traded in the market, who the players are, and how much each one trades.

Question: Why is LIBOR so extensively used in the derivatives market although we don't generally see it quoted otherwise?

Bautista: The use of LIBOR is a convention. It is the short-term interest rate or floating-rate instrument quoted in the Euromarkets and has the underlying credit of interbank dealers rather than of the U.S. government. Because swaps originated among dealers simply borrowing or lending interest rates to each other, LIBOR was used as the benchmark in swaps.

Question: Please explain counterparty risk. How should it be controlled? Should an investor set maximum limits per counterparty? How would you set them?

Mahabir: Because so many corporations have swaps and off-balance-sheet items on their books, you are affected by swap counterparty risk whether you are active in the derivatives market or not. Strong resources in fixed-income credit research are thus a valuable firm asset. A strong research department can address what type of exposures a corporation has on or off its books in terms of swap counterparty credit risk.

When you enter into a swap embedded in a structured note, you create a fire wall between the dealer and yourself. Only the issuer of the structured note is responsible for any payments to the investor. In selecting an issuer, it does not make any difference whether you have purchased a three-year yen inverse floater that is payable in dollars and is coupon linked or you have purchased a corporate bond in the secondary market; you have counterparty risk to the same issuer, and you are relying on that issuer to be good for the payments.

How much structured-note business you do with any one name is not an issue specific to the swap market. To determine what acceptable exposures are to individual names in the structured-note market, you have to apply the same credit research that you apply to evaluating names in the secondary market. Thus, spreading the risk around on a country-by-country basis makes sense; for example, you might not want to have all your structured notes that are linked to Sweden be issued by one particular issuer.

Another important issue is related to how much exposure you want in any one market. If you are trading in Japan, Sweden, or in a less liquid market, such as Finland, you want to make sure that you do not represent more of the outstanding interest in that market than you believe you can comfortably sell within an acceptable time. That period may depend on your institution. Fidelity, for example, does not want to be in any trade that we cannot exit very quickly. We want to be able to get out in about one day.

Keep in mind, also, that even though structured notes may move around a lot in price in times of high volatility in the markets, they are not typically subject to illiquidity in the sense of no one being out there to make a market. For any of the sales that we have wanted to make, we have had at least three dealers line up and make a market in them. We have been able to verify that the prices we got were extremely close to the previous night's closing price plus or minus whatever market movement occurred during that day. In addition, we can tell by looking at the screens where a derivative security should be priced, and that is the price, in fact, where we sell it.

Bautista: At Bankers Trust, we use a three-step process to evaluate our exposure to counterparties in a variety of markets. The first step is to determine the exposure today from a mark-to-market perspective. We need to know on a daily basis the value of the swaps we have outstanding with all our counterparties. The next step is to project where we think volatilities are in the markets in which we and the counterparties are involved, where we think the market could go—up or down in interest rates, for example—within the next year. With those two measures, we can tell how much our potential exposure is to the counterparty. The third step is to decide what we need to do—from a credit perspective, for example—to protect ourselves. If we think the expected exposure is a little high, then we might start negotiating collateral agreements or netting agreements or so on.

Question: Are the risks that have been highlighted by the financial publications real?

Bautista: The risk that the market will fall apart has been overblown. The market is definitely volatile these days, but that risk is slight.

Mahabir: Fidelity was pleased to see the recent attention the press paid to derivatives because that attention increases scrutiny of the market and, as a result, decreases the likelihood that any blowups will occur. From talking to different dealers, we understand all the attention that has been given to these issues has dried up activity from corporate treasurers—even though they are responsible for managing merely fixed-to-floating-rate swaps, not any exotic investments that could get them into trouble. In other words, the bread-and-butter type of business for which these treasurers are responsible has recently decreased substantially. This trend means that, everywhere around the country and the world, eyes are being focused inward to make sure the controls are in place. What should emerge from that process is a healthy and knowledgeable community of investors, hedgers, and dealers who will be active in the market.

Question: How can investors distinguish managers who know what they are doing with derivatives from those who do not? What disclosure of derivative use should a plan sponsor demand of a manager?

Mahabir: Because the area is so new, you cannot go to your local bookstore and buy a great book on the swap market or derivatives. The only way to evaluate managers is to follow the same intensive process you use in other areas: Ask the investment managers to come in, make a presentation, and educate you on the issues that will be relevant for the particular account.

The derivatives market offers many very good, very rich opportunities, but they must be properly classified in terms of suitability for different accounts. After you have determined the risk profile of the account in which you are interested, the next step is to call certain managers who are active in the marketplace. One way of identifying them is simply to call another dealer and say, "I know you deal with a lot of these people. It is in both our best interests for you to tell me who they are or give me a list of names so I can call them up myself and set up the appropriate presentation."

With respect to disclosure, once you have identified the risk profile of your account, the investment manager can present you with all the different instruments and combinations of those instruments that he or she believes will be most useful in providing the opportunities that are in keeping with that risk profile. Because the rate of innovation is so high, as you review accounts, you should keep in mind that new ideas will come up six months or one year later that you will want to explore. And because presenting new ideas and evaluating their suitability for an account can be a slow process, you might want to allow flexibility with derivatives for a rapid evaluation.

Question: The derivatives market is complex, but investors have to understand what is happening in it; what is the best way to go about figuring out this market?

Bautista: Investors should turn to dealers they know, respect, and trust and ask for an education on the market and market specifics. Concentrate on markets that you like and proceed slowly. You don't want to be presented with a structured note that seems interesting and seems like it will work if you don't understand the pricing of the underlying structure and the market in general.

Mahabir: First-time users need to make sure that the people with whom they are trading can provide daily mark-to-market data on everything purchased. (Actually, this approach would facilitate the use and safety of derivatives for all users or potential users.) You want to make sure that their execution is extremely good, that they can execute your trades inside or very close to what the screens say, and that their documentation and compliance department is fully developed and capable of providing you with all the required note documentation. You also want to make sure that they can line up a variety of potential issuers for you, because as you consider different trades and select an issuer, you will want to present your credit research department with several alternatives.

One particularly good way to learn about the market is to ask the dealers with whom you are working most closely to put their best ideas on paper. You can then form a portfolio based on those ideas and mark it to market yourself every week to see how their trades would perform. After a few months, you will have a good perception of who has the best ideas and who understands the risk profile you are trying to achieve. This approach is particularly useful if you are not comfortable initially with generating your own trade ideas and faxing them off to dealers for competitive bids.

A portfolio prepared by an experienced firm is a safe way to enter the market because that firm can make sure that all the things that can go wrong don't. As you review the product on a quarterly or monthly basis, you can ask the firm why it is doing certain things. You will learn what the best structures are, what the most effective asset allocations are, and how to trade in and out of those structures as market conditions change. The cost of this approach is low in relation to what you could lose on your own in one of these trades.

Global Relative-Value Analysis for Corporate Debt

John V. Malvey, CFA
Senior Vice President
Lehman Brothers

The major challenge for analysts working in the global fixed-income markets in the coming decade will be the development of a suitable relative-value framework for intermarket and intramarket analysis. Change in market structures, analytical tools, and speed, the globalization of markets, and the introduction of new products—all call for a more rigorous analysis of markets and issuers than in the past. Spreads remain the core of relative-value analysis for corporate debt, but investors need to consider other factors, and analysts need to develop multifactor models.

Economists have long debated the concept and measurement of "value," but fixed-income practitioners, perhaps because of the daily pragmatism enforced by the markets, have developed a consensus about its meaning. In the bond market, the meaning of "value"—or more precisely, "relative value"—is clear. "Relative value" refers to the ranking of fixed-income investments by sectors, structures, issuers, and issues in terms of their expected performance during some future interval. For the day trader, relative value may carry a maximum horizon of a few minutes. For a large insurer, relative value may have a multiyear horizon. Accordingly, "relative-value analysis" refers to the methodologies used to generate such rankings of expected returns.

The practice of relative-value analysis has improved greatly during the past decade. The evolution in methodologies was spurred by the widespread availability of inexpensive technologies that facilitate multihorizon and comparative analysis of portfolios and individual securities, the introduction of quantitative techniques to evaluate embedded options and risk–return trade-offs, and the proliferation of new fixed-income products (especially in the derivatives, mortgage-backed securities, and global bond markets), which stimulated demand for a comprehensive analytical framework. As a result, back-of-the-envelope methodologies have given way to rigorous techniques that allow comparisons of relative value throughout the global fixed-income markets.

Within the corporate bond market, "classic"

relative-value analysis is a dialectical process combining the best of top-down and bottom-up approaches. The approach is to pick the sectors with most upside potential, populate these favored sectors with issuers with the most upside potential, and select the structures (bullets, zero coupons, callables, putables) and the curve points that best reflect the outlook for the benchmark curve.

For many corporate investors, the use of classic relative-value analysis alone has been sufficient to ensure a measure of portfolio success. Although sector and issuer analyses remain the core of superior relative-value analysis, during the past decade, the increased availability of information and technology has transformed the analytical process into a complex discipline. Moreover, the broadening of the global corporate market has stimulated waves of new issuers. These two developments have raised the question of how best to meld classic relative-value analysis with new information and new techniques to construct the optimal relative-value decision.

As an illustration, consider the evolution in successful corporate-bond portfolio management during the early 1990s. In retrospect, the analytical challenge during that time looks easy. The keys to success were to operate at the high end of the credit-risk spectrum (especially in banks and industrials), ride the seasonal roller-coaster (avoid low-quality credits at the end of the third quarter and reverse direction before the end of the fourth quarter), and buy almost any new downgrade. By early 1994, however, this strategy appeared to have run its course. For the first time since 1983, corporate investors were confronted with the "burden of managing prosperity."

In early 1994, Federal Reserve Chairman Alan Greenspan testified to Congress that current economic prospects are the best in decades. I agree with his conclusion. Many investors, however, in view of the disappointing relative and absolute returns for corporate bonds during 1994, might prefer the economic angst of the early 1990s. Relative and absolute corporate returns were much more robust then, as shown in **Table 1**.

Now, a new phase of the corporate portfolio management cycle has begun. The arrival of comparative credit tranquility in concert with synchronized global economic expansion has compressed spreads and dampened spread volatility throughout the global corporate bond market. For many investors, the quest for total return maximization, the dominant corporate portfolio management goal of the early 1990s, has given way to a quest for preservation of capital and risk control. In addition, as signaled by reduced allocations to corporate bonds in many fixed-income portfolios, some total return investors have become defensive toward the global corporate-bond asset class.

In this difficult environment—difficult for managers accustomed to capitalizing on spread volatility—many practitioners have sharpened their relative-value tools in an attempt to bolster their performance.

Toward Comprehensive Total Return Analysis

The capital markets exhibit regular rhythms. For instance, the economic cycle is the major determinant of aggregate corporate spreads. During recessions, the escalation of default risk understandably widens spreads (which are, in effect, risk premiums over underlying, presumably default-free government securities). Economic prosperity reduces bankruptcies and tightens spreads.

Historical analogies can be taken to extremes. The stock market does not tumble every October. The "fourth-quarter effect" (the underperformance of low-quality corporate bonds compared with high-quality corporates in the fourth quarter) does not occur every year. Nonetheless, strategy is difficult to chart unless these technical patterns are taken into account; technical prophecies often become self-fulfilling during periods of below-average liquidity. Moreover, strategy formulation is difficult without an understanding of the historical underpinnings of corporate returns. Accordingly, thorough relative-value analysis begins with a dissection of past re-

turns and a projection of total returns.

Ibbotson Associates provides some data on corporate returns extending back to 1926, but comprehensive measures of fixed-income total returns (i.e., returns by sectors, durations, and credit quality) have a brief history compared with equity returns.[1] The comprehensive barometers of total return shown in **Table 2**, for investment-grade corporates, high-yield corporates, and dollar-denominated Eurobonds have, at most, only a two-decade history. Moreover, unlike the equity market, for which daily and even intraday pricing is available, corporate bond indexes report comprehensive pricing and returns only on a month-end basis.

Until the mid-1993 unbundling of corporate bond indexes into an equity-type, multisector template (i.e., categories of airlines, cable, Canadians, electric utilities, food, tobacco), inadequate categorization plagued the corporate bond market. Many analysts viewed the market in a limited 16-box grid: sectors for utilities, financial institutions, industrials, and Yankee bonds (Canadians, non-U.S. industrials and financial institutions, supranationals, and sovereigns) broken down by four generic ratings (Aaa, Aa, A, and Baa). This approach to corporate portfolio management produced erroneous inferences. For example, if an individual Baa/BBB credit like RJR Nabisco widened on Marlboro Friday (April 2, 1993—the day Philip Morris launched its Marlboro discount-pricing program), the market tended to conclude that weakness might envelop the entire Baa/BBB market.

Erroneous inferences may account for the persistence of certain anomalies that are contrary to conventional expectations. As an illustration, **Table 3** shows that duration-adjusted returns in the Eurobond market have exceeded their equivalently rated Aaa and Aa counterparts in the U.S. corporate market for each year since the inception of the Lehman Eurobond Index in 1987. In effect, global corporate investors have received a return premium in exchange for possibly less liquidity.

The information gap in the corporate bond market has inhibited systematic analysis by practitioners and academics of many key attributes of the market. Consequently, the impact of many capital market and economic variables on relative corporate returns is only partially understood or yet to be uncovered.

During the next decade, the global corporate market should become more efficient, and the information gap substantially reduced, by a growing cadre of researchers. The family of corporate bond indexes will be extended to cover the private-placement, preferred stock, floating-rate-note, and non-

---

[1]Ibbotson Associates, *Stocks, Bonds, Bills, and Inflation: 1991 Yearbook* (Chicago, Ill., 1991).

Table 1. Fixed-Income Total Returns, 1973 through March 1994

Year	Era	Investment-Grade Corporate	High-Yield Corporate	Eurobond	Government	Mortgage	Global	S&P 500 Index
1973	Oil embargo and	1.51%	NA	NA	3.08%	NA	NA	−14.77%
1974	recession	−5.86	NA	NA	6.57	NA	NA	−26.39
1975	Economic rebound	16.70	NA	NA	8.38	NA	NA	37.16
1976		19.34	NA	NA	12.36	16.31%	NA	23.84
1977		3.16	NA	NA	2.80	1.89	NA	−7.18
1978	Inflation, oil price	0.35	NA	NA	1.80	2.41	NA	6.56
1979	hike, and recession	−2.10	NA	NA	5.41	0.13	NA	18.44
1980		−0.29	NA	NA	5.19	0.65	NA	32.42
1981		2.95	NA	NA	9.36	0.07	NA	−4.91
1982	The "Golden Age"	39.20	NA	NA	27.75	43.04	NA	21.41
1983		9.27	5.84%	NA	7.39	10.13	NA	22.51
1984		16.62	9.70	NA	14.50	15.79	NA	6.27
1985		24.06	25.64	NA	20.43	25.21	NA	32.16
1986		16.53	17.45	NA	15.31	13.43	NA	18.47
1987		2.56	4.99	1.35%	2.20	4.29	15.93%	5.23
1988		9.22	12.53	9.12	7.03	8.72	4.49	16.81
1989	Slowdown and recession	14.09	0.83	13.54	14.23	15.35	6.67	31.49
1990		7.05	−9.59	8.84	8.72	10.72	12.30	−3.15
1991	Slow rebound and	18.51	46.08	16.49	15.32	15.72	15.34	30.45
1992	refunding blitz	8.69	15.75	8.17	7.23	6.95	4.51	7.61
1993		12.16	17.12	10.30	10.66	6.84	12.60	10.08
1994	Accelerating economic growth and higher rates							
First quarter		−3.52	−1.95	−2.63	−3.01	−2.32	−0.60	−3.79
Annualized yield to date		−13.36	−7.57	−10.13	−11.51	−8.98	−2.39	−14.33

NA = not applicable.
Source: Lehman Brothers Fixed Income Research.

Table 2. Means, Standard Deviations, and Coefficients of Variation for Fixed-Income Assets by Historical Era

Year	Investment-Grade Corporate	High-Yield Corporate	Eurobond	Government	Mortgage	Global	S&P 500 Index
Mean total return							
1973–79	4.73%	NA	NA	5.77%	5.19%	NA	5.38%
1980–89	13.42	11.00%[a]	8.00%[b]	12.34	13.67	9.03%[b]	18.19
1990–94	6.61	12.36	6.73	6.08	6.25	8.49	6.13
Standard deviation							
1973–79	8.84	NA	NA	3.44	6.48	NA	21.03
1980–89	11.17	7.80[a]	5.04[b]	7.32	12.18	4.96[b]	12.04
1990–94	10.73	20.25	8.93	9.21	8.28	6.53	14.93
Coefficient of variation							
1973–79	187	NA	NA	60	125	NA	391
1980–89	83	71[a]	63[b]	59	89	55[b]	66
1990–94	162	164	133	151	132	77	243

NA = not applicable.

[a]1983 through 1989.
[b]1987 through 1989.

Source: Lehman Brothers Fixed Income Research.

Table 3. Total Returns for Lehman Brothers Indexes, 1993 through March 1994

Year	Eurobond	Investment-Grade Corporate	Aaa	Aa	Global
A. Unadjusted returns					
1987	1.35%	2.56%	1.73%	1.76%	15.93%
1988	9.12	9.22	8.42	8.87	4.49
1989	13.54	14.09	14.20	14.34	6.67
1990	8.84	7.05	8.04	7.63	12.70
1991	16.49	18.51	16.39	18.89	15.34
1992	8.17	8.69	7.98	8.06	4.51
1993	10.30	12.16	11.41	11.70	12.30
1994	−2.63	−3.52	−3.38	−3.67	−0.60
January	1.38	1.94	1.56	1.78	1.11
February	−1.82	−2.36	−2.19	−2.38	−1.20
March	−2.18	−3.07	−2.73	−3.05	−0.50
Annualized yield to date	−10.13	−13.36	−12.84	−13.90	−2.39
Mean (1987–94)	7.21	7.37	6.92	7.17	8.69
Standard deviation (1987–94)	8.26	9.64	9.14	9.90	6.41
Coefficient variation (1987–94)	115	131	132	138	74
B. Duration-adjusted returns					
1987	0.34	0.40	0.31	0.27	3.23
1988	2.36	1.44	1.23	1.36	0.92
1989	3.35	2.18	2.20	2.13	1.33
1990	2.08	1.26	1.56	1.27	2.68
1991	4.12	3.29	3.05	2.84	3.13
1992	2.03	1.47	1.34	1.23	0.91
1993	2.31	1.92	1.95	1.83	2.35
1994	−0.67	−0.55	−0.53	−0.56	−0.12
January	0.34	0.30	0.26	0.27	0.21
February	−0.45	−0.37	−0.36	−0.37	−0.23
March	−0.55	−0.48	−0.43	−0.46	−0.10
Annualized yield to date	−2.64	−2.20	−2.11	−2.22	−0.47
Mean (1987–94)	1.74	1.22	1.19	1.09	1.76
Standard deviation (1987–94)	2.08	1.61	1.55	1.53	1.30
Coefficient variation (1987–94)	119	132	131	141	74

Source: Lehman Brothers Fixed Income Research.

dollar corporate markets. The enhancement of corporate pricing models by the index-reporting firms will allow the daily reporting of accurate returns. Moreover, the implementation of rigorous return-attribution models will improve understanding of the sources of total return among such factors as curve, spread, sector, structure (issue size, coupon, embedded options), and currency.

Strategic Implications of Changes in Market Structure

Given their legitimate preoccupation with sector,

issuer, and structure, portfolio managers often overlook market-structure dynamics in making their relative-value decisions. Because the pace of change in market structure is gradual, market dynamics have less effect on short-term, tactical investment decision making than on long-term strategy. To optimize long-term strategic decisions, investors must take into account changes in the structure of the global capital markets.

The changes have been vast. Medium-term note (MTN) origination has come to dominate the front end of the corporate curve. Rule 144 A bonds (quasi-private-placement bonds) have captured a growing share of Yankee and emerging market debt. Structured notes and index swaps have at long last heralded the introduction of derivative instruments into the global corporate market. The high-yield corporate debt market has been legitimized after being stress-tested in 1989 and 1990.

Although the growth of derivatives and high-yield instruments stands out, the most important development during the past decade was the globalization of the corporate market. The rapid growth of the Eurobond market since 1975 and the emergence of the Dragon bond market in the early 1990s have led to the proliferation of truly transnational corporate portfolios. From a broad viewpoint, the rapid development of the emerging debt market may be seen as a subset of this globalization process. Globalization will accelerate during the next decade as many high-quality European and Asian issuers, especially newly privatized entities, join the global community of corporate borrowers.

In the U.S. investment-grade corporate market, the dominance of capital-intensive utilities has been replaced by a more balanced distribution of issuers. Utilities currently account for 21 percent of outstanding corporate debt, down from 62 percent in 1973. Financial institutions hold a 25 percent market share, up from 12.6 percent 20 years ago. In that time, industrials have climbed from 25 percent to 36 percent. From a zero index representation in 1973, Yankee bonds have surged to 18 percent as of March 31, 1994.

Partially offsetting this proliferation of issuers, the global corporate market has become structurally more homogeneous during the past decade. Since the tremendous growth of MTN programs, the market resembles an extension of the commercial paper market. Specifically, from 1989 to April 1994, structures with embedded call options declined from 72 percent to 25 percent, and a reduction to about 20 percent is expected by the end of 1994.

Three reasons explain this convergence to structural homogeneity. The first is the continued shift away from utility issuers, who prefer long-dated maturities to fund long-term capital assets. The second reason is the attractiveness of origination at the front end of a historically steep yield curve to issuers seeking to minimize interest expense and to maximize fixed-charge coverages and ratings. Third is the emergence and tremendous growth of the swap market, which fosters convenient intermediate supply in the corporate bond market.

Nothing lasts forever. As the shape of the yield curve inevitably changes through time, more structural diversification may again become prevalent. Nevertheless, the supremacy of bullets in global high-grade markets is unlikely to change during the next decade.

The trend toward bullet securities does not pertain to the high-yield market, which remains call saturated. With the eventual improvement of credit quality, many issuers anticipate being able to refinance at lower rates.

What are the portfolio implications of this structural evolution? First, scarcity value must be considered in relative-value analysis. The dominance of bullet structures translates into scarcity value for structures with embedded call and put features. This aspect is not captured in option-valuation models. The steady decline in the percentage of electric utilities in the investment-grade markets helps to explain their robust valuations in the face of growing competition.

Second, long-dated maturities will decline as a percentage of outstanding corporate debt. All else being equal, this change will lower the effective duration of all outstanding corporate debt and reduce some sensitivity to interest rate risk. The possible overall dampening of interest rate sensitivity should also ripple through to reduce spread volatility. For asset/liability managers with long horizons, this shift of the maturity distribution suggests a rise in the value of long corporates.

Third, corporate derivatives are only in their adolescence. The maturation of corporate bond derivatives, whether on a stand-alone basis or embedded in structured notes, will give rise to new strategies for investors and issuers. As in moving from two- to three-dimensional chess, the growth of derivatives will increase the complexity, and the advantage, of sound relative-value analysis. Indeed, the integration of derivatives into a burgeoning global corporate market will be one of the principal relative-value challenges for practitioners in the next decade.

Credit Analysis: The Cornerstone of Corporate Relative-Value Analysis

Not surprisingly for this quasi-equity asset class, superior credit analysis and fundamental analysis have been and will remain the most important determinants of the relative performance of corporate bond portfolios. For too long, however, investors and dealers have learned the hard way that credit analysis has no shortcuts or model magic.

The credit analysis process is both unglamorous and arduous for many top-down strategists, those who focus primarily on macro variables. Genuine credit analysis encompasses actually studying issuers' financial statements, interviewing issuers' managers, evaluating industry issues, reading indentures and charters, and developing an awareness of (not necessarily concurrence with) the views of the rating agencies about various industries and issuers.

A long-term trend in the credit quality of investment-grade corporate bonds reversed in late 1993. **Figure 1** suggests that the credit quality has declined since 1973, but this picture is somewhat misleading. In the past 18 months, credit quality has been improving. During 1993, aggregate credit quality for U.S. issuers improved at both Moody's Investors Service and Standard & Poor's Corporation for the first time since 1984. This upgrade dominance may be repeated in 1994 and 1995 at Moody's, which would be the first consecutive three-year span of upgrades since the 1960s.

Figure 1. Quality Analysis of the Lehman Brothers Corporate Index, 1973 through March 31, 1994

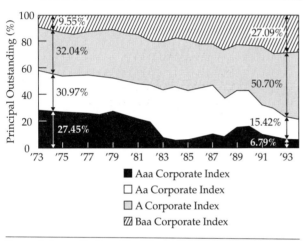

Source: Lehman Brothers Fixed Income Research.

The Baa/BBB sector has stabilized as such formerly high-yield issuers as Chrysler Corporation and McDonnell Douglas returned to the investment-grade ranks. Except for the automobile industry, the combination of issuers moving up from the speculative grades and issuers moving down from A ratings has reached a rough equilibrium. The eventual return of Chrysler Corporation and General Motors (the largest single issuer in the corporate market) to A ratings will provide an upward tilt to the outstanding rating distribution.

A strengthened economy and low interest rates have raised credit quality in the high-yield market during the past four years. As shown in **Figure 2**, B ratings accounted for 67 percent of the Lehman Brothers High-Yield Bond Index in 1987 but today represent barely 50 percent of the index.

Aside from the explicit incorporation of equity market signals in analysis (already a standard in the high-yield market), the art of analyzing an individual credit is unlikely to change substantively during the next decade. No new financial ratios are expected that will enhance the predictive capabilities

of analysts and portfolio managers. The rigor of the analysis, however (particularly at institutions attempting to outperform others with similar portfolio objectives and constraints), should vastly improve. Instead of merely relying on the rating agencies and a cursory glance at historical financial ratios, corporate bond analysts will develop their own operating and financial forecasts in the same manner as their equity and high-yield analytical brethren.

Unfortunately, the advantages of such analytical rigor may clash with the rapid expansion of the universe of global bond credits. Today, approximately 1,400 different credits exist in the dollar-denominated, public, corporate bond market alone. In a decade, with continued privatization of state enterprises, new entrants to the high-yield club, and the rapid growth of developing markets, this global roster of issuers could reach 2,000. An expected increase in U.S. portfolio managers' allocations to nondollar corporate debt will swell the universe of dollar and nondollar issuers even more.

Historically, many institutional participants in the corporate market have underallocated resources to credit evaluation because of a lack of analysts (credit evaluation is often considered merely a training position on the path to portfolio management). Such neglect must eventually undermine success, however, some credit calamity will neutralize the benefits of allocations to the riskier corporate instruments. Hopefully, the marketplace will not soon forget the lessons of the great credit crunch of the late 1980s and early 1990s. Given the increasing competitiveness of the asset management business, the goal of consistent returns will demand sufficient allocation to talented credit professionals.

Supply: A Counterintuitive Factor

The corporate bond market tends to be more reactive than proactive in examining relative values. Understandably, the primary market, especially in the high-yield and emerging debt markets, monopolizes investor attention. This focus can be hazardous for portfolio performance, however, because secondary issues often offer greater prospective returns and, sometimes, greater risks.

Primary-market myopia has intensified since 1990. The sharp descent of global yield curves generated a global refunding blitz that spawned gross origination records in 1991 through 1993 that may not be topped for a generation. The upward rotation of global yield curves in 1994 has already begun to choke the supply spigot, which has caused many portfolio managers, traders, and analysts (accustomed to a heavy daily dose of new supply) to make major adjustments.

Figure 2. Credit-Quality Composition of High-Yield Corporate Bonds by Par Value

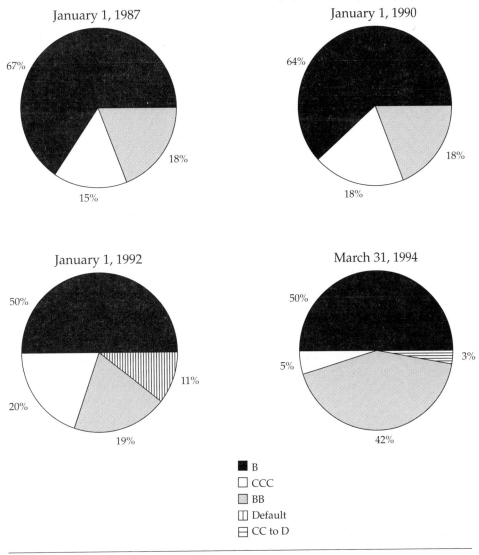

January 1, 1987

67% 18% 15%

January 1, 1990

64% 18% 18%

January 1, 1992

50% 11% 20% 19%

March 31, 1994

50% 3% 5% 42%

- ■ B
- ☐ CCC
- ▨ BB
- ▥ Default
- ⊟ CC to D

Source: Lehman Brothers High Yield Bond Index.

Supply is often a misunderstood strategic variable in short-term relative-value calculus. Prospective new supply causes many traders, analysts, and investors to advocate a defensive stance toward the overall corporate market as well as toward individual sectors and issuers. Unfortunately, this strategy has not been effective. In the first quarters of 1991, 1992, and 1993, the origination flurry was also associated with strong returns for corporate bonds relative to government securities. In contrast, the sharp supply decline during the first quarter of 1994 was accompanied by a major decline in both relative and absolute returns for corporates.

In the investment-grade corporate market, heavy supply helps relative returns as the new (often better) primary valuations validate and enhance secondary valuations. When primary origination declines sharply, secondary traders lose reinforcement from

the primary market and tend to lower their bids. In effect, Say's Law (supply creates its own demand) appears to hold. Counter to intuition, relative corporate bond returns tend to perform best during periods of heavy supply.

Over long periods, net supply (gross origination minus retirements) tends to track relative corporate valuations fairly well. Accordingly, the equilibrium spread level for issuers with large capital needs, such as communication firms and certain sovereigns, can be expected to climb relative to less capital intensive issuers.

Improved Liquidity

Trading boomed across the global capital markets in the past decade, and the corporate market was no exception. As shown in **Figure 3**, secondary trading

93

Figure 3. Average Daily Market Value of Corporate Debt Traded, May 1985 through February 1994

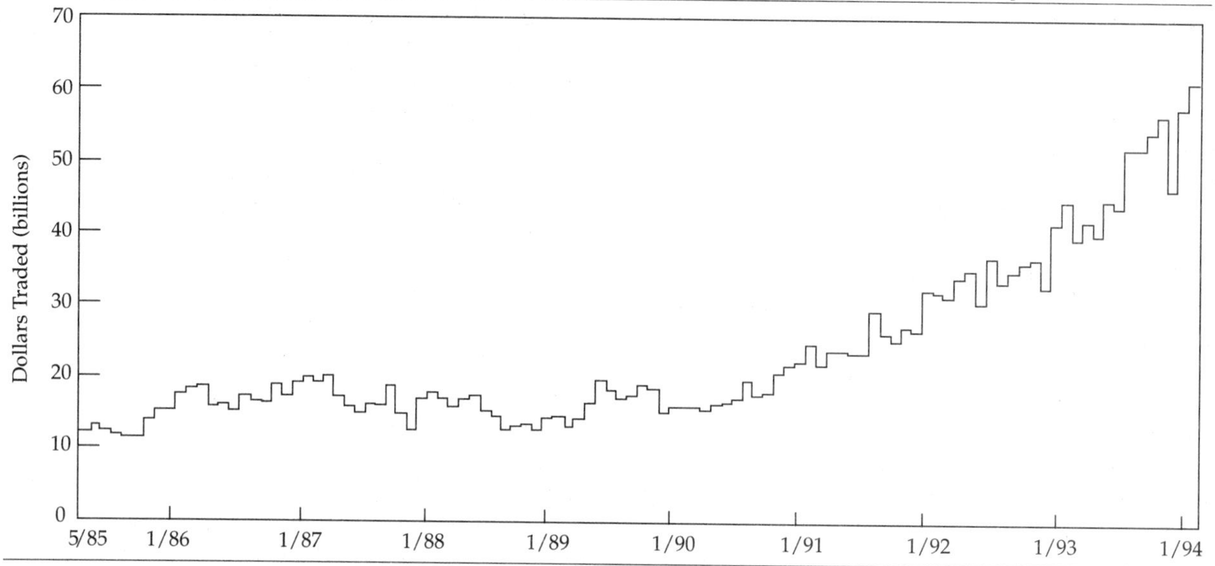

Source: Lehman Brothers Fixed Income Research, based on data from SIA Investor Activity Report.

activity in the U.S. corporate market has increased dramatically since May 1985 (the start of the data series). Note that this figure illustrates a trend, but the absolute magnitude of the amounts is incorrect because of significant double and triple counting of transactions recorded by Depository Trust Company.

This secular expansion in secondary trading stems from an accumulation of factors: the great refunding blitz of the early 1990s; the resulting multiplier effect of record origination as most new issues were sold partially on swap against existing issues; the market volatility triggered by the 1990–91 recession; a variety of secular sector opportunities (such as banks in the early 1990s); and the effects of the descent of the yield curve as investors sought call protection in bullets, some defense against the yield curve in put structures, and short-term yield maximization in high-coupon callables. Moreover, active portfolio managers increasingly approached management of bond portfolios as equity managers handle their portfolios.

In Lehman Brothers' view, corporate trading volume probably peaked in early 1994 and will slow in the mid-1990s, in concert with reduced origination and more stable spreads. Nonetheless, corporate liquidity, buttressed by new commercial bank dealers, should remain ample to facilitate the fine-tuning of corporate portfolios by both active and passive investors.

This secular rise in liquidity and decline in transaction costs, even allowing for some cyclical vulnerability, accentuates the demand for superior relative-value analysis. Leaving aside the special objective of indexers, the relative returns generated by the more activist investors have been subsidized by classic buy-and-hold investors, such as long-term asset/liability managers. A growing awareness of this phenomenon has already begun to spur a more activist posture by traditional corporate investors.

Spread Analysis: Its Primacy and Some Caveats about Current Practices

By custom, some segments of the high-yield and Eurobond markets prefer bond price or bond yield to spread as the measure of value. In the past decade, however, nominal spreads (the yield differences between corporate and government bonds of similar maturities) have become the basic units of both price and relative-value analysis throughout the global corporate market. Lehman Brothers believes the high-yield and Eurobond markets also will switch completely to spreads in the next several years. Unlike the mortgage-backed security market, the corporate market has not adopted and is not likely to adopt option-adjusted spreads as measures of price/value, for two reasons. First, most Eurobonds, most MTNs, and a growing percentage of U.S. investment-grade corporate debt (69 percent) are bullet securities that do not feature embedded options. Second, the standard one-factor binomial models in use today do not take into account credit-spread volatility.

Although spreads are the mainstay of corporate relative-value analysis, corporate investors should avoid spread myopia in making relative-value decisions. Spread movements are a key but not the exclusive determinant of relative returns. Coupon, maturity, and structural differentials often can more than counter spread movements—even movements in the entire corporate market. Spreads tightened in

April 1993, but the nominal total return difference between investment-grade corporates and governments was zero thanks to the negative effects of a rising benchmark curve on the (longer duration) corporate market versus the (shorter duration) government market. In August 1993, the exact converse occurred: Spreads widened in some sectors, but corporates outperformed governments because of the sharp descent of the yield curve.

Investors should have a firm understanding of the strengths and weaknesses of the common spread and relative-value tools. In addition to nominal spreads, corporate relative-value analysis also includes an examination of quality spreads, the yield difference between low- and high-quality credits. Not surprisingly, based on the current strong economic environment, **Figure 4** shows that industrial quality (Baa–Aaa yields) have stabilized and are the lowest since the last economic boom in the 1980s. This analysis may tempt some investors to upgrade the quality of their portfolios in anticipation of the next recession. An upgrade rotation does not make sense, however, unless a recession is fairly imminent. Moreover, Baa/BBB industrial spreads have been tighter for extended stretches at many intervals during the post-World War II era, as shown in **Figure 5**.

Percent yield spread analysis (the ratio of corporate yields to government yields for securities of similar duration), shown in **Figure 6**, is another popular technical tool with some investors. Lehman Brothers has major reservations about this method-

ology, however. Percent yield spread is more a derivative than an explanatory or predictive variable. Our data show that yields and spreads do not always move in the same direction. The economic cycle is the main determinant of overall spreads. A recession in a low-yield environment may precipitate high percent yield spreads. Strong economic growth accompanied by inflation, indicating a higher benchmark Treasury curve, would generate low percent yield spreads.

Another common tool for analyzing spreads among individual securities and across industry sectors is mean-reversion analysis. **Figure 7** illustrates this measure for the retail sector. We also have major reservations about this methodology. The mean is highly dependent on the interval selected, and no market consensus on the appropriate interval exists. Over the years, we have observed investors who use 3-, 5-, 10-, and even 20-year means to judge relative value. Why should a somewhat arbitrary mean exert a mysterious gravitational effect on current spreads? More importantly, the timing of supposed reversion is completely uncertain. In the absence of macroeconomic changes or sector/issuer-specific fundamental developments, spreads tend to persist for long periods. For example, consolidation in the retail sector during the late 1980s, mainly debt financed, elevated the mean for the interval under review, but portfolio managers who sold retail debt in April 1992 would have missed out on further spread tightening.

Current spread compression and the immediate

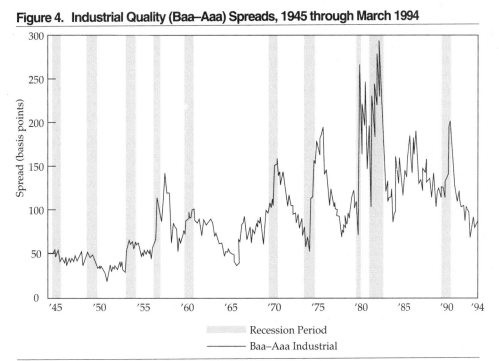

Figure 4. Industrial Quality (Baa–Aaa) Spreads, 1945 through March 1994

Note: Benchmark is 10-year Treasuries until February 1977 and 30-year Treasuries thereafter.

Source: Lehman Brothers Fixed Income Research, based on data from Moody's Investors Service.

Figure 5. Baa Industrial Spreads, 1945 through March 1994

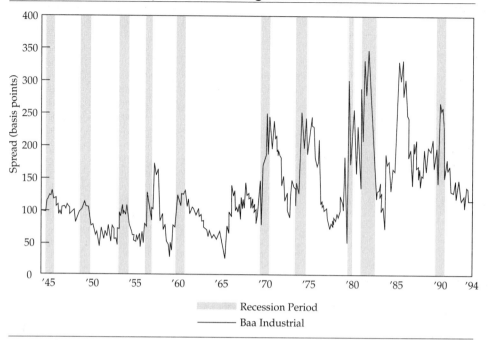

Recession Period

——— Baa Industrial

Note: Benchmark is 10-year Treasuries until February 1977 and 30-year Treasuries thereafter.

Source: Lehman Brothers Fixed Income Research, based on data from Moody's Investors Service.

prospect for low spread volatility have inspired an understandable eruption of curve and structure infatuation by some investors in corporate debt. In the hope of compensating for the dearth of potential spread contractions, some total return investors have deployed their government-curve tools in the corporate bond market. This practice seems to be least prevalent among asset/liability managers (insurance companies and pension funds), who have long horizons. Aside from transactions at the margin, the

Figure 6. Baa Industrial Percent Yield Spread, 1945 through March 1994

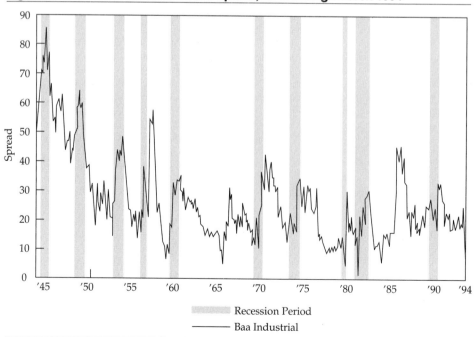

Recession Period

——— Baa Industrial

Note: Benchmark is 10-year Treasuries until February 1977 and 30-year Treasuries thereafter.

Source: Lehman Brothers Fixed Income Research, based on data from Moody's Investors Service.

Figure 7. Thirty-Year Retail Spreads, December 31, 1987, through March 31, 1994

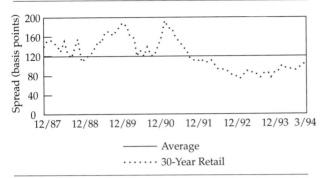

Source: Lehman Brothers Fixed Income Research.

asset/liability investor class —the real controllers of market valuation for investment-grade corporates— appear content to balance yield optimization with targeted credit-risk tolerances and durations. Moreover, even if such long-term investors seek to emulate the market nimbleness of short-term total return maximizers, the constraining combination of portfolio size, accounting adjustments, and transaction costs will limit curve hopscotch within the corporate market.

Those managers with a focus on curve analysis may benefit from an understanding of how different segments of the corporate curve respond to rate changes. As an illustration, the actual performance of corporate bonds relative to government bonds is presented in **Figure 8**.

Rich–cheap analysis is another favorite diagnostic tool. **Figure 9** presents an example of this tool applied to utility debt at the end of the first quarter of 1989. Users should be wary, however. Rich–cheap measures are static snapshots of market valu-

Figure 8. Corporate-Bond Total Return versus Government-Bond Total Return by Maturity for 1993 and First Quarter 1994

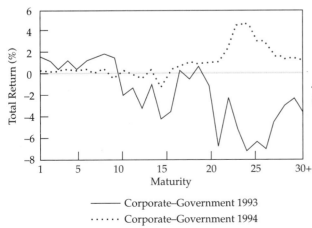

Source: Lehman Brothers Fixed Income Research.

ations. Such findings do not necessarily indicate whether a security will become richer or cheaper. El Paso Funding (ELPF), for example, turned up as cheap in 1989, but this issue became much cheaper when El Paso Electric, its ultimate credit support, entered Chapter 11 three years later. Panhandle Eastern Pipe Line (PANL) and Texas Eastern Transmission (TET) also subsequently became cheaper, before sharply rebounding in the early 1990s.

In the mid-1980s, option-adjusted spread (OAS) analysis became extremely popular throughout the global bond market, but its popularity has waned during the 1990s. Lehman Brothers believes OAS analysis has a major problem; *ex ante* OAS rankings do not correlate well with *ex post* total return rankings in the corporate market. We ranked baskets of structurally homogeneous utility securities by OAS ratings (using a binomial model) at the end of 1987. We then studied returns for the subsequent five years. In general, the OAS-to-return rankings were very weak.

This study certainly had some flaws. For one thing, to expect OAS rankings at one point in time to map total returns for the next five years is somewhat unfair. Moreover, the option models of 1987 were not as refined as the models of 1994. We have tried other models and other corporate sectors, however, without additional success. Therefore, analysts should be cautious about using OAS models as a guide to expected total returns. A one-factor model does not offer much help in predicting spread/return volatility in the subsequent year or two.

Multifactor option valuation will eventually mitigate these weaknesses. In the interim, practitioners are forced to rely on heuristic techniques such as variation of issuer-specific spread curves to gauge reasonably effective duration, effective convexity, and OAS.

In the next decade, analysts will develop models that incorporate the full richness of the factors that shape valuation. These multifactor models will include valuation sensitivities not only to curve changes but also to structure, sector, equity valuations, spread volatility, issue liquidity, and indenture differences.

Conclusion

Abetted by the persistence of outmoded portfolio constraints on many institutional investors, the development of a suitable relative-value framework for intermarket and intramarket analysis is the major challenge for the global fixed-income markets. Analysis has improved greatly during the 1990s, but regional and product biases persist. For example, some European strategists and managers ignore U.S.

Figure 9. Actual Yield Spread off U.S. Treasury versus Utility Quality Score

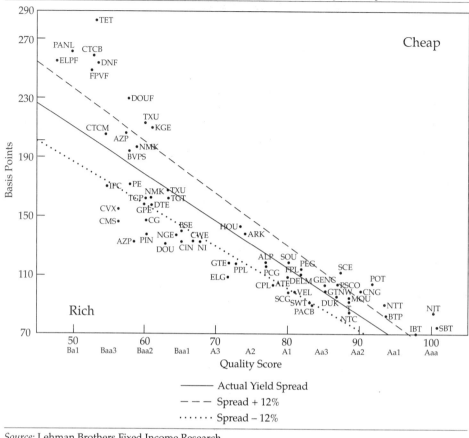

Source: Lehman Brothers Fixed Income Research.

spread products, and many U.S. strategists do not fully take into account nondollar products. Because of either internal constraints or the absence of an analytical framework, many investors confine their search for relative value to varying subsets of the global bond markets.

Therefore, fixed-income managers have many questions for which they really do not yet have good answers. These questions concern

- the reliability of economic forecasts (in light of the quickening of geopolitical change in the mid-1990s);
- the economic and credit implications of an acceleration of global environmental remediation;
- the escalation of health care costs in developed markets as populations age;
- the effects of rapid technological innovation in such industries as communications, computers, and financial services;
- the likelihood of rising inflation;
- the possibility of balance sheet releveraging in the late 1990s;
- the spread of shareholder activism to bondholders;

- the convergence or divergence of global yield curves;
- the possible convergence of the emerging and high-yield markets;
- the development of a high-yield corporate market for non-U.S. origination;
- the constraints (capital or issuers) for low-quality origination;
- the sources of the differences in credit risk evaluation;
- the evolution of rating philosophy at the global rating agencies and the resulting ripple effects on corporate valuations;
- the likelihood of non-U.S. institutions improving infrastructures for analyzing credit risk;
- the best ways to hedge low-quality debt;
- the growth of the derivatives market;
- the optimal means to incorporate derivative strategies in corporate portfolios; and
- the development of improved systematic tools to identify relative-value anomalies across the global corporate bond market.

Clearly, a fascinating road lies ahead for fixed-income analysts.

Question and Answer Session

John V. Malvey, CFA

Question: Can the necessary analytical work be accomplished without the cost of creating and maintaining internal research capabilities? Would sitting down with Street analysts from several firms (so that their biases offset each other) be an acceptable alternative?

Malvey: You need dedicated in-house analytical staff to check and balance the information you receive. In-house staff can also provide additional analytical input based on internal requirements. From my observations, the investors who fare best in the corporate bond market have internal analytical resources. A number of tears have been shed over the years by those who don't have the internal resources to analyze corporate bonds.

Question: Could equity analysts use any parts of the fixed-income credit analysis you described?

Malvey: Yes, they could. Equity analysis and debt analysis have been converging in many respects during the past ten years. In particular, equity analysts and portfolio managers have imported several key analytical processes from their fixed-income brethren: rating-agency awareness and the effects of ratings on cost of funds and dividends (i.e., in the financial institution sector); debt indenture (covenant familiarity, especially in the high-yield sector); and greater focus on the balance sheet and analysis of its effects on debt and equity valuations.

By the same token, many debt analysts have learned much from their equity counterparts. Unlike a decade ago, and similar to equity analysts' approach, fewer buy-side and sell-side debt analysts are attempting to cover the entire market. Specialization and rigorous analysis has finally arrived in fixed income.

Question: Why has the derivatives market developed only in the mortgage area and not around corporate bonds?

Malvey: Arguably, corporate bonds are the last frontier for the derivatives market. Derivative use has become commonplace in government bonds, municipal debt, equities, and foreign exchange, as well as in mortgages. Derivative use has also blossomed among corporate end users in the swap market. So far, however, corporate investors have been slow to embrace the limited derivatives offered (excluding the burgeoning structured-note market). Many factors contribute to the lag in derivative use, including lack of regulatory and tax incentives, market dominance by long-term asset/liability managers (who are accustomed to controlling risk through broad diversification), the limited availability of corporate derivatives because of costs (when compared with other fixed-income derivatives), and lack of analytical tools. Despite these drawbacks, as the transaction costs decline and analytical tools improve in the next decade, derivative use by corporate bond investors should expand rapidly.

Creating Low-Variability Global Portfolios

Theresa A. Havell
Partner and Managing Director
Neuberger & Berman

Global fixed-income securities can enhance portfolio returns, but only if investors are careful to assess all the risks—concentration, foreign exchange, credit, and duration—and limit or balance them according to their risk preferences. Derivative securities are beneficial vehicles for altering portfolio risks, but they can be misused. They also introduce basis risk and can be costly. Investors can reduce the costs by using customized rather than packaged derivatives.

Investors in the global bond markets seem to be always looking for a free lunch—high return and low risk. But there is no free lunch in fixed income. Consequently, some investors have lost a great deal of money.

Part of the problem is semantics. Investors typically equate "short term" with "low risk." They also think that "insured" means low risk and that "market neutral" means low risk. These terms do not necessarily assure that risks are low, however, because they apply to only limited aspects of risk; they do not define risk comprehensively.

For example, short-term world money market funds were the hottest items in the market in 1992. That year, assets surged to more than $30 billion on the basis of the funds' high current yields. The funds, being short term, were thus also thought to be low risk. When the Exchange Rate Mechanism collapsed in 1992, however, the money flowed out of the funds, most of which posted negative returns for the year. In 1994, as a category of funds, these "low-risk" funds lost about 2 percent on average. The worst performing of the short-term funds declined more than 6.5 percent. The asset category has less than $12.5 billion in it today and many very disappointed investors.

The global bond markets, in general, have had a wide range of returns. In 1993, global funds as a category had a spectacular year. The global mutual fund category returned more than 17 percent, with the best performing fund up more than 51.5 percent, which indicates more than simply diversified investing, and with the worst performing fund down 4.9 percent. In the first quarter of 1994, in aggregate, the funds were down 5.11 percent; the worst performing funds were down about 21.2 percent. In this category of 100 funds, the No. 1 and No. 2 performing funds in 1993 finished No. 99 and No. 100 in the first quarter of 1994. Thus, even so-called nonrisky assets have tremendous variations in returns.

The aim of this presentation is to offer managers some practical approaches, in light of the semantic pitfalls, to controlling risk when investing through global fixed-income portfolios. As part of analyzing risk control, the presentation will also provide some words of wisdom about derivatives.

Approaches to Risk

Bond managers have typically identified risk in their portfolios by measuring credit risk and market risk. Traditionally, those two parameters could indicate whether a portfolio was in control. Today, managers need to adopt a more complex approach to managing fixed-income portfolios.

The recommended approach has four facets. It begins with the two traditional, basic considerations—the portfolio's credit risk and market risk. The third facet is the portfolio's volatility risk. Volatility has become a concern mainly because of the proliferation of derivative securities—in the direct form of futures and options and in a package form—and the introduction and widespread use of foreign-denominated securities with their attendant foreign currency risk. A fundamental problem in the derivatives market is that funds do not currently post their volatility; thus, investors cannot truly judge the funds' riskiness. A portfolio that cannot be measured for volatility does not allow a focus on the fourth facet of modern management of global fixed-income portfolios, namely, the full portfolio.

To achieve a low-variability global portfolio, managers must not only strictly control the risk of each individual security, they must control risk in the aggregate portfolio to ensure that the portfolio remains consistent with its low-volatility mandate.

What investors traditionally view as low volatility and high volatility is an interesting study. Investors have three basic choices in their investing—eat well, sleep well, or a combination. **Figure 1** illustrates the annualized return and risk profile of various alternative investments. In an eat-well portfolio, stocks are the vehicle of choice because they provide good returns over long periods of time, averaging 11.63 percent a year from 1951 to 1993. Their standard deviation, however, has been significantly higher than that of fixed-income securities. Despite their superior performance over long periods of time, equity portfolios often have quarters with negative returns. In the past thirty years, the S&P 500 Index had negative returns in almost 40 percent of the quarters. Fixed-income securities of an intermediate term, such as two- and five-year Treasury instruments, have provided good returns (6.10 percent and 6.24 percent, respectively) with modest standard deviations, particularly compared with long-term government bonds.

The sleep-well approach to investing produces safe, rather dull, low-risk portfolios, such as a portfolio of two-year T-bills. During the past thirty years, two-year notes had negative returns in less than 5 percent of the quarters. As shown in **Figure 2**, the

longer the T-bill's maturity, the higher the risk of a negative quarter or year. One-year to five-year notes have not had negative annual returns, but they have had some negative quarters. Ten-year notes had negative annual returns for 14 percent of the observations, and twenty-year and thirty-year bond returns have been negative about a third of the time.

A domestic combination of the eat-well and sleep-well approaches would balance U.S. equity and T-bills to produce a rate of return and standard deviation that a specific investor can live with.

Controlling Risk

Investors can view investment outcome in the global fixed-income market as being built on four factors: concentration, currency, credit, and interest rates. By managing these four factors effectively, investors can decrease portfolio risk.

For example, risk increases with concentration within the market. Some of the global funds that did the best in 1993 and the worst in early 1994 were concentrated in the riskiest sector of the market— emerging markets. Emerging markets declined about 20 percent in that period.

Foreign exchange positions also increase risk, which was the problem for the world money market funds in 1992. These funds had high levels of exposure to nondollar securities. When the dollar rose, the securities declined; their high foreign currency exposures created unacceptable levels of volatility in investors' portfolios.

Figure 1. Risk–Return Profile of Various U.S. Securities, 1951–93

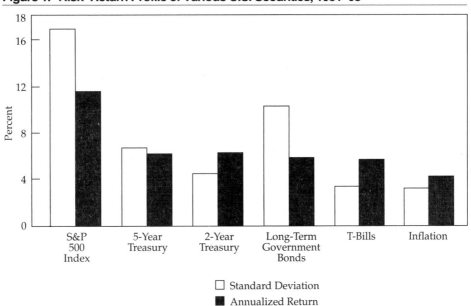

Note: Inflation is the consumer price index.

Source: Neuberger & Berman.

Figure 2. U.S. Treasuries: Negative Quarters and Years at Constant Maturities, 1973–93

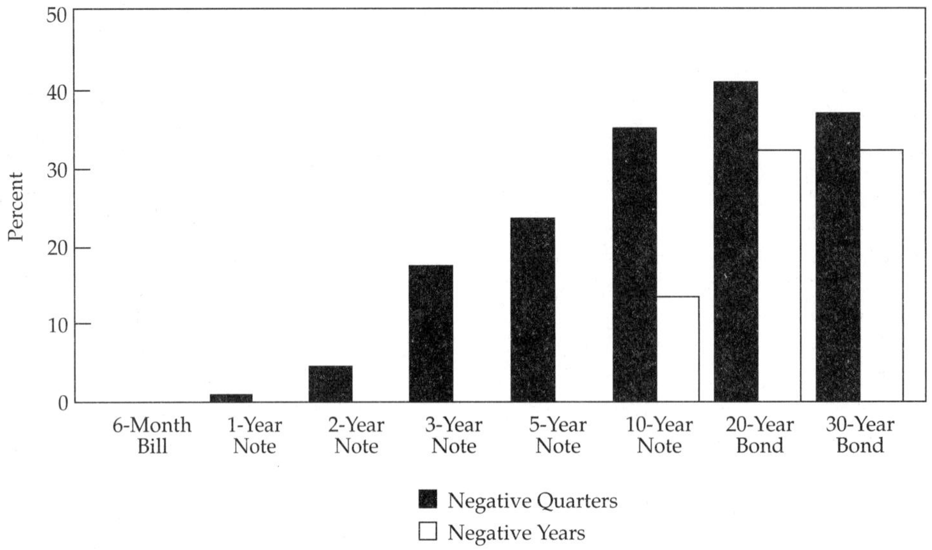

Source: Neuberger & Berman.

Another factor that increases risk is low credit quality, which can arise directly or through a derivative security.

Finally, long duration also increases risk. Most fixed-income managers are comfortable measuring duration, but obtaining an accurate number for everything is tricky, particularly when a manager uses such securities as mortgages, which have options embedded in them.

Investors can use a global portfolio to increase the returns available from U.S. securities because of the global portfolio's diversification features and the abundance of worldwide market opportunities. Moderation, however, is vital. The four factors must be in proportion in the portfolio. Managers can lower the credit quality or increase the duration in a few securities or maybe even concentrate in one area or another or have some extra foreign exchange exposure in a certain market; the aggregate, however, should bring the portfolio into equilibrium.

Derivative Securities

Derivatives play an important beneficial role in today's global fixed-income market, but they also have introduced some problems. Derivatives allow an investor to alter market and credit risk in a portfolio but without changing the underlying assets, which is a desirable option for managers. The real problem arises when investors buy derivative securities with the belief that they have obtained something for nothing. A derivative may offer flexibility, but it will not substitute for a correct prediction of the market. For example, if investors know that U.S.

interest rates will rise or that the rates in Japan will fall, then they can buy derivatives or cash securities to take advantage of that knowledge.

Because derivatives have the ability to alter the structure of a portfolio fundamentally without making the change explicit in the securities themselves, however, derivatives provide a dangerous means to circumvent the guidelines and objectives of a portfolio. This aspect has been the most fundamental problem with the use of derivatives in the fixed-income markets, and the problem has plagued individual, corporate, pension, and mutual fund portfolios.

Also, all derivatives carry basis risk, and the basis risk can be significant. Investors have no guarantee that the derivative security will perform along the lines of the cash security.

Derivative securities in package forms are the most costly way to participate in the market. A Christmas fruit basket serves as an appropriate analogy. If a consumer buys a Christmas fruit basket, what he or she receives for the money is six pears, three bananas, a couple of fancy jars of jelly, some cellophane, and a ribbon. The cost of the individual contents is about $12.95, but the cost of the package is about $80.00. In the same way, derivative products are the most costly way to use derivatives. If investors really know what they want to do, they should buy exchange-traded options or futures and create their own packages.

Packaged derivative securities must be analyzed carefully. Take, for example, a AAA-rated bank security that was widely sold late in 1993 while the emerging market mania was under way. It had a one-year maturity and a 3.95 percent coupon, which at the time was well above what a floating-rate note or a one-year security offered. The deceptive feature of this security is that its performance (i.e., its principal) was linked to the spread in yield between a 30-year Mexican par bond and a 30-year Treasury bond. At maturity, if the spread did not change, the repayment would be 100; investors would get back 100 percent of their principal (a logical outcome in fixed-income securities). If the spread were to widen, however—and remember, this security was sold at the absolute all-time narrow spread for Mexican par bonds to 30-year T-bonds—then the principal repayment would be less than 100. So, a one-year fixed-income security would be returning less than 100 percent of principal back at par. Prior to the concept of derivatives, the only reason investors would receive less than 100 percent of principal at maturity would be in the event of a default. In the case of this packaged derivative security, however, merely a widening spread would cause less than 100 percent principal repayment.

An alternative that would create the security much more cheaply than buying the packaged derivative would be to buy the 30-year Mexican par bond and to sell the U.S. Treasury. Many mutual funds or other clients believed, however, that their customers would never allow them to buy 30-year Mexican par bonds but would allow them to buy a 1-year cash security that was linked to a AA-rated

bank. The deceptive aspect of the derivatives market is precisely that dodge. Managers who use derivatives to alter perceptions about a security may find themselves in trouble, particularly with their clients.

Another example is a recently offered collared floating-rate note with embedded options that create a cap and floor. A bank rated AAA issued this ten-year subordinated note at a six-month LIBOR minus 25 basis points, even though such a security would typically trade at a higher rate than LIBOR minus 25. This security was sold as a six-month floater, but it has the variability of a 30-year T-bond. It moved down more than ten points on a one-point move in interest rates. Investors who bought this security were truly fooling themselves; they paid a high price for the option in this security.

Conclusion

Global fixed-income securities offer investors the opportunity to enhance returns moderately if investors take only moderate risks. Global fixed-income securities will not, however, create a duration-neutral strategy that will return 15 percent year after year with no negative quarters. The amount of concentration, foreign exchange exposure, credit risk, and duration in the global fixed-income portfolio should be consistent with an investor's preference between sleeping well and eating well.

Question and Answer Session

Theresa A. Havell

Question: Do you use derivatives?

Havell: We use only exchange-traded futures and options, and we use them to change the duration characteristics of our portfolios. The duration of the portfolio, however, has to remain within the parameters mandated by the portfolio philosophy. We use derivatives strictly on an unleveraged basis and not necessarily for hedging. We have not used any packaged derivatives because, when we examine them, we have found that every package was more expensive than what we ourselves could assemble.

Question: Please comment on Brady bonds, especially in light of the recent sell-off.

Havell: Many technical adjustments have occurred in the emerging fixed-income markets, but securities such as Argentine par bonds have moved from 46 to 70 and then back to 50—some rather extraordinary moves. So, emerging markets are cheap now; if they bounce back up again, the investor's ride may be very different from what it was in the past, however, because much of the investor base has been shaken.

These securities are still sensitive to interest rates, so investors or managers must make a bet on interest rates if they want to buy a floating-rate bond. If the investor thinks interest rates at 7.5 percent for long-term bonds are attractive, the Argentine fixed-rate instruments probably carry the best value because they will trade on Argentine credit—that is, primarily on how well market liquidity recovers. They will also trade to some extent, however, on U.S. interest rates.

Question: Please explain parallel hedging and the risk–return trade-offs involved.

Havell: Parallel hedging carries basis risk. It is similar to saying, "We will hedge gold with silver." Every time investors leave a cash market and substitute a proxy or parallel market, they incur basis risk ranging from very small to very great.

Question: If we try to control the risk of individual securities in a portfolio and control overall portfolio risk, aren't we practicing too much risk control?

Havell: Not to my mind. You could take the approach of saying, "Well, as long as the aggregate is all right, the risk level is fine," but if you have too many individual securities spinning out of control, if you have too many pork bellies in your portfolio, you will not be able to bring the aggregate into control. The philosophy behind most well-thought-out portfolios is to limit the risk of each individual security as a way of keeping aggregate risk down to the desired level.

Global Bond Management

Michael R. Rosenberg
Managing Director, International Fixed Income Research
Merrill Lynch & Company

Foreign bonds have in the past provided fixed-income portfolios with diversification and higher returns than domestic bonds. Realizing the benefits of foreign bonds, however, depends on careful portfolio construction and, in particular, active management. In the future, the benefits will be reduced if the links among global interest rates tighten.

The purpose of this presentation is to describe how the international fixed-income investment game is being played today and how the game is likely to evolve in the future. The presentation addresses both theoretical issues and practical problems facing the global fixed-income manager.

Analysts' views about the benefits of international fixed-income diversification are changing, and the reason is that interest rates around the world are apparently becoming more tightly linked than they were in the past. If they are, that development has enormous implications for the benefits of passive global diversification and, more importantly, for actively managing a global bond portfolio. For example, if interest rates are becoming more tightly linked, will incremental value in running a global bond portfolio come more from currency selection than from bond selection? Should currencies be viewed, then, as a separate asset class?

The discussion will also tear down some myths that have crept into the business of global bond management in recent years. In particular, this presentation will show that neither high-yield foreign bonds nor currency-hedged foreign bonds provide a free lunch.

The Role of Foreign Bonds in a Fixed-Income Portfolio

Foreign bonds can no longer be ignored by U.S. portfolio managers. These bonds, constituting more than 26 percent of the entire asset pool, are the single largest component of world wealth.

Globalization in the bond market is a fairly new phenomenon. Until 1990, despite the enormous role foreign bonds play in the world portfolio, U.S. investors had only a tiny chunk of their total assets in foreign bonds, as **Table 1** shows; even in 1994, the percentage is small. For Canadian investors, the percentage is even smaller. Germany's participation in the foreign bond market increased greatly in the 1980s, but at 10 percent, it is still small relative to what it would be if German investors held a market-capitalization-weighted allocation in foreign bonds. Japan and the United Kingdom had regulations on capital outflows until about 1980. As these regulations were relaxed, both countries' percentages invested in foreign bonds increased enormously.

To assess the contribution foreign bonds can make to a U.S. fixed-income portfolio, the issue of whether the theory of uncovered interest rate parity holds must first be addressed. This theory states that the expected change in the exchange rate over time will equal the domestic–foreign interest rate differential. For example, if U.S. interest rates are higher than those overseas, the expectation would be for the dollar to decline at a rate equal to the interest rate differential; otherwise, investors would earn an excess return by owning U.S. bonds. Interest rate parity means that what investors can earn in one market is essentially on a par with what they can earn in another market after adjusting for changes in exchange rates. **Figure 1** shows how uncovered interest rate parity works. If the U.S. yield curve is higher than the foreign yield curve, then the value of the foreign currency would be expected to appreciate against the U.S. dollar over time.

If uncovered interest rate parity holds at all times, one cannot possibly make a case for international fixed-income investing because investors in the foreign market would earn the same rate as they earn in the U.S. market. If foreign bonds offer a risk premium over and above what investors can earn in the U.S. market, perhaps a case can be made for

105

Table 1. International Investment Positions as a Percent of GDP

Country	1975	1980	1985	1990
United States	1.8	2.2	2.7	4.0
Canada	2.4	2.7	3.6	3.6
Germany	1.5	1.9	5.9	10.3
Japan	0.8	1.8	9.2	16.8
United Kingdom	5.4	7.9	27.1	33.3

Source: Linda Tesar, "Home Bias in International Portfolios," National Bureau of Economic Research Working Paper No. 4218 (Cambridge, Mass.: November 1992).

getting involved in international fixed-income investment. If no risk premium exists, this case cannot be made.

The evidence indicates that, since the beginning of floating exchange rates in 1973, foreign bonds have historically outperformed U.S. bonds, as shown in **Figure 2**, which suggests that uncovered interest rate parity has not held. If this history is broken down into periods, however, uncovered interest rate parity has held for substantial periods. **Figure 3** shows the 1973–85 period and **Figure 4** shows the period from 1988 through early 1994; both indicate that uncovered interest rate parity held in the U.S. and foreign bond markets for significant periods. The exception was the 1986–87 period (not shown in Figures 3 and 4), when the dollar collapsed. When that unusual episode is excluded, the cumulative return on foreign bonds, over time, pretty much matches the cumulative return on U.S. bonds.

Uncovered interest rate parity did not hold for every week and every month of these periods; indeed, the deviations were often quite large. From 1973 to about 1981, foreign bonds outperformed U.S. bonds, and then the U.S. market quickly caught up from 1981 to 1985. Thus, tremendous opportunities existed to move in and out of foreign bonds. In the long run, however, the expected return on U.S. and foreign bonds was roughly the same.

Figure 1. Yield-Curve Slopes and the Expected Path of Exchange Rates in the Long Run

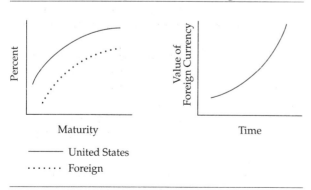

United States
⋯⋯ Foreign

Source: Merrill Lynch & Co.

Figure 2. Total Return Performance of U.S. and Foreign Bond Markets in U.S.-Dollar Terms, 1973–94

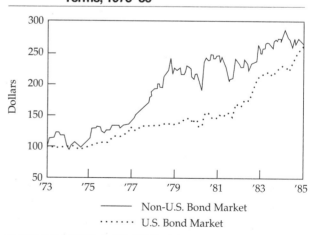

Non-U.S. Bond Market
⋯⋯ U.S. Bond Market

Note: U.S. bond market for 1973–78 period is U.S. corporate and government bonds; for 1978–93 period, U.S. T-bonds.

Source: Merrill Lynch & Co.

If this parity holds true for the future, persuading U.S. investors to diversify internationally may prove to be difficult. That is, if uncovered interest rate parity holds in the long run, it will be difficult to argue that foreign bonds are a unique asset class that can make a valuable contribution to risk performance. From a total return standpoint, foreign bonds do not make a contribution to an already well-diversified portfolio; therefore, the case for considering foreign bonds as a separate asset class is weak.

In that case, the next basic question for investors is: Do foreign bonds contribute in terms of risk

Figure 3. Total Return Performance of U.S. and Foreign Bond Markets in U.S.-Dollar Terms, 1973–85

Non-U.S. Bond Market
⋯⋯ U.S. Bond Market

Note: U.S. bond market for 1973–78 period is U.S. corporate and government bonds; for 1978–85 period, U.S. T-bonds.

Source: Merrill Lynch & Co.

Figure 4. Total Return Performance of U.S. T-Bonds and Foreign Bonds in U.S.-Dollar Terms, 1988–94

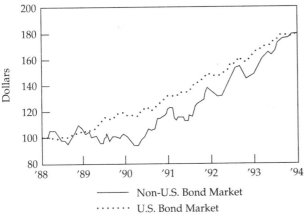

Non-U.S. Bond Market

U.S. Bond Market

Source: Merrill Lynch & Co.

reduction? Unfortunately, the amount of risk reduction gained by investing in foreign bonds is almost insignificant. The risk–return profile of foreign and domestic U.S. bonds for the 1975–93 period is shown in **Figure 5**. Although foreign bonds are not highly correlated with U.S. bonds, foreign bonds are more volatile when measured in U.S.-dollar terms because of currency volatility. That volatility offsets the lower correlations, and therefore, the amount of portfolio risk reduction gained by investors in foreign bonds is modest.

Figure 5. Risk–Return Profile of Passively Managed International Fixed-Income Portfolios, 1975–93

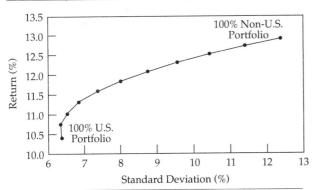

Source: Merrill Lynch & Co.

Much research has examined what foreign bonds bring to an already well-diversified U.S. fixed-income portfolio from a passive standpoint. In 1990, Burik and Ennis summed up the research conclusions by noting that, in the absence of superior active management, foreign bonds "make only a modest contribution to domestic portfolios that hold domes-

tic fixed-income securities and already enjoy efficient international common stock and real estate diversification." Therefore, the authors determined, "Many investors will conclude that foreign bonds constitute a diversification opportunity they can afford to pass up."[1]

Managing a Global Bond Portfolio

Given the limited diversification benefits that foreign bonds offer, foreign bonds should not be promoted as a unique, separate asset class. Instead, foreign bonds should be promoted as a subset of a broad asset class entitled "global fixed income." This subset should be viewed as an "opportunistic asset," and indeed, many investors are now viewing foreign bonds in this light.

Active versus Passive Management

Because domestic and foreign bonds offer the same returns in the long run and the amount of portfolio risk reduction is modest, to make a compelling case from a passive standpoint for international fixed-income diversification is difficult. Thus, when an investor is considering setting up a global bond portfolio, an indexed nondollar bond portfolio makes no sense. No long-run excess return and no significant reduction in portfolio risk can be achieved through that approach. Therefore, throughout the investment community as a whole, with all the mandates that have been granted for foreign bonds from the pension fund community, only 4 percent of the total mandates have been for passively managed portfolios, whereas 96 percent have been for actively managed portfolios.

A stronger case can be made for active than for passive international diversification because the differences in annual total return performance among the major government bond markets, shown in **Figure 6**, are strikingly large; on average, 3,500–4,000 basis points (bps) separate the lowest and highest performing markets in the world on an annual basis. Unlike the U.S. market, the foreign markets provide potential for substantial incremental return. Because of the striking differences in annualized total returns, U.S. fund managers may use foreign bonds as an alternative to U.S. cash to help them outperform their domestic benchmarks, not for the purpose of outperforming some global or nondollar benchmark.

A simple illustration of how the game may be played follows: Assume a manager allocates 100 percent of a portfolio to U.S. bonds and zero to

[1]Both quotations are from Paul Burik and Richard M. Ennis, "Foreign Bonds in Diversified Portfolios: A Limited Advantage," *Financial Analysts Journal*, vol. 46, no. 2 (March/April 1990):31–40.

Figure 6. Total Return Performance of Major Government Bond Markets in U.S.-Dollar Terms

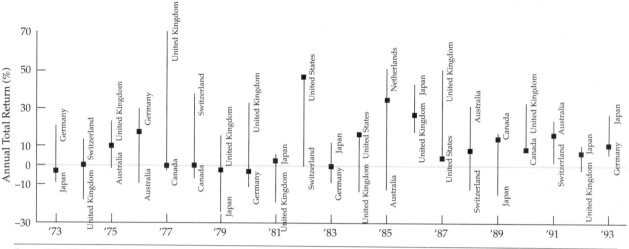

Source: Merrill Lynch & Co.

foreign bonds when he or she is bullish on the dollar, then allocates 80 percent to U.S. bonds and 20 percent to foreign bonds when he or she is bearish on the dollar. In this example, a U.S. manager playing this game will never be more than 20 percent invested in foreign bonds and will never have less than 80 percent invested in U.S. bonds.

As an illustration of the opportunistic strategy, consider the following trading rule: Managers will be bullish on the dollar when the trade-weighted dollar moves above its 12-month moving average and will be bearish on the dollar when the dollar falls below its 12-month moving average; this rule will dictate whether the portfolio is 100/0 or 80/20 invested in U.S./foreign bonds. Had a manager followed this simple rule from the beginning of floating exchange rates until now, he or she would have outperformed the total return performance of a passive U.S. domestic fixed-income portfolio by 150–200 bps, as shown in **Figure 7**.

Using the dollar as the basis for moving in and out of foreign bonds is only one approach; many other strategies can be used to take advantage of changes in yield spreads, yield curves, and so on. What this simple example illustrates is that foreign bonds can be used by U.S. fund managers to help them substantially outperform their domestic benchmarks and, in turn, their competitors.

Global Interest Rates

The problem with actively managing foreign bonds is that long-term global interest rates are becoming more tightly linked than in the past. Therefore, even active management may not be able to continue achieving above-average returns from foreign bond investing.

Short-term rates are not highly correlated; the correlation for the United States and Japan is only 0.05; for the United States and Germany, 0.12. These low correlations essentially reflect the fact that countries' central bank policies differ over time. For example, the United States is presently in a tightening mode, whereas German monetary policy is presently in an easing mode.

Long-term rates, however, have had much higher correlations, and these correlations are actually increasing, as shown in **Table 2**. One reason for these greater correlations is that the world financial markets have become increasingly liberalized and deregulated. A second reason is that most central banks around the world have adopted a long-run anti-inflationary resolve. A third, particularly important, reason is the stable expectations regarding the long-run percentage changes in exchange rates.

Figure 7. Total Return Performance of an Actively Managed Global Bond Portfolio versus a 100 Percent U.S. Treasury Portfolio

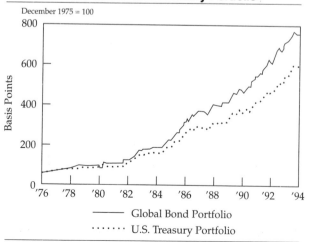

Source: Merrill Lynch & Co.

**Table 2. Correlation of Monthly Changes in
Long-Term Interest Rates**

Period	United States–Germany	United States–Japan
1973–79	0.22	0.11
1980–88	0.57	0.49
1989–93	0.58	0.74

Source: Merrill Lynch & Co.

For example, the U.S. dollar has historically moved in big trends against the German mark, as shown in the two currencies' exchange rates in **Figure 8**. This phenomenon could have been exploited through a trend-following trading rule, but as shown in Figure 8 and in detail in **Figure 9**, the exchange rates have stabilized since the Louvre Accord in 1987. (The Louvre Accord established the desire by the Group of Seven nations—Canada, France, Germany, Italy, Japan, the United Kingdom, and the United States—to maintain greater exchange rate stability among the key currencies versus the U.S. dollar.) The U.S. dollar:German mark exchange rate, the pivotal exchange rate in the world today, has been fluctuating between 1.60 and 1.80 about 70 percent of the time. That is, the dollar has been moving into what could be called a de facto target zone against the German mark.

Figure 8. German Mark:U.S. Dollar Exchange Rate, 1973–94

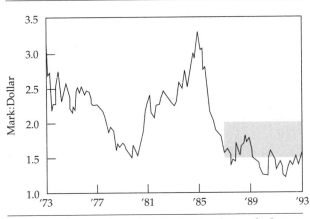

Note: Shaded area is the de facto trading band since the Louvre Accord.

Source: Merrill Lynch & Co.

In addition to stabilization in exchange rates and the increasing correlation of global bond markets, the yield levels in the United States have aligned more closely than previously with the yield levels throughout Europe, as graphed in **Figure 10**. **Figure 11** indicates that the U.S.–German ten-year bond yield spread during the past few years has gravitated

Figure 9. German Mark:U.S. Dollar Exchange Rate since Louvre Accord: Mean and Mean plus/minus One Standard Deviation

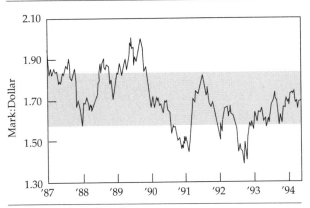

Source: Merrill Lynch & Co.

around zero.

The changes noted in yield spreads, correlations, and exchange rates raise questions about how investors should analyze interest rate differentials. Interest rate differentials reflect two factors: the mean expected change in exchange rates and the variance in the distribution of expected changes in exchange rates. The mean expected change may be zero, but if the variance around zero is large, the market may want to build in a risk premium to reflect that variance. The more credible the target zone, the more the interest rate differential will approach zero. In fact, in a world of credibly fixed exchange rates, in which the expected short-run and long-run changes in the exchange rate are zero, the expected change in the exchange rate in the short run will equal the short-term spread and the expected change in the exchange rate in the long run will equal the long-term spread. In both cases, the short-term spread will be zero and the long-term spread should be zero. If credibility is complete, domestic and foreign yield curves will sit on top of one another. In the absence of complete credibility, investors may expect the system to stay stable in the short run, but if the foreign currency is expected to weaken in the long run, then yield spreads will have to reflect that expectation (see **Figure 12**). So, expectations of exchange rates for the short and long run have a major bearing on how yield curves are configured globally.

In Europe, the yield spreads for France and Germany indicate that the Exchange Rate Mechanism (ERM) was not very credible in the late 1980s but became more credible in the early 1990s. As **Figure 13** shows, in 1988, French long-term rates were 300 bps higher than German long-term rates. In other words, the market was pricing in a 3 percent a year depreciation of the French franc for the next ten

Figure 10. Nominal Long-Term Interest Rates in the United States and Europe as of March 28, 1994

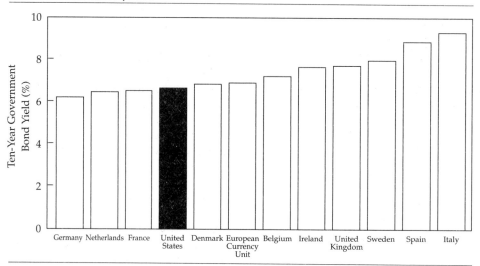

Source: Merrill Lynch & Co.

years. The franc proved to be considerably more stable, however, than the market anticipated. As a result, the link between the French franc and German mark has become more credible over time. Therefore, the spreads of France relative to Germany recently reached a point at which they hovered

Figure 11. U.S. minus German Ten-Year Government Bond Yields, 1990–94

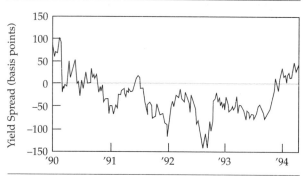

Source: Merrill Lynch & Co.

around zero. Lately, however, the spreads have begun to widen again, as shown in **Figure 14**, possibly reflecting some concern that the credibility of the system may not be as strong as previously thought.

If the stability in the German mark:U.S. dollar exchange rate continues, the yield spread between the United States and Germany may echo the France–Germany experience. If yield spreads gravitate toward zero and the German mark:U.S. dollar exchange rate experiences little change in the long run, U.S. investors may question whether being involved in foreign bonds of the developed markets pays. This disillusionment may, in turn, provide an

impetus for investors to look to other markets, such as the emerging markets, where they can still achieve incremental returns.

In short, U.S. fixed-income investors are generally finding more stable exchange rates, similar yield levels, and increased correlations around the developed bond markets in the world today. If the case for U.S. diversification into European bonds is thereby weakened, U.S. investors may move increasingly into the emerging markets.

Figure 12. Short-Run versus Long-Run Credibility of Fixed Exchange Rate Regimes

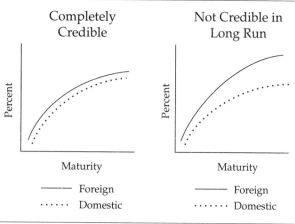

Source: Merrill Lynch & Co.

High-Yield Foreign Investments

One of the myths permeating the bond industry is that high-yield foreign investments offer a free lunch (risk reduction with no loss of total return). In truth, they do not. The uncovered interest rate parity equation is

$$\%\Delta S_t = b_0 + b_1(i_H - i_L) + \varepsilon_t,$$

where

S_t = spot exchange rate
i_H = interest rate in high-yield market
i_L = interest rate in low-yield market

Figure 13. French–German Ten-Year Yield Spreads, January 1988 to June 1993

Source: Merrill Lynch & Co.

In the case of a consistently high-yielding foreign market and a consistently low-yielding foreign market, the low-yielding market's currency would be expected to rise over time relative to the high-yielding market's currency by the amount of the interest rate differential. Therefore, in theory, b should equal 1. In fact, evidence indicates that b is much less than 1, and furthermore, b has often been found to be less than zero in many empirical studies. The conclusion is that, historically, interest rate differentials have not been offset by changes in exchange rates. In other words, although high-yield currencies are expected to decline, they do not decline as much as theory would suggest. Therefore, high-yielding markets tend to outperform low-yielding markets, and some analysts argue that investors would do better if they consistently overweighted the high-yielding markets in their portfolios.

Figure 14. French–German Ten-Year Yield Spreads, June 1993 to March 1994

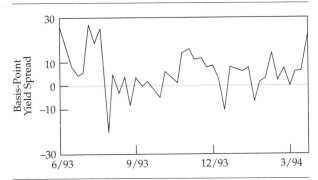

Source: Merrill Lynch & Co.

Why have high yielders outperformed low yielders? Does a free lunch await high-yield investors? The superior performance has four possible explanations. The first can be illustrated by what economists call the "peso problem," which dates back to the 1970s when interest rates in Mexico were about 20 percentage points above U.S. interest rates but the peso did not weaken. Why was the market pricing in a weaker peso when, in fact, the weakening did not occur?

Yield spreads sometimes reflect two possible outcomes—one, with a weight w, in which a big devaluation is expected and another, with weight $1 - w$, in which no change in the exchange rate is expected. The market may assign a high probability of a large devaluation, but over a particular time horizon that devaluation does not occur. Often, the devaluation expectation is correct but the devaluation is postponed, so for the period in which yield spreads and exchange rate changes are tested, the high yielders appear to outperform the low yielders.

A second explanation is that high-yield investments are riskier and, therefore, should command a higher return in the long run. A third explanation is that the monetary authorities in high-yield countries may maintain high interest rates to resist the depreciation of their currencies. Finally, the high yielders may have outperformed the low yielders simply because the market consistently gets it wrong; that is, the market systematically underestimates the strength of the high-yielding currency.

Rationally, high-yielding markets cannot always and consistently outperform low-yielding markets. Consider the following relationships, where interest rates in the high- and low-yielding markets are broken down into a real rate and an expected inflation rate:

$$i_L = r_L + p_L^e$$

and

$$i_H = r_H + p_H^e,$$

where

i_L = interest rate in low-yield market
r_L = real return in low-yield market
p_L^e = expected inflation of low-yield market
i_H = interest rate in high-yield market
r_H = real return in high-yield market
p_H^e = expected inflation of high-yield market

For both the low-yield country and the high-yield country, the country's interest rate equals its real rate plus the expected inflation differential:

$$i_H - i_L = (r_H - r_L) + (p_H^e - p_L^e).$$

In order for the high-yield market to outperform the

111

low-yield market consistently, real rates in the high-yield market would have to lie consistently above the low-yield market's rates. If they did, the result would be weak growth in the high-yield country for the long run, and eventually, an easing of policy in the high-yield country would be required. After that easing, exchange rates would adjust and long-run interest rate parity would be realized. The only other way that high-yield markets could consistently post superior performance would be if the inflation rate was consistently higher in the high-yield country than in the low-yield country and no offsetting exchange rate change occurred. In that case, the result would be an increasingly overvalued currency in the high-yield country. The end would be a serious deterioration in the high-yield country's competitiveness; eventually, a devaluation would be required, which would then equalize the two returns in the long run.

In the past, many analysts proposed that investors could earn a free lunch by going long the Italian lira and shorting the German mark. The argument was that investors should bet on the European Monetary System staying intact, with the lira staying pegged to the mark. A whole industry sprouted up in the late 1980s and early 1990s to capitalize on this supposed free lunch. Indeed, for a considerable period, Italian investments outperformed German investments. Because the lira was linked to the German mark, the currencies stayed relatively in line with one another and investors were able to earn the higher return on Italian bonds than on German bonds. The free lunch fell apart in September 1992, however, when the system of fixed exchange rates in Europe broke down. **Figure 15**, which depicts the total return performance of Italian and German money market investments from 1987 to 1994, shows the yield on Italy to be far above the yield on Germany for much of the period, but that incremental return was washed away in one fell swoop with the devaluation of the lira in September 1992.

Thus, uncovered interest rate parity holds in the long run. High-yield markets provide no long-term free lunches.

To Hedge or Not to Hedge

Plan sponsors are generally reluctant to invest large sums in unhedged foreign bonds if they already own unhedged foreign equities for two reasons. One is that foreign bonds tend to underperform foreign equities (which could also be said about U.S. bonds and equities). The second, and perhaps more important, reason is that unhedged foreign bonds are highly correlated with unhedged foreign equities; the correlation is 0.60. (On a hedged basis, the correlation is only 0.17.) The foreign bond

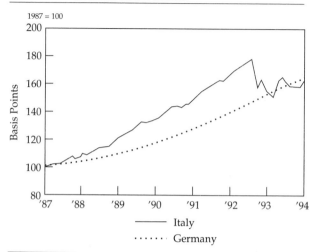

Figure 15. Total Return Performance of Italian and German Money Market Instruments in German-Mark Terms

Note: Three-month Eurolira and Euromark deposits.
Source: Merrill Lynch & Co.

and equity markets are highly correlated on an unhedged basis because currency movements tend to increase the comovement of foreign bonds and equities. A hedge reduces the correlation by eliminating the currency element.

Managers have heard much about the benefits of currency hedging. By separating and removing currency volatility from total return volatility, hedging the currency can remove a major source of foreign bond volatility. If the international bond position is viewed in isolation, significant risk reduction is associated with currency hedging, but if the international bond position is viewed in the context of a total portfolio, the actual risk reduction accomplished by hedging is found to be quite small. For modest allocations to international investments (U.S. investors' allocations to non-U.S. investments will probably never exceed 10–20 percent of a total portfolio), the net risk reduction through currency hedging is generally so small that investors must seriously question whether hedging is worth doing at all.

If one is considering hedged-versus-unhedged foreign bonds in isolation from other assets, hedged foreign bonds are less volatile than unhedged foreign bonds, as **Figure 16** shows. The reason is that hedging foreign bonds leaves investors with only local-market volatility, which is relatively small. If the forward discount that investors incur to hedge their currency exposure equals the expected change in the exchange rate in the long run, then the same return can be earned on either a hedged or unhedged foreign bond but with less risk for the hedged foreign bond.

The evidence on hedging suggests that U.S. in-

**Figure 16. Hedged Foreign Bonds versus Unhedged
Foreign Bonds**

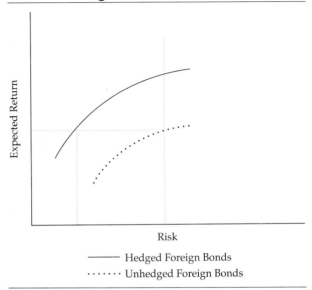

Source: Merrill Lynch & Co.

**Figure 17. U.S. Domestic Bonds versus Hedged and
Unhedged Nondollar Bonds: Historical
Risk–Return Trade-Off**

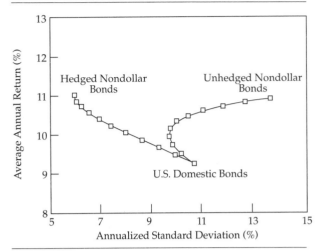

Source: Merrill Lynch & Co.

vestors can have a free lunch if they invest in hedged foreign bonds. As illustrated in **Figure 17**, U.S. bonds have historically had an average annualized return of about 9.0 percent with a volatility of slightly more than 10.5 percent. Hedged foreign bonds have had a higher average return, almost 11.0 percent, with an overall volatility of about 6 percent. Therefore, investors in hedged foreign bonds could achieve lower volatility with higher returns than with U.S. bonds; investors in unhedged foreign bonds could achieve a higher return than with U.S. bonds but with greater risk.

Much of the purported benefit of hedging, however, is time dependent. The evidence on which the free lunch argument for unhedged foreign bonds is based stems largely from the 1978–87 period. The 1988–93 period paints a strikingly different picture, as shown in **Figure 18**. U.S. bonds actually posted a

higher return than hedged foreign bonds. Although hedged foreign bonds are still less volatile than U.S. bonds, because foreign markets have been less volatile than U.S markets, the difference in volatility for the 1988–93 period is much smaller than it was in the 1978–87 period. U.S. volatility has come down sharply while many foreign markets have seen an increase in their respective volatilities.

In theory, the expected returns and volatilities of U.S. bonds and hedged or unhedged nondollar bonds should be roughly the same. The theoretical relationships are shown in **Figure 19**, which indicates how investors should view U.S. and foreign bonds.

The chief disadvantage of currency-hedged foreign bonds is that the removal of currency risk removes an important source of diversification. In an examination of the correlation of hedged or unhedged foreign bonds with U.S. bonds, one aspect stands out: Hedged foreign bonds are more highly

**Figure 18. U.S. Bonds versus Hedged Foreign Bonds: Historical Risk–Return
Trade-Offs, 1978–87 and 1988–93**

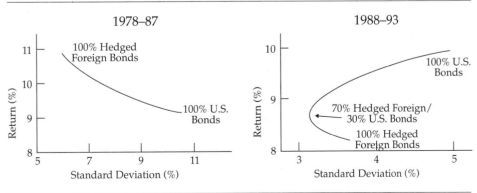

Source: Merrill Lynch & Co.

Figure 19. Theoretical Long-Run Expected Return and Risk of U.S. Domestic, Hedged Nondollar, and Unhedged Nondollar Bonds

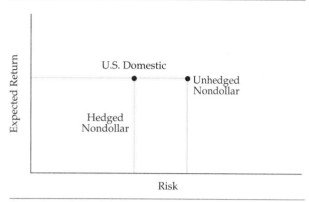

Source: Merrill Lynch & Co.

Figure 21. Benefit from Currency Hedging by Share of Total Portfolio Allocated to Foreign Investments

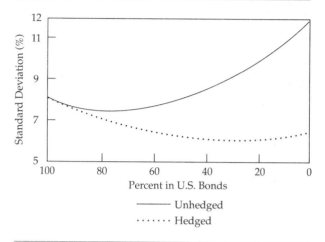

Source: Merrill Lynch & Co.

correlated with U.S. bonds. Hedged foreign bonds are less volatile, but unhedged foreign bonds are more efficient diversifiers in a portfolio context. Mixing U.S. bonds with unhedged foreign bonds reduces risk more than using hedged foreign bonds in the mix, as shown in **Figure 20**.

Even if the foreign markets were to be forever less volatile than the U.S. bond market and an investor were to put up to 10–15 percent of his or her entire portfolio in hedged foreign bonds rather than unhedged foreign bonds, the amount of risk reduction to the entire portfolio would be insignificant, as shown in **Figure 21**. The only way hedged foreign bonds can begin to have an important impact on the overall riskiness of the portfolio is for the percentage in U.S. bonds to drop and the percentage in the foreign bonds to increase. Most U.S. fund managers, however, will never put a large portion of their portfolios in hedged foreign bonds.

Therefore, in a world free of transaction costs,

the amount of risk reduction available from international diversification in the long run is largely independent of whether the currency risk is hedged or is not hedged. Unfortunately, transaction costs cannot be ignored, and managing an always-hedged foreign bond portfolio can at times be quite expensive—as high as 6 bps. Rolling over the hedges creates settlement costs, execution costs, and management fees. Accordingly, in the real world, managers may actually achieve a higher return by mixing U.S. bonds with unhedged foreign bonds.

Currency Overlay Management

Most global fixed-income managers have developed a strong bent for currency management, and many have branched into currency overlay management—that is, the active management of currency exposures—which separates currency decisions from bond market decisions. This separation assigns securities management to asset-selection specialists and currency management to currency specialists. Investors use currency overlay managers to determine a portfolio's optimal net currency exposure, which may indeed be very different from the underlying asset position.

Technical analysis has repeatedly and consistently proved to provide above-average returns in currency overlay management. Levich and Thomas recently concluded, "Active currency risk management, based on a simple application of technical trading signals, can substantially improve the risk–return opportunities for investors in comparison to passive currency strategies." More importantly, they stated that following a selective currency hedging strategy that uses technical trading rules can lead to "superior results when compared to never hedg-

Figure 20. Theoretical Diversification Benefits from Portfolio Combinations of U.S. and Hedged or Unhedged Foreign Bonds

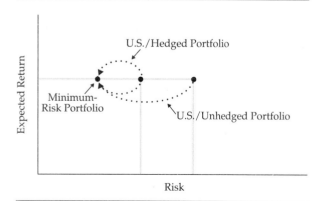

Source: Merrill Lynch & Co.

ing or to always hedging."[2]

In fact, in studies of the profits of technical trading rules, a buy-and-hold strategy yields little or no long-run return—which confirms the theory of uncovered interest rate parity. **Table 3** shows a technical rule that moves an investor in and out of currencies using a 1–5-day moving average, a 5–20-day moving average, or a 1–200-day moving average, each of which provides substantial superior performance relative to a buy-and-hold strategy. Such results are consistently found in all studies that have been conducted on the profitability of technical trading rules in the foreign exchange markets.

Table 3. Profits of Technical Trading Rules in Currency Futures Markets, 1976–90

Strategy	German Mark	Yen	Canadian Dollar
Buy and hold	0.3%	1.8%	0.5%
1–5-day moving average	6.4	7.3	3.3
5–20-day moving average	11.2	10.6	2.7
1–200-day moving average	8.1	9.2	2.3

Source: Levich and Thomas, "Internationally Diversified Bond Portfolios."

Because currencies can be traded using technical trading rules, currencies should be viewed as an opportunistic asset; they do not truly fit the traditional definition of an asset class. If interest rate parity holds for currencies in the long run, merely holding currencies over the long run provides no excess return.

If some currencies offer a risk premium, one could argue that some foreign currencies should constitute a separate asset class. That is, currencies can be viewed as a separate asset class if Jensen's inequality is valid. Jensen's inequality, demonstrated in **Table 4**, is a simple mathematical property in terms of looking at the percentage change of a fraction and the percentage change of the reciprocal of that fraction. Assume the German mark:U.S. dollar exchange rate is 2.00; the U.S. dollar:German mark rate, then,

[2]Both quotations from Richard M. Levich and Lee R. Thomas, "Internationally Diversified Bond Portfolios: The Merits of Active Currency Risk Management," National Bureau of Economic Research Working Paper No. 4340 (Cambridge, Mass.: April 1993).

Table 4. Jensen's Inequality: Excess Returns from Holding a Portfolio of Dollars and Marks

	Exchange Rate		Percent Change
	At Time t	At Time $t+1$	
German mark: U.S. dollar	2.00	2.08	+4.00%
U.S. dollar: German mark	0.50	0.48	−3.85
Excess return			+0.15

Source: Merrill Lynch & Co.

is the reciprocal, 0.50. If the dollar rises by 4 percent against the mark, to 2.08, the reciprocal would be 0.48, which means that the mark has weakened by 3.85 percent against the dollar. In this case, an excess return is available from holding a portfolio of dollars and marks: An investor who owned both one unit of dollars and one unit of marks, when the dollar went up 4 percent and the mark went down 3.85 percent, would earn an excess return of 0.15 percent. Mathematically, in fact, the bigger the change in the exchange rate, the bigger the excess return from holding a basket of currencies. The inequality works because simple arithmetic measures of percentage change are used. (If the logarithm of the percentage change were used, the changes would be +4 and −4 percent and Jensen's inequality would not hold.)

When investors hedge their underlying currency positions, they are basically hedging away the gain they can expect from Jensen's inequality. Therefore, the optimal portfolio would be one that is less than fully hedged.

Conclusion

The global bond business provides no free lunches. In addition, no glaring inefficiencies persist in the international bond markets that can be exploited by U.S. investors. Because the benefits of passive international diversification are limited, enhanced returns can be earned only from active management. The best way to achieve enhanced return through active management is by taking a top-down approach—focus on getting the currency and duration right and deemphasize individual security selection.

Question and Answer Session

Michael R. Rosenberg

Question: Please comment on the risk environment regarding proxy or parallel hedging.

Rosenberg: In a parallel hedge, if investors want to be long Italian bonds and short lira, they may choose to carry out this strategy by selling German marks forward because hedging by selling lira forward is expensive. The hope is that the lira:mark exchange rate will be stable and, therefore, the mark hedge can serve as a proxy for a lira hedge. In today's world, under the ERM, in which exchange rates are much more unstable than in the past, a parallel hedge is much more dangerous than it used to be—as many investors learned in the 1992–93 period.

Question: Given the low correlations among short-term rates, should diversification gains be expected for short-term portfolios?

Rosenberg: More diversification opportunities exist at the front end than at the back end of the curve; therefore, investors should be mining the front ends, not the back ends of the respective yield curves.

Question: If global fixed-income instruments were to be considered an asset class, what would be the relevant benchmark?

Rosenberg: U.S. bonds. The objective of the investor in foreign bonds is to outperform his or her domestic bogey.

Question: Are real interest rates important in analyzing non-U.S. bonds?

Rosenberg: Real interest rates vary over time, but in the developed countries, they tend to move together, so when U.S. real rates are increasing, real rates are normally increasing in Germany, Japan, and elsewhere. The movements of real rates are important for currency trends. Merrill Lynch's modeling work shows that trends in real interest rate differentials have a decisive impact on the direction of currencies; thus, if U.S. real rates are rising relative to Germany's, even though both may be moving up, the dollar will move higher, and vice versa.

Question: Please comment on the observation that correlations in bonds of the developed countries seem to rise at the worst times (i.e., in highly volatile environments).

Rosenberg: We are finding, perhaps with a little hindsight, that the foreign markets had already begun four or five years ago to become highly correlated with the U.S. market. The correlation level of rates in the bull bond market globally at the time was more than 90 percent for most major markets. Correlations remain high in the current bear market. Clients ask me, "Where do you see value today?" I answer, "In a bear market, cash is king." The problem is that investors' choices are few. They could buy German bonds hedged into U.S. dollars as an alternative to owning U.S. bonds outright, but German bonds have been hit as hard as U.S. bonds in 1994. So far, at least, owning hedged German bonds as an alternative to owning U.S. bonds has been of little benefit in 1994.

Analyzing Emerging Market Debt

Isabel Saltzman
Vice President
Scudder, Stevens & Clark, Inc.

The emerging bond markets have three characteristics that make them potential positive contributors to a portfolio: geographical diversity, asset diversity, and a large and liquid market. Historically, this market has provided high yield, and the potential exists for capital appreciation. Risk assessment is critical in these markets, however, and should encompass global economic factors, political or sovereign risks, and market risks.

The investor who is interested in emerging market debt as part of a global bond portfolio needs to address four key issues: investment opportunities, characteristics of the markets, risk, and construction of the debt portfolio.[1]

Investment Opportunity

The opportunity for investing in emerging markets springs from two market traits: high yield and the potential for capital appreciation. Much of the opportunity for U.S. investors in these debt markets is provided by the large amounts of debt in Brady bonds, restructured debt allowed by the Brady plan beginning in 1989.[1]

The yields on Mexican par bonds (PARs) at 10.6 percent and Argentine PARs at slightly more than 11 percent are representative of opportunities in this market. Yields are even higher on Moroccan, Brazilian, and Venezuelan bonds. Relative to U.S. Treasuries, these yields are phenomenal. For example, on April 18, 1994, the Mexican PARs were yielding 295 basis points (bps) above U.S. Treasuries. Other sample spreads as of that date (in bps) were as follows:

Argentine PAR	418
Czech National Bank 7%	130
Merrill "BBB"	120
Nigerian PAR	748
Philippine PAR	263
Venezuelan PAR	605

[1] *Editor's Note:* The Brady plan offers debtor nations some relief from their debt through partial debt forgiveness, lowered interest rates, and extended maturities. In return, the countries agree to reduce their inflation rates, public-sector borrowing, and trade deficits. Brady bonds are Euro-issues, not custodied in the country of issuance, and the majority of the bonds are denominated in U.S. dollars. The cost of trading Brady bonds is low in comparison with most emerging market debt.

The spreads have not always been as wide as these current figures. For example, before the North American Free Trade Agreement (NAFTA) was passed in November 1993, the Mexican PAR was trading at only 170 bps above Treasuries, and the spread narrowed to as little as 140 following the passage of NAFTA, before widening to current levels.

The potential for capital appreciation is illustrated by an analysis of total return for the J.P. Morgan Emerging Markets Brady Bond Index (EMBI). For January 31, 1992, through April 15, 1994, the total return on the index, which is composed primarily of Latin American debt, was 24.06 percent. In 1993, the index had a total return of 43.4 percent.

These returns are not achieved without risk, however. By April 1994, the index's total return had dropped below 20 percent. This decrease is attributed to a technical correction; that is, no fundamental changes occurred in the credit quality of the major emerging market debt countries. Factors contributing to the drop in total return included concern about increases in U.S. interest rates and the fact that emerging market debt was a part of highly levered positions in the debt portfolios of mutual funds, institutional clients, and small, retail, Latin American investors. Another important factor was that trading desks with large inventories of emerging market debt chose to sell off positions as prices started to decline. The last factor involves Japanese banks. Japanese banks with huge gains in emerging market debt also chose to realize gains prior to the end of their fiscal year in March. The result was significant sell-offs in the emerging debt markets.

Market Characteristics

The emerging bond markets have three characteristics that make them potential positive contributors to a portfolio: geographical diversity, asset diversity, and a large and liquid market.

With more than 160 countries classified by the World Bank as emerging economies, the geographical choices for investment are extremely wide. As shown in **Figure 1**, emerging market countries are scattered throughout the world.

Asset diversity—from dollar-denominated bonds to domestic-currency obligations—is quite broad. Investors can participate in bank loans, convertibles, structured instruments, and derivatives. They can also structure a portfolio to contain fixed- and floating-rate obligations.

Total dollar-denominated assets in emerging market debt are $360 billion. Of that total, bank loans account for $190 billion, Eurobonds for $60 billion, and Brady bonds for $110 billion. The Brady bonds tend to be the most liquid bonds. Liquidity is such that investors can easily buy and sell blocks of $10 million at bid–offer spreads of no more than a quarter of a point without affecting price. Therefore, emerging market debt has become more liquid than emerging market equities.

Risk Assessment

In assessing the risks in emerging markets, an important initial consideration is global economic factors—global liquidity, interest rates, and the worldwide demand for dollars.

A study of the countries themselves and sovereign risk analysis are also important. Foremost to be considered is political risk, because what actually moves prices in big swings in emerging markets is not the economic fundamentals so much as political factors. In 1994, for example, two major emerging countries, Mexico and Brazil, are undergoing presidential elections, which will certainly contribute to market volatility.

The second aspect to be studied is the country's current macroeconomic situation, the economic fundamentals. How sound are public finances? What is the monetary policy? What is the status of the external accounts and of the financial markets? Finally, the country's ability to sustain long-term growth should be assessed. Specifically, how is it achieving stabilization policies and structural reforms? What is the attitude toward and status of foreign investment? After deriving both the political risk and the economic fundamentals, the analyst can assign ratings to the countries.

The third area that should be considered when assessing risks is market risk. Several factors affect market risk, including the demand–supply balance in the market, liquidity, and the volatility of individual bonds. Investors need to assess new sources of supply and demand. In the spring of 1994, for example, the issuance of Brady bonds in Brazil caused a tremendous bulge in the supply of emerging market debt. As the market digested this enormous supply, prices began to fall. Investors will also want to investigate changes on the demand side. Are new

Figure 1. Geographical Diversification of Emerging Markets

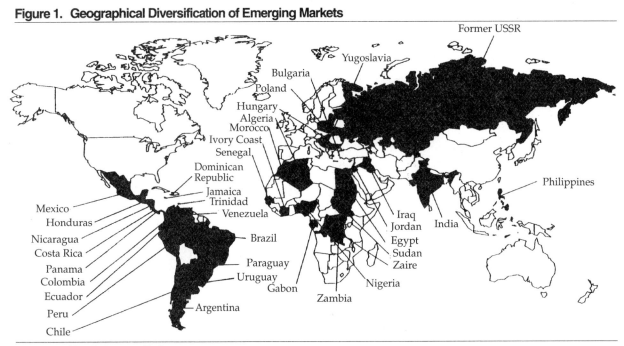

Source: Scudder, Stevens & Clark.

institutional clients appearing? Are the hedge funds coming back into the market? Are international bond portfolio managers allocating a certain percentage of their assets to emerging market debt?

Table 1 illustrates the volatility of individual issues relative to the market. In 1993, the volatility of the EMBI was considerably lower than the volatility of its component bonds. One year later, volatility was considerably higher for the index than for the individual bonds. The index's volatility increased as a result of closer correlations within these markets when concerns about U.S. Treasuries became the primary fuel for the debt markets' collapse.

Table 1. Annualized Monthly Volatility of EMBI Index and Various Bonds

Index/Bond	March 30, 1993	March 30, 1994
J.P. Morgan EMBI	6.10%	23.15%
Argentine FRB	12.71	23.15
Argentine PAR	10.62	31.92
Brazilian IDU	12.88	24.91
Mexican PAR	4.58	26.97
Mexican discount bond	9.60	22.35
Venezuelan DCB	23.03	32.95
Venezuelan PAR	10.72	33.94

Source: Scudder, Stevens & Clark.

An investor considering these markets will want to look closely at current and expected correlations. Studies indicate historically very weak correlations between dollar-denominated and local-currency emerging market debt, but these correlations change, as Table 1 shows.

The last element to consider when assessing market risk is the counterparties. Not all instruments settle cash on delivery; therefore, investors must carefully check out the credit status of those with whom they are dealing.

Portfolio Construction

A combination top-down/bottom-up approach to portfolio construction is advisable in the emerging market debt area. The top-down portion is an analysis of sovereign risk and market risk; the bottom-up portion consists of scenario and security analysis. The goal is to identify
- the issuers with the best relative prospects for improving creditworthiness,
- the technical factors affecting the market, and
- the securities that offer the best relative value.

An important element is establishing the objectives for including emerging market debt in the fixed-income portfolio. The goals of Scudder,

Stevens & Clark are to pursue superior total return, reduce volatility through diversification, and emphasize high current income. High current income is not a goal of every emerging debt portfolio. If the objective is primarily capital appreciation, the investor can buy nonperforming loans. Peruvian loans sell at 49 cents on the dollar, for example; Russian loans at 27 cents on the dollar.

The potential for capital appreciation within a one-year horizon is illustrated by the current and expected spreads in Table 2. The assumptions behind these figures are important—in particular, the conservative assumption of a return to pre-NAFTA spreads for the major (most liquid) bonds in the emerging economies' debt markets, namely, the Mexican PARs, Argentine PARs, Brazilian exit bonds, and Venezuelan FLIRBs (front-loaded interest-reduction bonds). Another significant assumption is that U.S. Treasuries will stay at current levels. Instability in U.S. interest rates would cause continued turmoil in emerging market debt, as well as in many other global fixed-income markets.

Table 2. Actual and Potential Spreads: One-Year Horizon (in bps)

Bond	November 1993 Spread above Treasuries	April 18,1994, Spread above Treasuries	Expected Spread above Treasuries
Mexican PAR	170	295	170
Argentine PAR	263	418	270
Brazilian exit bond	606	953	620
Venezuelan FLIRB	593	1,263	620

Note: The following assumptions have been made: U.S. Treasury yield curve remains unchanged; Mexican PARs return to November 1993 level; Argentine PARs trade at 100 bps above Mexican PARs; Brazilian exit bonds and Venezuelan FLIRBs trade at 350 bps above Argentine PARs.

Source: Scudder, Stevens & Clark.

On the basis of the spreads shown in Table 2, the potential for total return from these bonds is attractive. Assuming a stabilization in interest rates and a return to pre-NAFTA spreads, returns could be sizable, as shown in Table 3. The significance of the income component is interesting; even if prices do not move from their currently depressed levels, an investor can earn approximately 10 percent from income alone.

Another strategy based on price appreciation would be to place a credit-quality bet on deep-discount long-term floaters. Table 4 and Table 5 illustrate the potential total return from three floating-rate bonds (FRBs): an Argentine FRB, which is currently trading at 71 cents on the dollar; a Brazilian interest due and unpaid (IDU) bond, which is currently trading at 72 cents on the dollar; and a Vene-

Table 3. Potential Total Return as of April 18, 1994: One-Year Horizon

	Mexican PAR	Argentine PAR	Brazilian Exit Bond	Venezuelan FLIRB
Current price	64.00	51.38	47.50	57.00
Coupon rate	6.25%	4.25%	6.00%	7.00%
Return terminal price	71.80	58.80	56.64	73.61
Income	9.77%	8.27%	12.63%	12.28%
Capital gains	12.19	14.45	19.24	29.14
Total return	21.96%	22.72%	31.87%	41.42%

Source: Scudder, Stevens & Clark.

zuelan debt-conversion bond (DCB), which is currently trading at about 52 cents on the dollar. The

Table 4. Actual and Potential Spreads for Floating-Rate Bonds: One-Year Horizon (in bps)

Bond	November 1993 Spread above Treasuries	April 18, 1994, Spread above Treasuries[a]	Expected Spread above Treasuries[a]
Argentine FRB	390	738	390
Brazilian IDU	658	1,001	690
Venezuelan DCB	666	1,229	690

Note: The following assumptions have been made: the U.S. Treasury yield curve remains unchanged; the Argentine FRB returns to November 1993 level; the Brazilian IDU and Venezuelan DCB trade at 300 bps above the Argentine FRB.

[a]Swapped spread.

Source: Scudder, Stevens & Clark.

coupon rates on these bonds are tied to LIBOR, but the spreads in Table 4 do not include changes in LIBOR. Obviously, the income return would increase if LIBOR increased. As shown in Table 5, the potential total returns for the bonds in Table 4 are attractive. Five-year and eight-year floaters may be trading at significant discounts—thus carrying the potential for capital appreciation without the investor needing to give any thought to interest rates.

Historically, portfolio volatility can be reduced through country and bond diversification. Prior to 1994, these markets were somewhat weakly correlated with each other, which highlights the importance of diversifying among countries at that time. In the first quarter of 1994, however, enormous positive correlations have been found. All the emerging countries suffered a downturn, and all asset classes suffered as well. Volatility can also be reduced by adding local-currency exposure to the portfolio.

Conclusion

Emerging market debt can offer both excellent opportunities for yield and potential for capital appreciation. Prior to investing in emerging market debt, however, investors must study the risks involved in these markets.

Table 5. Potential Total Return for Floating-Rate Bonds as of April 18, 1994: One-Year Horizon

	Argentine FRB	Brazilian IDU	Venezuelan DCB
Current price	71.13	72.13	51.75
Coupon rate	5.00%	4.31%	4.31%
Return terminal price	84.12	79.91	65.04
Income	7.03%	5.98%	8.33%
Capital gains	18.25	10.74	25.68
Total return	25.28%	16.72%	34.01%

Source: Scudder, Stevens & Clark.

Question and Answer Session

Isabel Saltzman

Question: How has the analysis of emerging market debt changed in the past few years?

Saltzman: The analysis has become more sophisticated, and today, analysis is of critical importance. Deep research, both on sovereign and corporate bonds, will be very important in the future. Because of the market turmoil, not one corporate bond has come into the market this quarter. Although many companies need to raise capital, they have neither sold equity nor gone to the debt markets. Investing is thus going to be tough, which is why differentiation and research will continue to be important. In the future, we will probably see differentiation in credit quality.

Question: Would you suggest using specialized management firms for exploring investment in emerging markets?

Saltzman: Emerging markets are quite complicated. At Scudder, we look at emerging markets as a unique asset class and have a research group dedicated to it. We have made a large research commitment; we have two economists performing sovereign risk analysis in Latin America alone. If a firm does not want to commit heavily to research in this area, then it should go outside.

Question: Is the correlation between the emerging debt and equity markets high?

Saltzman: Not really. Looking at equity flows is certainly important in trying to understand the debt markets, but the markets do not necessarily move in tandem. Emerging market debt has recently suffered significantly, whereas emerging market equities have not. Consider Latin American debt and equity, for example. Latin American emerging market debt represents the bulk of the issues in the J.P. Morgan EMBI, so the Latin American part of the index returned about the same as the index, 19 percent. Equities in Latin America, however, had not experienced any significant movement through March 1994.

Question: Why have the Argentine PAR and the FRB acted so similarly even though they have large differences in duration (see Table 1)?

Saltzman: The Argentine PAR is a fixed-rate bond with a 30-year life to maturity. It is a bullet. The FRB is a floater with roughly a 10-year average life. If it is a floater, you might argue, it should have a six-month duration, so why has it dropped 16 percent? In looking at these markets, you cannot look merely at interest duration; you

need to look at credit duration, which is a whole different topic. Note that the PAR dropped even farther than the FRB, more than 20 percent.

All the deep-discounted securities, whether floaters or fixed-rate instruments, were hurt in the recent economic turmoil. When people needed to sell assets, the floaters, unfortunately, were sold off. Floaters will outperform fixed-rate bonds in an environment of rising interest rates, however; so although the investor in floating-rate bonds may have been hurt in the short run, in the future, the floaters will outperform.

Question: Please comment on the prospects of the Philippine Brady bonds.

Saltzman: The Philippines has a small issue of Brady bonds that was hurt less than other emerging market debt, primarily because investors were not focusing as much on the Philippines as on other countries. The Philippine bonds are attractive when they are trading at the same levels as Argentine Brady bonds. The Philippine bonds are currently trading at spreads similar to Mexico's. Argentine Brady bonds, therefore, which are trading at a much wider spread than the Philippine bonds, afford better relative value at this point.

Market-Value Accounting: The Effects of FAS No. 115

John F. Tierney, CFA
Senior Vice President, Fixed Income Research
Lehman Brothers

Financial Accounting Statement No. 115 restricts the trading of fixed-income securities to those held in trading and available-for-sale accounts and requires that these securities be marked to their market values. A primary concern in managing available-for-sale portfolios is measuring and managing market risk, but in managing the firm's total portfolio, maximizing net interest margin remains the most important aim.

Financial Accounting Statement (FAS) No. 115 is a major current concern, especially for banks and insurance companies, and the adjustments to it will continue for some time to come. This presentation addresses why FAS No. 115 is different from other accounting standards, how investors and companies have responded to it, and whether or not FAS No. 115 is important. The presentation closes with some thoughts on how managers might manage their securities portfolios under FAS No. 115.

According to academic accountants, the Financial Accounting Standards Board (FASB) has two goals in setting accounting standards: (1) to improve the quality of information to investors and (2) to provide standards so that decision makers can focus more on economic criteria and less on bookkeeping criteria. Whether FAS No. 115 is helping achieve the first goal is debatable. Regarding the second goal, no one who is dealing with this issue has said that his or her ability to manage a portfolio has improved because of FAS No. 115.

Development of the Standard

FAS No. 115 differs from other accounting standards in that its genesis involved an interaction between government regulators and FASB. The process of developing FAS No. 115 began in 1989 when the Office of Thrift Supervision (OTS) issued the *Investment Portfolio Policy and Accounting Guidelines*. In the view of many, these guidelines virtually mandated that the thrift industry switch to mark-to-market accounting for securities portfolios.

The only body that backed the OTS was the SEC,

which has continued to support the idea. The SEC holds strongly to the view that market-value accounting is the only way to deal with a securities portfolio.

After a massive outcry against the OTS mandate from the accounting profession and the thrift industry, the OTS tabled the proposal. Then, the American Institute of Certified Public Accountants (AICPA) agreed to address the issue. It spent about a year and a half, through the end of 1990, struggling unsuccessfully with the topic, trying to come up with a workable proposal.

In early 1991, the AICPA kicked this issue over to FASB, which did nothing for about six or seven months. Then, at a summer FASB meeting, SEC representatives pressed FASB to add a project to its agenda on the subject of market-value accounting for securities. FASB acquiesced.

At about the same time, the SEC started taking a number of actions against banks and thrifts. For example, institutions that had filed registration statements to issue stocks or bonds found the SEC analyzing their investment portfolios. In a number of cases, the SEC found significant amounts of trading activity and turnover and told the institutions that such activity was inconsistent with what they were supposed to be doing with their investment portfolios. The SEC would not allow the firms to register to sell securities unless they reclassified their securities in held-for-sale accounts and accounted for them on the lower of cost or market basis. Several institutions had no choice but to reclassify most of their investment portfolios into the held-for-sale category.

The message was clear: If FASB did not step up and do something on the market-value accounting issue, the SEC would. FASB worked on the issue during the next two years and, by mid-May 1993, had developed FAS No. 115.

According to FAS No. 115, debt securities and marketable equity securities must be assigned to one of three portfolios: a held-to-maturity (HTM) portfolio in which securities are accounted for at historical costs, similarly to the investment portfolio prior to FAS No. 115; an available-for-sale (AFS) portfolio in which securities are marked to market and unrealized gains and losses affect equity but not the income statement; and a trading portfolio in which unrealized gains and losses affect both income and equity (similarly to the way trading portfolios were treated before FAS No. 115).

Application of FAS No. 115

FAS No. 115 has drastically changed how investors manage securities that are carried at book value. Prior to FAS No. 115, investors held securities in the investment portfolio and accounted for them at book value as long as they intended to hold them for the foreseeable future. As economic conditions or business plans changed, investors might restructure their investment portfolios.

Under FAS No. 115, the conditions under which securities can be sold out of the HTM portfolio are very restrictive and sales may be made only in response to

- a major acquisition/divestiture,
- a change in the tax status of the security,
- a deterioration in the credit quality of the security (e.g., to below investment grade),
- a change in regulatory requirements that affects what is a suitable security or what can be held, and
- the occurrence of "isolated, nonrecurring, and unusual" circumstances.

Liquidity-related reasons are not acceptable reasons to sell assets out of an HTM portfolio. Even if a property and casualty insurance company needs cash to respond to a major natural disaster, for example, it cannot sell securities out of its HTM portfolio. Such an event would be considered a normal business risk. If a new management team wants to change the company's business strategy, in most cases, it does not have the option of restructuring the HTM portfolio. Also, securities cannot be sold because of a change in interest rates or in prepayments.

When it was first introduced, many people did not appreciate how tough FAS No. 115 is. Historically, many of them had done little trading out of

their investment portfolios and thus figured that FAS No. 115 would not affect them.

That attitude changed in November 1993 when FASB issued guidance to banks on accounting for collateralized mortgage obligations (CMOs). When banks want to buy a CMO, regulations enforced by the Federal Financial Institutions Examination Council (FFIEC) require them to subject the CMO to a three-part test. The bank must continue to test the security while it is held. If the security was initially placed in the HTM portfolio and if at some point it fails part of the test, the FFIEC in the past required the bank to transfer the CMO out of the HTM into the AFS portfolio—with mark-to-market accounting. (Regulators have since rescinded the transfer requirement.)

In November 1993, FASB issued a statement saying that, because of this FFIEC regulation, even though a bank may *intend* to hold a security to maturity, it does not have the *ability* to hold it to maturity. Many people suddenly realized the seriousness of FAS No. 115 and the utter inflexibility of the HTM portfolio concept. They also realized that the accounting profession intended to enforce FAS No. 115, as accountants began laying down strict guidelines on what companies could and could not put in their HTM portfolios.

The CMO issue was eventually resolved. In April 1994, the FFIEC eliminated the transfer requirement for CMOs that failed the suitability tests, but it retained ultimate divestiture authority; that is, regulators had the authority to force banks and thrifts to sell securities out of an HTM portfolio. In July 1994, the FFIEC further agreed that it would require divestiture of securities out of the HTM portfolio only if they threatened the safety and soundness of the institution. For its part, FASB stated that it had not intended that the existence of the regulators' general divestiture authority would automatically impair an institution's ability to hold securities to maturity, and it withdrew the November 1993 guidance, effective July 1994.

Investor Response to FAS No. 115

Little quantifiable data have appeared with respect to the response of investors—specifically, banks and insurance companies—to FAS No. 115. FAS No. 115 went into effect for financial years beginning after December 15, 1993. Regulatory financial filings for the first quarter of 1994, which would be the first reporting period to reflect FAS No. 115, were not available when this presentation was prepared. Thus, this section provides anecdotal information.

Some 40–70 percent of banks and insurance companies' securities have apparently been assigned to

AFS portfolios. In only a few cases are AFS portfolios 90 percent of holdings or higher. One of those cases involves a securities portfolio of very short durations (e.g., floaters), so the mark-to-market risk is small. The other situation involves a handful of banks that have chosen to manage their securities portfolios under a mark-to-market discipline. Either securities are a fairly small proportion of their total assets, or they have significant capabilities in risk management and handling derivative securities.

Some 30–50 percent of securities have ended up in HTM portfolios. This percentage represents a big change from the first few months after FAS No. 115 was released, when many companies thought an AFS portfolio might be a fourth of their total securities and the rest would be assigned to the HTM portfolio.

Companies generally have sought to put mortgage securities in the HTM portfolio and Treasuries in the AFS portfolio. Treasuries are the more liquid securities, and if companies want a trading instrument or want to use something to actively manage their portfolios, they tend to do it with Treasuries rather than mortgages. Part of the reason why the regulatory–FASB dissonance over CMOs has been such a major issue for banks is that the banks have been hoping fervently that resolution of the issue would allow them to put CMOs in an HTM portfolio.

Large operations with sophisticated risk management systems generally seem confident about what they are doing in response to FAS No. 115. Many other financial institutions are simply trying to be as flexible as possible while they search for ways to manage their securities portfolios under FAS No. 115.

The Importance of FAS No. 115

Some security analysts argue that FAS No. 115 does not matter much in the general scheme of things. The basic argument is that most of the information that FAS No. 115 is designed to reveal has already been disclosed in footnotes to the financial statements. Most financial institutions now provide a significant amount of mark-to-market disclosure about their security portfolios, and FAS No. 107 fair value disclosures have also been helpful. The argument is that FAS No. 115 should not, therefore, affect the financial institutions' stock prices.

One interesting point in favor of this argument is that, in the big bond-market sell-off during February through April 1994, bank stocks generally performed in line with the market. For individual banks that have done worse than the market, the performance was usually attributable to factors other than FAS No. 115. I have not heard of any bank being hurt significantly in stock price because it had a huge AFS portfolio and took a big mark-to-market hit.

The other side of the argument is that FAS No. 115 matters very, very much. One reason is the monitoring of banks' capital by the bank regulators. If a bank's capital (measured according to generally accepted accounting principles [GAAP]) falls below certain trigger points, regulators are required by statute to take certain supervisory actions against the institution. Although a bank's economic capital may not change with a change in market values (because of offsetting changes in the market value of liabilities), if the bank's risk-based capital falls below 8 percent or if its GAAP capital falls below about 4 percent, regulators must take supervisory action even if they know the institution is sound.

The second reason FAS No. 115 matters is the "USA Today effect." Assume, for example, that a company is reporting its earnings in the newspapers and states that it achieved, say, a 20 percent increase from the prior year's period. The second paragraph states that, because of unrealized losses on its securities portfolio, its capital declined by 30 percent. Then the next paragraph says that security analysts shrugged off the capital loss, saying that the duration of assets and liabilities is well matched and its assets are more convex than its liabilities; so, on an economic basis, it probably has more capital than it ever had. In the next paragraph, the reporter attempts to explain duration and convexity. What will the person in the street make of this report, and what action will he or she take? The aftereffects of bad publicity may linger indefinitely.

In the meantime, banks and insurance companies that are wrestling with this issue have a deep uncertainty about just how much the potential market value and capital volatility caused by FAS No. 115 matters. Companies are wondering how much they should be focusing on the economics of the business versus managing what amounts to bookkeeping risk.

The uncertainty and tension are particularly pronounced for life insurance companies, which generally have assets of very long durations and portfolios with very large securities. Most life insurance companies are moving as best they can to comply with FAS No. 115 and have decided to focus on the economics of the business rather than worry much about the issue of capital volatility. Insurance companies, especially life insurance companies, have been making efforts to educate people and have been using FAS No. 107 types of disclosures and any other measures needed to make people understand that the cause of capital volatility lies in bookkeeping, not economics.

Managing a Securities Portfolio under FAS No. 115

Financial institutions need to focus carefully on what has and has not changed under FAS No. 115. Before this statement, managing investment portfolios in an asset/liability framework was comparatively simple. As indicated in Equation 1, return was a matter of a coupon rate earned on assets, some cost for liabilities, and overhead:

$$\text{Return} = (r \times A) - (c \times L) - \text{G\&A}, \qquad (1)$$

where

r = coupon income on assets
c = cost of liabilities
A = assets
L = liabilities
G&A = general and administrative expenses

Over time, a positive spread would probably be generated, which would translate into earnings, positive return on equity, growth of capital, and so on.

FAS No. 115 makes this equation more complex, as shown in Equation 2, because it involves three portfolios (HTM, AFS, and trading), each generating a return (r):

$$\begin{aligned}\text{Return} = {}& (r \times \text{HTM}) + (r \times \text{AFS}) + (r \times \text{Trading}) \\ & + (\text{AFS}_t - \text{AFS}_{t-1}) + (\text{Trading}_t - \text{Trading}_{t-1}) \\ & - (c \times L) - \text{G\&A}, \qquad (2)\end{aligned}$$

where AFS is the market value of the available-for-sale portfolio, and Trading is the market value of the trading portfolio. In addition to coupon income on the three portfolios, the return includes the changes in value of the AFS and the trading portfolios.

One approach to coping with FAS No. 115 is to look at the HTM portfolio as one problem and the AFS as another. (Trading portfolios are generally very small and do not require discussion here.)

Managing a Held-to-Maturity Portfolio

The ultimate goal in managing HTM portfolios is to select assets and manage liabilities so as to maintain a positive spread during the life of the assets. The HTM portfolio continues to be a spread game. Managers must be careful about how they select those assets because, in most cases, they do not have the option of restructuring that asset portfolio. Companies need to focus on managing the liabilities side of their balance sheets more actively than they have in the past. Banks, if they are not already doing so, will be making more use of swaps.

Managing an Available-for-Sale Portfolio

A primary factor in managing an AFS portfolio is market risk, because unrealized gains and losses will affect companies' GAAP capital. A simple way to measure market risk is duration (a measure of the percentage change in the value of a security or portfolio given a 100-basis-point shift in interest rates). In a leveraged operation, such as a bank or insurance company, the duration of the securities portfolio should be considered, but so should the duration of the portfolio equity or GAAP equity. The following equation describes the duration of portfolio equity:

$$D_e = D_{\text{AFS}} \times \frac{(\text{AFS})}{A} \times \frac{A}{E}, \qquad (3)$$

where

D_e = duration of shareholder equity
D_{AFS} = duration of AFS portfolio
A = total assets
E = shareholder equity

The relationship between leverage and the durations of the AFS portfolio and duration of portfolio equity can be seen in **Table 1**. For example, if the leverage ratio is 10 and the AFS portfolio has a duration of 4 years and is half of total assets, duration of the portfolio equity is 20 percent. In other words, a 100-basis-point shift in weights would change the AFS portfolio's value by 4 percent and portfolio equity by 20 percent. At lower and higher levels of leverage, the multiplier relationship between AFS duration and portfolio equity duration declines and rises, respectively.

Table 1. Duration of Portfolio Equity

AFS Share (percent)[a]	One Year	Four Years	Seven Years
25	2.5 years	10.0 years	17.5 years
50	5.0	20.0	35.0
75	7.5	30.0	52.5

Note: Leverage (total assets/equity) is 10 percent.

[a]AFS portfolio as a percentage of total assets.

Source: Lehman Brothers.

Management Approaches

Looking at HTM and AFS portfolios separately introduces certain problems. One is that managers may tend to create an AFS portfolio that is relatively small or has a short duration and an HTM portfolio that is quite large and has a larger duration. If managers view these two portfolios separately, they may lose sight of other risks being taken—yield-curve risk and the risk of a mismatch between the cash flows of assets and liabilities. They may also fail to take advantage of the benefits of diversification in managing and controlling risk.

A more comprehensive approach to the problem is to think in terms of unbundling the sources of return and sources of risk in a portfolio. This approach can be illustrated by rearranging Equation 2 into a component representing net interest margin and a component representing market risk or opportunity:

$$
\begin{aligned}
\text{Return} &= (r \times \text{HTM}) + (r \times \text{AFS}) + (r \times \text{Trading}) \\
&\quad + (\text{AFS}_t - \text{AFS}_{t-1}) + (\text{Trading}_t - \text{Trading}_{t-1}) \\
&\quad - (c \times L) - \text{G\&A} \\
&= \{[r \times (\text{HTM} + \text{AFS} + \text{Trading}) - (c \times L)] \\
&\quad + [(\text{AFS}_t - \text{AFS}_{t-1}) + (\text{Trading}_t - \text{Trading}_{t-1})]\} \\
&\quad - \text{G\&A} \\
&= \text{Net interest margin } + \text{Market risk or} \\
&\quad \text{opportunity} - \text{G\&A}. \tag{4}
\end{aligned}
$$

Given the leverage at which banks and insurance companies operate, relatively little of the spread between assets and liabilities (net interest margin) has to reach the bottom line to generate quite attractive return on equity. Net interest margin has been and will continue to be the driving force behind bank or insurance company earnings. Managers should thus continue to think in terms of maximizing net interest margin, except now they must do so across three portfolios. In other words, the portfolio manage-ment problem today is similar to that of the past but more complex because of FAS No. 115. Over time, net interest margin will provide a capital cushion to absorb market risk in the AFS and trading portfolios. The AFS and trading portfolios should be viewed as providing an additional opportunity for portfolio managers to add value by taking advantage of relative value opportunities in the market.

Conclusion

It remains to be seen whether FAS No. 115 disclosures will affect stock prices. Meanwhile, FAS No. 115 is a serious event and one that is changing the behavior of portfolio managers at banks and insurance companies. Perhaps the most important thing to keep in mind is that FAS No. 115 allows far less flexibility than in the past for managing the HTM portfolio (formerly, the investment portfolio). A second point is that, even though FAS No. 115 will lead to relatively large AFS portfolios, managers should be careful not to become overly focused on the market risk element of the AFS portfolio. FAS No. 115 has not changed the underlying economics of managing a securities portfolio in an asset/liability framework. In the future, however, it may provide them with additional opportunities to add value.

Question and Answer Session

John F. Tierney, CFA

Question: For sales from an HTM portfolio, what constitutes a significant credit deterioration? What evidence is required?

Tierney: Banks are not allowed to hold securities below investment grade; so a security that goes from investment grade to below investment grade constitutes a clear case that the asset has deteriorated in quality.

With respect to insurance companies, under risk-based capital requirements, securities rated A or higher receive a relatively small capital charge; then, as they go from BBB to BB ratings and so on, the capital charges rise quite sharply. When a security moves from one capital bucket to a lower one, you probably have a good case for finding unanticipated deterioration in credit quality and for removing that security.

Question: Do these rules apply to mutual companies without GAAP reporting requirements? Do mutual companies need to be concerned at this point?

Tierney: Mutual companies do not have to issue a GAAP statement to the public because they are not publicly held. FASB has ruled, however, that mutual companies will have to report GAAP-like statements beginning in 1995; so mutuals soon will have to deal with FAS No. 115.

In addition, just because mutuals are not publicly held and just because GAAP accounting is less of an issue for them, mutual companies are not insulated from the issue. In many cases, a mutual is relying on a bank for a line of credit, and the bank obviously wants to look at the mutual's fi-

nancial statements each quarter. If mutuals produce financials that are not in accordance with GAAP, they may have trouble dealing with their banks.

Question: What happens if a company sells an HTM security or moves it to another basket?

Tierney: If the action is for any reason other than the five reasons considered acceptable, the company is running the risk of having part or all of its portfolio made subject to the mark-to-market rule. That is, it runs the risk of its accountants or regulators questioning the status of comparable securities. They may say, "You did not have the intent or the ability to hold that security to maturity; how do we know that you have the intent to hold the comparable securities to maturity?" Some accountants seem to be willing to take a commonsense approach, saying that only similar securities could be tainted. Others seem to be taking a hard line: If you sell a security out of the HTM portfolio, you have to transfer everything out of the HTM. The answer to your question will be worked out on a case-by-case basis, but be prepared for the extreme.

Question: Has FAS No. 115 rolled through completely, or is a shift in demand ahead of us that will affect values in the bond market?

Tierney: Banks and insurance companies have recently shown a strong preference for securities with short maturities. They have to hold relatively large AFS portfolios, and they are concerned, es-

pecially now, about the mark-to-market risk and how much investors will pay attention to it. The strong preference for short-duration securities is evident by spreads that have tightened in the short end of the sector and widened somewhat in the long end of the sector. How much of that trend is attributable to the backup in interest rates and how much of it to FAS No. 115 is not clear.

The tendency toward strong demand for the short sector and less for the long sector is likely to continue. Companies that do not have to worry about FAS No. 115 will thus find value opportunities in the long sector of the market.

Up to now, a popular transaction for many institutions has been to acquire CMO floaters, then to do CMO swaps or indexed amortizing swaps (receive fixed-rate cash flows for 3–7 years and pay LIBOR), and link them to the floater for accounting purposes. This approach provides a means of extending duration. Under FAS No. 115, if these transactions are linked to CMO floaters that are held in the AFS portfolio, the combined position (with its longer duration) will be subject to mark-to-market accounting.

Few companies have been going the other way—acquiring a longer duration fixed-rate cash instrument and converting it into a floater using swaps. In the future, companies managing AFS portfolios will probably be investigating that kind of transaction more closely than at present, especially if spreads are wide in the five-year, seven-year, and ten-year sectors. Why not buy the cash instrument, shorten its duration via a swap, and try to capture some of that value?

Question: Does FASB have any plans to address the liability side in terms of marking the liabilities to market?

Tierney: The staff at FASB is thinking about the issue and studying it, but marking liabilities to market is not a specific project on FASB's agenda and will not happen soon. FASB will probably address the issue when it gathers enough information and when the market evolves to the point that we have an acceptable way to put a mark-to-market value on bank certificates of deposit, core deposits, insurance policies, and so forth.

Question: What have we learned from the way FAS No. 115 developed? Was there a better way to move to a mark-to-market environment?

Tierney: If the SEC had not pushed the issue, we would not have FAS No. 115. FAS No. 115 is really a response by FASB and the accounting profession to the threat that a regulatory body would come in and start setting accounting policy. Even though FASB voted 5 to 2 to approve FAS No. 115, nobody on the board was happy with it.

Question: What will happen if a bank or insurance company moves a security from an HTM to another basket for reasons they

believe are consistent with FAS No. 115? Do they immediately have to mark that security to market?

Tierney: Yes. If the security is moved to the AFS portfolio, unrealized gains or losses are reflected in capital but not income. If it is transferred to the trading portfolio, unrealized gains and losses are reflected in both income and capital.

Question: Does FAS No. 115 apply to loans and private placements?

Tierney: FAS No. 115 does not apply to loans. It does apply to private placements that are debt instruments.

Self-Evaluation Examination

1. The result of liquidity mismatch in the municipal bond market is:
   a. Reduced overall liquidity.
   b. Reduced volatility.
   c. Spikes in volatility.
   d. Lower credit ratings on municipal bonds.

2. According to Kaplan, the key elements in a stochastic, or statistical, method of interest rate forecasting are:
   a. Expected interest rate behavior and economic output.
   b. Expected interest rate behavior and the stock market.
   c. Historical interest rate and stock market behavior.
   d. Historical interest rate behavior and volatility.

3. A good bellwether for the bond market is:
   a. The automobile sales-financing industry.
   b. The utility industry.
   c. The banking industry.
   d. None of the above.

4. In deciding and revising bond ratings, Moody's Investors Service analyzes:
   a. The issuer's regulatory environment.
   b. The issuer's financial data.
   c. The issuer's strategic plan.
   d. All of the above.

5. The mortgage-backed securities (MBS) market now represents almost 50 percent of the taxable fixed-income market.
   a. True.
   b. False.

6. The least predictable reason borrowers prepay their mortgages is:
   a. Death or divorce.
   b. Refinancing opportunity.
   c. Moving.
   d. All three are equally unpredictable.

7. The duration and convexity of an MBS is similar to that of a noncallable fixed-income security.
   a. True.
   b. False.

8. The objective of a prepayment model is to:
   a. Predict the values of mortgage securities.
   b. Compare the values of mortgage securities.
   c. Hedge the values of mortgage securities.
   d. All of the above.

9. According to Patruno, the prepayment pattern of groups of mortgages carrying the same interest rate does not vary significantly as a result of loan sizes.
   a. True.
   b. False.

10. A credit rating on a mortgage pass-through security will typically address:
    a. Timely payment of interest and principal.
    b. Return of principal according to schedule.
    c. The prepayment assumption.
    d. A and b above.

11. Because of their negative convexity characteristic, first mortgages appear less attractive than home equity asset-backed securities.
    a. True.
    b. False.

12. Because of its size, the municipal bond market is not seriously affected by shifts in the mix of municipal bond holders.
    a. True.
    b. False.

13. A primary advantage of OTC derivatives is
    a. A central market for trading.
    b. Customization and flexibility.
    c. Lack of credit risk associated with a counterparty.
    d. Standardization of product.

14. Because of the proliferation of issuers, the global corporate market has become structurally more homogeneous during the past decade.
    a. True.
    b. False.

15. Malvey's relative-value analysis for corporate debt is based on:
    a. Spreads.
    b. Coupon.
    c. Maturity.
    d. All of the above.

16. In addition to foreign exchange risk, global fixed-income analysts should assess:
    a. Credit risk.
    b. Concentration.
    c. Duration.
    d. All of the above.

17. According to Rosenberg, uncovered interest rate parity:
    a. Has held throughout since 1973.
    b. Has held for substantial periods since 1973.
    c. Has not held for substantial periods since 1973.
    d. Has never held since 1973.

18. If interest rate parity holds for the future:
    a. U.S. investors will be less likely than in the past to diversify internationally.
    b. U.S. investors will be more likely to diversify internationally.
    c. U.S. investors will be indifferent about international diversification.
    d. Non-U.S. investors will be more likely to diversify internationally.

19. In assessing the risks in emerging markets, an important initial consideration is:
    a. Global liquidity.
    b. Global interest rates.
    c. Worldwide demand for dollars.
    d. All of the above.

20. Financial Accounting Standard No. 115:
    a. Restricts the trading of fixed-income securities to those held in trading and available-for-sale accounts.
    b. Requires that securities to be traded be marked to their market values.
    c. Is a major current concern for banks and insurance companies.
    d. All of the above.

Self-Evaluation Answers

1. c. See Trainer.

2. d. See Kaplan.

3. a. Grant argues that the U.S. auto market is a laboratory of financial innovation and improvisation.

4. d. See Abbott.

5. b. Lipton states that the MBS market has reached almost $2 trillion and represents almost a third of the taxable fixed-income market.

6. b. According to Lipton, demographic reasons—such as death, divorce, or moving—are relatively stable and easy to predict.

7. b. The prepayment option in an MBS causes duration and convexity of a mortgage security to be different from those of a noncallable fixed-income security.

8. d. Patruno believes that a prepayment model can reasonably be expected to do all three tasks.

9. b. Patruno states that prepayment patterns do vary significantly as a result of loan sizes.

10. d. Jones warns that ratings carry slightly different meanings for different securities and that a rating for a mortgage pass-through security does not address repayment of principal according to a particular schedule.

11. a. See van Eck.

12. b. As Jacobs shows, the municipal bond market is very susceptible to the shift in the mix of bondholders and to the cycles of mass redemptions by individual investors and bond funds.

13. b. See Bautista–Mahabir.

14. b. According to Malvey, the global fixed-income market has become more homogeneous *despite* the proliferation of issuers.

15. d. Malvey states that analysts should avoid spread myopia in making relative-value decisions. Coupon, maturity, and structural differentials often can more than counter spread movements.

16. d. See Havell.

17. b. Rosenberg shows that uncovered interest rate parity has held during the 1973–85 and 1988–94 periods but not for every week during those periods and not for the entire 1973–94 period.

18. a. According to Rosenberg, if interest rate parity holds, analysts will have difficulty making the argument that foreign bonds are a unique asset class that can improve the risk performance of a well-diversified U.S. portfolio.

19. d. See Saltzman.

20. d. See Tierney.

Order Form₀₄₃

Additional copies of *Fixed-Income Management: Techniques and Practices* (and other AIMR publications listed on page 133) are available for purchase.   Simply complete this form and return it via mail or fax to:

PBD, Inc.
P.O. Box 6996
Alpharetta, Ga. 30239-6996
U.S.A.
Telephone: 800/789-AIMR • Fax: 404/442-9742

Name _____

Company_____

Address _____

_____ Suite/Floor _____

City_____

State _____ZIP _____ Country _____

Daytime Telephone _____

Title of Publication	**Price**	**Qty.**	**Total**
_____	_____	_____	_____
_____	_____	_____	_____
_____	_____	_____	_____

SHIPPING/HANDLING CHARGES: Included in price of book for all U.S. orders. Surface delivery to Canada and Mexico, add $12 if value of books purchased is less than $50, or 18% of the total if value is between $50 and $100. Priority (air) delivery to Canada and Mexico, add $25 if value of books is less than $50, or 33% of the total if value is between $50 and $100. Other international purchasers should call or fax PBD for a shipping quote.
DISCOUNTS: Students, professors, and university libraries, 25%; CFA candidates (ID #_____), 25%; retired members (ID #_____), 25%; 50 or more copies of the same title, 40%.

Discount	$_____
4.5% sales tax (Virginia residents)	$_____
8.25% sales tax (New York residents)	$_____
7% GST (Canada residents, #124134602)	$_____
6% sales tax (Georgia residents)	$_____
Shipping/handling	$_____
Total cost of order	$_____

❑ Check or money order enclosed payable to **PBD, Inc.**
Charge to: ❑ VISA   ❑ Mastercard   ❑ American Express   ❑ Discover

Card Number: ⟦⟦⟦⟦⟦⟦⟦⟦⟦⟦⟦⟦⟦⟧

Signature:_____ Expiration date: _____

Selected AIMR Publications*

Blending Quantitative and Traditional Equity Analysis, 1994 . . . . $30
H. Russell Fogler, *Editor*

Investment Policy, 1994 . . . . $30
Jan R. Squires, CFA, *Editor*

Investing Worldwide V, 1994 . . . . $30

Analysts' Earnings Forecast Accuracy in Japan and the United States, 1994 . . . . . $20
Robert M. Conroy, Robert S. Harris, and Young S. Park

The Automotive Industry, 1994 . . . . $30
Theodore Shasta, CFA, *Editor*

The Telecommunications Industry, 1994 . . . . $30
Randall S. Billingsley, CFA, *Editor*

Managed Futures and Their Role in Investment Portfolios, 1994 . . . . $30
Don M. Chance, CFA

Fundamentals of Cross-Border Investment: The European View, 1994 . . . . $20
Bruno Solnik

Good Ethics: The Essential Element of a Firm's Success, 1994 . . . . $30
H. Kent Baker, CFA, *Editor*

A Practitioner's Guide to Factor Models, 1994 . . . . $30

Quality Management and Institutional Investing, 1994 . . . . $30
Keith P. Ambachtsheer, *Editor*

Managing Emerging Market Portfolios, 1994 . . . . $30
John W. Peavy III, CFA, *Editor*

Global Asset Management and Performance Attribution, 1994 . . . . $30
Denis S. Karnosky, Ph.D., and Brian D. Singer, CFA

Franchise Value and the Price/Earnings Ratio, 1994 . . . . $30
Martin L. Leibowitz and Stanley Kogelman

Investing Worldwide, 1993, 1992, 1991, 1990 . . . . $30 each

The Modern Role of Bond Covenants, 1994 . . . . $20
Ileen B. Malitz

Derivative Strategies for Managing Portfolio Risk, 1993 . . . . $30
Keith C. Brown, CFA, *Editor*

Equity Securities Analysis and Evaluation, 1993 . . . . $30

The CAPM Controversy: Policy and Strategy Implications for
Investment Management, 1993 . . . . $30
Diana R. Harrington and Robert A. Korajczyk, *Editors*

---

*A full catalog of publications is available from AIMR, P.O. Box 3668, Charlottesville, Va. 22903; 804/980-9712; fax 804/980-3634.